Multiple-Choice & Free-Response Questions
in Preparation for the
AP Computer Science Examination

NINTH EDITION

by

Leon Schram

John Paul II High School
Plano, Texas

ISBN # 978-1-934780-34-3 / 1-934780-34-0

Preface

This book has been prepared with one purpose in mind: to help students prepare for the Advanced Placement Computer Science Examination. It should be clear from the start that students will have to respond to both multiple-choice and free-response questions on the AP examination. Our focus is on the multiple-choice area. Students of Computer Science frequently get the kind of practice they need in developing algorithms and writing programs through programming assignments during the course of the year. But all too often there is not enough time for teachers to practice multiple-choice questions at the AP Computer Science Examination level. This book seeks to serve that purpose. There are a total of 354 multiple-choice questions, providing a vast array of practice for the examination. Additionally, there are four free-response questions in each sample examination for a total of 366 questions in the ninth edition.

The questions you will find within have been specifically chosen to give students a review experience over a wide range of topics covered on the AP Computer Science Examination. The difficulty level of the questions aims to be as varied and challenging as those on the exam itself, and deliberately more challenging in specific areas.

The ninth edition consists of two major parts. The first part contains 17 individual chapters with twelve review questions for each topic at the end of each chapter. There is an additional chapter on snooker questions, devoted to helping students with tricky questions. This chapter covers 15 major topic areas and provides 2 questions per topic. The second part consists of three sample exams. Each examination contains 40 multiple-choice questions and four free-response questions.

For the teacher of Advanced Placement Computer Science, this book is designed to provide you and your students with additional practice materials. For the student of computer science, I hope this book helps you achieve continued success in an exciting and important field.

All communication concerning this book should be addressed to the publisher and distributor:

D&S Marketing Systems, Inc.
1205 38th Street
Brooklyn, New York 11218

www.dsmarketing.com

Foreword to the 9th Edition

The most important requirement for review materials is that the questions cover the range of topics that will be tested, so that strengths and weaknesses in test preparation can be identified. Another requirement is to gain familiarity with question style. In creating this ninth edition I have relied heavily on my experience with the AP Test Development Committee and the test philosophy of the College Board. Additionally, I have used the AP Course Description in Computer Science, workshops I have taught and attended and communication with many teachers who are active with the College Board and AP Computer Science.

The AP Computer Science Examination language is still Java and has not changed, but this preparation book has changed from the previous edition to reflect the new curriculum starting with the 2014-2015 school year.

The GridWorld Case Study will no longer be tested and all questions on that topic have been removed. The previous edition had GridWorld questions included in the three sample exams. These questions are all replaced. In the place of the GridWorld Case Study are three AP Labs. These will not be explicitly tested, but the topics they cover are part of the AP Exam.

For many years questions on the previous *Marine Biology* and *GridWorld* case studies covered two-dimensional array topics. With the removal of GridWorld, many of the replacement questions have focused on two-dimensional arrays. This edition also presents array questions that emphasize the fact that a two-dimensional array is in fact an array of arrays. This is a new emphasis starting with the 2015 AP Exam.

Advanced Placement teachers face a classic *no-win situation* as they prepare students for an AP examination. A teacher can give students a sample examination that is very rigorous and hope that students will be relieved that the real exam is not as difficult as the practice test. The problem with this approach is that some students will be discouraged and select not to take the examination. A teacher can also give a relatively easy examination to motivate students and give them a sense of success. This approach also has a problem since it can result in a serious *cold shower* during the real AP examination.

Many teachers prefer a compromise and like to give a practice examination that is neither too hard nor too easy and represents the difficulty level of the actual examination. Such is a lofty goal that is easily mentioned but difficult to attain. Multiple-choice examinations are not released on a yearly basis and the difficulty level of exam questions are hard to predict.

The main purpose of the three sample examinations in this book is to help prepare students for the *real thing*. I have decided to fault on the side of difficulty. Students often find many questions on the AP examination that are long and time-consuming to read. Normally, students have not received many *full-page* questions during the school year. The three sample examinations in this review book have a heavy dose of long questions. The long questions include many preconditions and postconditions that are time-consuming to read, but will also appear throughout the actual AP Computer Science Examination.

Students must budget their time wisely as they take difficult, time-controlled tests. The sample examinations in this book intentionally contain many time-consuming questions to alert students to the reality of time budgeting. There are a variety of questions that involve selecting the correct solution for some incomplete method. These *complete-the-method* questions are intended not only to prepare students for the multiple choice part of the examination, but also for the free-response section. I have noticed with my own students that the biggest problem with the long questions is that students skip them. Students think these questions are too long and too complicated. In reality, the long *complete-the-method* style questions are quite manageable, and experience has shown that students handle such questions very well with sufficient exposure. The spirit of the sample examination is to give students sufficient exposure and prepare them to succeed on the real test. I hope these questions will satisfy that goal.

Leon Schram
Royse City, Texas

Table of Contents

Chapter 1 Review
Control Structures

Before the actual review of control structures starts, you need to understand clearly what to expect from this review and the reviews of future chapters. This book is designed to prepare you for the upcoming AP Computer Science Examination, which will be abbreviated as APCS Exam from this point forward. This manual is not a substitute for a text book which introduces and explains each of the computer science topics. Each review section consists of three parts.

First, there is a review of the significant points that you must clearly understand before you approach any of the questions. Keep in mind that the topics are presented not as a first introduction, but as a review which assumes you have seen this information earlier. If in fact you come to a chapter where the review makes it very clear that you have never studied the given topic, then you must seek help from your teacher, a text book or whichever resource can provide you with a good first introduction. Certain Computer Science topics, like control structures, which have proven to present few understanding problems, provide very little review. Topics which have a record of poor test performance will be presented in greater detail.

Second, you will receive information that will be tested on the APCS Exam. The College Board has established an AP Subset, which is a set of topics that may be tested. This preparation manual only focuses on those topics that will be tested and the questions will likewise only focus on those topics. For example, the Java post-condition `do...while` *loop is not in the AP Subset. This means that* `do...while` *will not be reviewed in this section. It also means there will not be sample questions on post-condition loops in the question section. It is very possible that the* `do...while` *loop is in your textbook and you may have seen questions on this topic in a chapter test. However, this manual will strictly focus on those topics and sub-topics that are listed in the College Board Course Description.*

Third, you need to be aware how easily somebody with a clear understanding on a given topic can still answer questions incorrectly. This means you need to understand test-taking strategies by topic. Each topic has its own, subtle, little pitfalls that can be overlooked. Students, who are not aware of these problems, may feel good about their performance on the APCS Exam. Later, they are quite unpleasantly surprised when an unexpected low score arrives in the mail.

If you are using this test preparation manual as part of the course curriculum, your teacher will specify what the class needs to do and when to do it. On the other hand, it is possible that you, and perhaps a small number of fellow students, are given this manual and told to study and prepare for the test. How should you proceed in such a scenario? I am now assuming that you have access to the solutions manual. It really is pretty much impossible to work on your own if you do not know the accuracy of your solutions.

I suggest the following approach. After the chapter review do the twelve questions that follow and check your answers. It is very important that you do not guess on any questions. Leave a question blank if you are confused. It is possible that you answer a question correctly with lucky guessing. In such a case you may erroneously conclude that you understand the material. Therefore, it is very important that you carefully identify questions into several categories.

- You know the topic well and you have the question correct.
- You know the topic, but you selected the wrong answer.
  When you see the answer you know that you made a careless error.
- You know the topic, but you selected the wrong answer.
  When you check the explanation of the solution you realize your mistake and you understand this type of question better.
- You thought you understood the question, but you have the wrong answer.
  The solution manual does not help to clarify the confusion.
  This means that you must seek help on this topic.
- You skipped the question and you know that you must seek help for this topic.

There are very few problems that test control structures directly on the APCS Exam. The scope of topics in AP Computer Science guarantees that there cannot be many questions on any one topic. Control structures can also be overlooked as a fundamental topic, which does not compare in complexity to many other topics in computer science. This may all be true, but the simple reality is that control structures appear everywhere in any program and they will appear in many APCS Exam questions. A question may focus on inheritance, sorting, searching, parameter passing, algorithmic analysis or other topics, but still include one or more control structures. This can easily bring about the following problem.

APCS Examination Alert

Students frequently answer questions incorrectly about a variety of topics, even though they have solid knowledge on these topics. The wrong answer is selected due to handling control structures incorrectly.

The problem described here is analogous to mathematics. Students may have a good understanding of advanced mathematical concepts and yet answer many questions incorrectly because of arithmetic errors.

It was mentioned earlier that not all Java features are tested on the APCS Exam. You will see evidence of this in this introductory chapter since not all control structures are tested. The rationale for inclusion or exclusion of topics is not a concern in this APCS Exam review book. The AP Computer Science Test Development Committee makes decisions about the inclusion of topics and makes questions based on included topics. The focus of this review book will be strictly on those topics that are going to be tested. This pattern is already evident in this first chapter. The review questions presented do not use all of the Java primitive data types.

APCS Examination Alert

The College Board has published an **AP Java Subset** of Java features that may be tested on the AP Computer Science Examination. Whenever appropriate, you will receive alerts to those items that are tested.

A *simple* or *primitive* data type holds a single value. Java's primitive data types that are in the AP Java Subset are:

int   **double**   **boolean**

The three primary control structures are *simple sequence*, *selection* and *repetition*. Program logic, in any language, dictates that a program executes in the sequence that program statements are presented. Line after line the program is executed unless some control structure causes the program flow to jump to another sequence of instructions. During program execution, conditional statements are encountered. These conditional statements will always be either true or false, and they are used in both selection control structures and repetition control structures. The Java syntax of the different control structures will be reviewed in various program examples that will be shown later in this chapter. Not all of the Java control structures will be tested.

AP Examination Alert

One-way selection with **if** and two-way selection with **if...else** are part of the AP Java subset.

Multi-way selection with **switch**, **case** and **break** is not part of the AP Java subset.
Multi-way selection logic will be tested with nested **if...else** statements.

Fixed iteration with **for** and pre-condition iteration with **while** are part of the AP Java subset.

Post-condition iteration with **do...while** is not part of the AP Java subset.

Many APCS Exam questions require determining the output of a program segment. Students are used to working on their computers. The compiler detects syntax errors, and the program execution displays the actual program output. It is a different matter when no computer is available and the program is printed on paper. Now you need to be the compiler and program executor. Playing computer requires that you keep track of the variable values as they change. You need to do a *variable trace*. Many students think that it is possible to perform variable tracing in their heads. Please take the time to write down changing variable values in columns. The best students, all with solid computer science knowledge, can easily lose track when there are multiple variable values, which change throughout a large variety of repetitions.

AP Examination Alert

There are no computers available during the APCS Exam. You must perform all program executions on paper. Scratch paper and calculators are not allowed during the examination. All writing, including the multiple-choice segment, must be done on the test paper. It is vital to use *variable traces* whenever questions require the program segment output or variable values.

The program segment in **Example 1.1** shows a typical problem that requires tracing. The segment combines a loop control structure with a selection control structure. Two variables change during program execution. Some students may have the mental concentration to handle this problem. The anxiety people feel on an important test makes it more difficult to keep track of multiple details. The program segment is followed by a *variable trace table*.

Example 1.1

```java
int count = 0;
for (int k = 1; k < 5; k++)
{
    if (k % 2 == 0)
        count += 2;
    else
        count += 3;
}
System.out.println(count);
```

k	count	Output
	0	
1	3	
2	5	
3	8	
4	10	10

Control Structure Pitfalls

The review sections are placed at the start of each chapter before you tackle a dozen or more sample questions on a specific topic. After completing all of the topics, you can then test yourself with various sample APCS Exams. Some chapters, like this chapter, present less review because of their fundamental nature. It can be argued that any student who does not comprehend control structures may encounter serious difficulties during the challenging APCS Exam. On the other hand, even the brightest students may have difficulties with subtleties that are easily overlooked and result in selecting the wrong answer. Keep in mind that the committee who creates the APCS Exam intentionally includes *distracters* (wrong answers), which seem correct if the subtleties are ignored. Perhaps the biggest benefit of each review section is a summary of pitfalls that are common for the given topic.

The most common control structure error is the OBOB. OBOB means *Off By One Bug*. It may appear that OBOBs are only a problem with control structure questions. Since there are not that many control structure questions, you might argue that this is not a big deal. The reality is that control structures are found everywhere in a program. It does not matter what the focus of a certain topic is; control structures can still be used. During the multiple choice segment of the APCS Exam, you will need to evaluate many types of methods and program segments. This allows many OBOB opportunities. Likewise, during the free response section of the APCS Exam, you need to write your own code. The code you write may be almost correct because you overlook a boundary case.

AP Examination Alert

An OBOB is an **Off By One B**ug.

OBOBs occur frequently because the program code may appear simple and may be considered unworthy of serious attention.

Failure to consider borderline conditions causes many OBOBs.

This review will conclude with a set of programs that demonstrate examples of OBOB situations. The first program segment in **Example1.2** is an example of a program that determines how many times the loop structure executes. You need to determine the value of count by checking how many times the loop repeats. A quick look at the loop condition k < 5 makes a surprising number of students conclude that the loop repeats five times. Keep in mind that a loop body executes only if the loop condition (k < 5 in this case) is true. This means that the loop will not execute the fifth time. The next program segment, in **Example1.3** makes a small change and now the loop repeats five times.

Example 1.2

```
int count = 0;
for (int k = 1; k < 5; k++)
{
    count++;
}
System.out.println(count);
```

The program examples in **Example1.2** and **Example1.3** use almost identical loop control structures. In both cases the loop control variable (LCV) is initialized to **1**. In both cases the **LCV** increases by one after each execution of the loop body. The difference is the loop condition, which determines if the loop body will be executed. As long as the loop condition is true, the loop will be executed. Make sure you watch out for the <= operator. In this case it means that the segment in **Example1.3** will repeat once more than the segment in **Example1.2**.

Example 1.3

```
int count = 0;
for (int k = 1; k <= 5; k++)
{
    count++;
}
System.out.println(count);
```

The two previous examples are subtle enough to be missed by many students. The common mistake presented in **Example 1.2** does happen often enough, but it tends to be a mistake of students new to computer science or students who do not pay attention. Frequently, students who are very confident, or perhaps impatient, quickly look at a problem and pick the answer. The simpler the problem, the lesser the concentration on that problem and the greater the likelihood of picking the wrong answer.

Sometimes program output occurs during the loop execution. This presents a different type of OBOB. **Example1.4** starts the loop execution by incrementing `count`, followed by an output display. This results in an output display of 1 2 3 4 5. The loop repeats five times and five times the value of `count` is displayed.

Example 1.4

```
int count = 0;
for (int k = 1; k <= 5; k++)
{
    count++;
    System.out.print(count + " ");
}
```

The output in **Example1.5** is also displayed five times. The exact same loop structure is used, which repeats five times. There are still five numbers that will be displayed, but they are not the same five numbers. In this example the value of `count` is first displayed and then incremented. You now have a classic OBOB opportunity. The first value displayed will be 0 and the last value is 4. The complete output display is 0 1 2 3 4. You can be sure that any multiple choice question will include distracters such that the answer is *off by one*.

Example 1.5

```
int count = 0;
for (int k = 1; k <= 5; k++)
{
    System.out.print(count + " ");
    count++;
}
```

You now come to the main chapter section. It is your turn to demonstrate your understanding. Look at each of the twelve questions that follow and create a variable trace. It is possible that these questions are assigned for homework. It is also possible that you are working independently preparing for the APCS Exam. In either case, it is very simple to place the question code in an actual computer program to determine the correct output or value. If you do that, congratulations, you have proven your word processing skills of copy and paste. Please have the maturity to realize that getting the answer by any means should not be your goal. You need to realize what you know and what you do not know.

Chapter 1 Questions
Control Structures

01. Consider the following code segment.

```
int p = 0;
while (p < 5)
{
    int q = 0;
    while (q < 4)
    {
        p += q;
        q++;
        System.out.println(p + "   " + q);
    }
}
```

What is the last output when the segment executes?

(A) 0   1
(B) 1   2
(C) 3   3
(D) 6   4
(E) 10   5

02. Consider the following code segment.

```
int count = 5;
for (int p = 0; p < 7; p++)
{
    if (p % 3 == 0)
        count--;
    else
        count ++;
}
System.out.println(count);
```

What is printed as a result of executing the code segment?

(A) 4
(B) 5
(C) 6
(D) 7
(E) 8

03. Consider the following code segment.

```
int x = <some integer greater than zero>
int n = 100;

if (x < 1000)
{
    if (x > 1000)
        n = 200;
    else
        n = 300;
}
else
{
    if (x < 1000)
        n = 400;
    else
        n = 300;
}
System.out.println(n);
```

What is printed as a result of executing the code segment?

(A) 100
(B) 200
(C) 300
(D) 400
(E) 200 or 400

04. Consider the following code segment.

```
int x = 0;
for (int y = 1; y <= 12; y++)
{
    while (x <= y)
    {
        if (x % 2 == 0)
            x += 2;
        else
            y -= 2;
    }
}
System.out.println(x);
```

What is printed as a result of executing the code segment?

(A) 11
(B) 12
(C) 13
(D) 14
(E) 15

05. Consider the following code segment.

```
int q = 0;
for (int p = 0; p < 5; p++)
{
    q = q + p;
}
System.out.println(q);
```

What is printed as a result of executing the code segment?

(A) 1
(B) 3
(C) 6
(D) 10
(E) 15

06. Consider the following code segment.

```
int q = 0;
for (int p = 0; p < 10; p++)
{
    q++;
    p += q;
    System.out.print(p + " ");
}
```

What is printed as a result of executing the code segment?

(A) 1 4 8 13
(B) 1 4 8 13 19
(C) 1 3 5 7 9
(D) 1 3 5 7 9 11
(E) 0 2 4 6 8 10

07. Consider the following code segment.

```
int q = <some integer value greater than 0 >
int p = <some integer value greater than q >
while (p > q)
{
    if (p % 2 == 0)
        p--;
    else
        q++;
}
System.out.println(q + "   " + p);
```

What kind of values are printed when the segment executes?

(A) Two positive integers, such that p equals q
(B) Two positive integers, which are the initial values of p and q
(C) Two positive integers, such that p is greater than q
(D) Two positive integers, such that p is lesser than q
(E) Two positive integers, such that p equals q + 1

08. Consider the following code segment.

```
int k = 0;
for (k = 1; k <= 5; k++)
{
    k++;
}
k++;
System.out.println(k);
```

What is printed as a result of executing the code segment?

(A) 5
(B) 6
(C) 7
(D) 8
(E) 9

09. Consider the following code segment.

```
int count = 0;
for (int p = 0; p <= 5; p++)
{
    for (int q = p; q <= 5; q++)
    {
        count++;
    }
}
System.out.println(count);
```

What is printed as a result of executing the code segment?

(A) 3
(B) 6
(C) 10
(D) 15
(E) 21

10. Consider the following code segment.

```
int n = 6;
int count = 0;
for (int p = 1; p <= n-1; p++)
    for (int q = 0; q < p; q++)
        count++;
System.out.println(count);
```

What is the value of count when the code segment finishes executing?

(A) 10
(B) 15
(C) 21
(D) 28
(E) 36

11. Consider the following code segment.

```
int p = 10;
int q = 5;
while (p > 0 && q > 0)
{
    p++;
    if (p % 2 == 0)
        q--;
    System.out.println(p + "   " + q);
}
```

What is the last output when the segment executes?

(A) 16   2
(B) 17   2
(C) 18   1
(D) 19   1
(E) 20   0

12. Consider the following code segment.

```
int p = 10;
int q = 5;
while (q != 0 && p/q > 0)
{
    p--;
    System.out.println(p + "   " + q);
    q--;
}
```

What is the last output when the segment executes?

(A) 7   3
(B) 6   2
(C) 5   1
(D) 4   0
(E) An ArithmeticException error message due to division by zero

Chapter 2 Review
Methods and Parameters

Reviewing methods presents a *chicken or egg* problem. Methods are members of a class and a class has members that include methods. Should methods be presented in the context of an Object Oriented Programming (**OOP**) review which includes classes and methods? In four, separate, later chapters, Object Oriented Programming will be reviewed, and at that time classes and their members will get closer scrutiny. At this stage, methods and parameters will be considered without the bigger OOP picture. With a better understanding of the building blocks used by classes, it will be easier to handle questions about classes and program design.

A method is nothing more than a group of program statements placed between a set of opening and closing braces **{ }** . The method has a heading with a name that is used to execute the program statements in the method body. Up to this point it can be argued that working with methods is pretty simple if you understand the control structures that are likely to be used inside the method body.   The essence of understanding methods depends upon a clear understanding of how information is passed to methods and returned from methods.

Methods can be categorized in various types. Most fundamentally, especially for information passing, is the distinction between a `void` method and a `return` method. Method `sum` in **Example 2.1** is a return method. Method `sum` computes and then *returns* the sum of the two calling or *actual parameters*, n1 and n2. The method heading parameter, or *formal parameter* x, receives the value 100, which is passed by method call parameter n1 and likewise method heading parameter y receives the value 200, which is passed by method call parameter n2. It is easy to identify a `return` method. The conspicuous keyword `return` takes care of passing information back to the "calling" program statement, which in this case will display 300. Note that variable `result` is an `int` and that is also the `return` type of method `sum`.

Example 2.1

```
public static void main(String args[])
{
    int n1 = 100;
    int n2 = 200;
    System.out.println(sum(n1,n2));
}

public static int sum(int x, int y)
{
    int result = x + y;
    return result;
}
```

Java makes method distinctions easy. `Return` methods include the keyword `return` and `void` methods include the keyword `void`. In **Example 2.2,** method `displayMax` compares parameters `x` and `y` for equality and then displays the result. There is no value returned, and in this example the parameter information is used to display the result of some desired process. The `return` type of a `return` method is required in the heading. If the method does not return a value, the `return` type is `void`, which is indicated in the same location where the data type normally is located.

Example 2.2

```
public static void main(String args[])
{
    int n1 = 100;
    int n2 = 200;
    displayMax(n1,n2);
}

public static void displayMax(int x, int y)
{
    if (x == y)
        System.out.println(x + " equals " + y);
    else if (x > y)
        System.out.println(x + " > " + y);
    else
        System.out.println(x + " < " + y);
}
```

Calling Return Methods and Void Methods

A **return** method is called by using the *returned value* in a program statement. This can be output, assignment or comparison, like ...

```
System.out.println(computeSum(n1,n2));
int result = computeSum(n1,n2);
if (computeSum(n1,n2) > 100)
```

A **void** method call becomes a *stand-alone* program statement, like ...

```
displaySum(n1,n2);
centerString(title);
```

Methods and Parameters Pitfalls

It is easy to make mistakes in determining the values processed by a method. Such mistakes are not method errors. They are control structure errors, which were discussed in the previous section. There are problems, which are unique to method handling. First, it is important to remember the fundamental parameter rules.

Fundamental Rules About Using Methods With Parameters

The parameters in the method calls are called *actual parameters*.

The parameters in the method headings are called *formal parameters*.

The number of actual parameters must match the number of formal parameters.

The corresponding actual parameters and formal parameters must be the same data type.

The sequence of the actual parameters must match the sequence of the formal parameters.

The actual parameter identifiers may be the same identifiers as or different identifiers from the formal parameter identifiers.

There exists a subtle misunderstanding about parameter passing that can have serious logic error consequences in a program. Primitive data types, like `int`, `double` and `boolean`, store the actual data values. Objects store references to memory locations, where the actual data information is stored. Methods use both primitive data types and objects for parameter passing. This means that passing primitive data type values and object values seem to be different. The problem is that there is both a similarity and a difference, which is frequently misunderstood.

The problem at hand applies to `void` methods. What happens to the calling parameter values? `Return` methods do not share this confusion. With `return` methods, parameters provide necessary values for the processing of the `return` method and the requested result is returned.

Consider a `swap` method. Two parameters are passed, and the goal is to exchange the parameter values. A `return` method can only return a single value and is no help for a swapping routine. Perhaps a `void` method will do the job. The program in **Example 2.3** passes two integer values to method `swap` where the parameter values are exchanged. The variable values are displayed before the method call, inside the method body and after the method call.

Example 2.3

```
public class Example23
{
    public static void main(String args[])
    {
        int x = 10;
        int y = 20;
        System.out.println(x + "   " + y);
        swap(x,y);
        System.out.println(x + "   " + y);
    }

    public static void swap(int p, int q)
    {
        int temp = p;
        p = q;
        q = temp;
        System.out.println(p + "   " + q);
    }
}
```

Program Output

```
10   20
20   10
10   20
```

The program output displays the original `10 20` values in the `main` method before the `swap` method call. The output statement inside the `swap` body proves that the parameter values are swapped. However, when the `main` method variables are displayed after the `swap` call, there is no change in the values. The `swap` method in **Example 2.3** is proof that the values of primitive data type variables cannot be changed by a method in this manner.

The logic of the swapping or lack of swapping, is caused by the fact that the `main` method variables x and y each have memory locations, which are separate from method variables. The values of these memory locations are passed to the `swap` method and copied to `swap` parameters p and q. Both p and q have memory locations different from x and y. When method `swap` exchanges the values of p and q, it has no impact on the original values of x and y.

In **Example 2.4** the `swap` method still exchanges values, but these values are now objects. For simplicity they are objects of the `String` class. The output results are identical to the previous example with integers. There exists a simple rule in Java, *actual parameters cannot be altered*. Remember, actual parameters are the parameters in the calling method and they are fixed. The values of the actual parameters are passed to the formal parameters in the method heading. In the case of object parameters, references are passed, but back in the actual parameter's location those references will not change.

Example 2.4

```
public class Example24
{
    public static void main(String args[])
    {
        String name1 = "Tom";
        String name2 = "Sue";
        System.out.println(name1 + "   " + name2);
        swap(name1,name2);
        System.out.println(name1 + "   " + name2);
    }

    public static void swap(String s1, String s2)
    {
        String temp = s1;
        s1 = s2;
        s2 = temp;
        System.out.println(s1 + "   " + s2);
    }
}
```

Program Output

```
Tom   Sue
Sue   Tom
Tom   Sue
```

At first glance it may appear that it does not matter what the parameters are. It seems that both primitive data values and object values behave in the same manner. Look at the method body and changes that occur with the copies of the actual parameters. Now return to the calling program segment, and the values of the actual parameters remain unchanged.

When working with an object, you must be aware that it has a *shallow value* and a *deep value*. The shallow value is the memory address reference being stored by that object. The deep value is the actual data stored at the memory address being referenced by the shallow value.

The program in **Example 2.5** demonstrates that it is possible to alter the deep values of an actual parameter. This is accomplished by changing method swap drastically. The earlier swap method stated something like: *temp = object1; object1 = object2; object2 = temp;* That approach does not touch the deep values that are stored. It only swaps the shallow values.

Now in the method of **Example 2.5**, the swap routine digs *deeper* and goes straight to the attributes of each object. Two exchanges are performed. First the name attributes are swapped, and then the age attributes follow. When method swap is finished, the actual parameters of the Student objects are not altered; however, the *deep* values certainly have been altered.

Example 2.5

```java
public class Example25
{
    public static void main(String args[])
    {
        Student student1 = new Student("Tom",16);
        Student student2 = new Student("Sue",15);
        student1.showData(); student2.showData();
        System.out.println("\n\n");
        swap(student1,student2);
        student1.showData(); student2.showData();
        System.out.println("\n\n");
    }

    public static void swap(Student s1, Student s2)
    {
        int tempAge = s1.getAge();
        s1.setAge(s2.getAge());
        s2.setAge(tempAge);
        String tempName = s1.getName();
        s1.setName(s2.getName());
        s2.setName(tempName);
    }
}

class Student
{
    private String name;
    private int age;

    public Student (String n, int a)
    {
        name = n;
        age = a;
    }

    public int getAge()            { return age;  }
    public String getName()        { return name; }
    public void setAge(int a)    { age = a;      }
    public void setName(String n){ name = n;     }

    public void showData()
    {
        System.out.print(name + "   " + age + "     ");
    }
}
```

Program Output

```
Tom   16     Sue   15
Sue   15     Tom   16
```

Java Parameter Notes

Java passes information to a method with parameters.

A copy of the <u>calling, actual</u> parameters are assigned to the <u>receiving, formal</u> parameters in the method.

In the case of a simple/primitive data type, a copy of the variable's value, like **23**, '**A**', or **true**, is sent by the parameter. Any changes are changes to a <u>copy</u>, which makes no changes to the <u>original</u>.

The same thing actually happens in the case of an object; however, with an object the value is the <u>memory address</u> of the object itself. If this is changed, it does not alter the memory address of the original object.

The values of actual parameters cannot be altered.

The only way changes made in a method impact the original calling object, is with a **return** method or if changes are made to the attributes of the object.

A Special Note For Students With C++ Knowledge

In C++ parameters can be *passed by value* or *passed by reference*.

In C++ when parameters are *passed by value*, a copy is made, and any change to the copy will not alter the value of the actual parameter.

In C++ when parameters are *passed by reference*, both the actual parameter variable and the formal parameter variable share the same memory location. Passing the reference of the actual parameter indicates where the values are stored. Any change to the formal parameter will change the actual parameter.

In Java parameters are only *passed by value*. It is true that objects store references, but the value of the reference is passed, and variables do not share the same memory location. The confusion comes from the fact that Java uses references for objects, even though parameters are passed by value only.

Chapter 2 Questions
Methods and Parameters

01. Consider the following method.

```java
/** Precondition: p > 0
 */
public static int method0201(int p)
{
    int count = 1;
    for (int q = 1; q < p; q++)
    {
        count += count;
    }
    return count;
}
```

What value is returned as a result of the call `method0201(n)` ?

(A) n
(B) 2n
(C) n^2
(D) 2^n
(E) $2^{(n-1)}$

02. Consider the following method.

```java
/** Precondition: p > 0
 */
public static int method0202(int p)
{
    int count = 1;
    for (int q = 1; q < p; q++)
        count += count;
    return count;
}
```

What value is returned as a result of the call `method0202(5)`?

(A) 5
(B) 7
(C) 8
(D) 15
(E) 16

03. Consider the following code segment and method.

```
for (int n = 1; n <= 10; n++)
    System.out.print(method0203(n) + "   ");

public static int method0203(int n)
{
    int temp1 = 0;
    int temp2 = 1;
    int temp3 = 1;
    for (int k = 3; k <= n; k++)
    {
        temp3 = temp1 + temp2;
        temp1 = temp2;
        temp2 = temp3;
    }
    return temp3;
}
```

What is printed as a result of executing the code segment?

(A) 55   34   13   8   5   3   2   1   1
(B) 1   1   2   3   5   8   13   34   55
(C) 1   1   1   2   3   5   8   13   21   34
(D) 34   21   13   8   5   3   2   1   1   1
(E) 0   1   1   2   3   5   8   13   21   34

04. Consider the following method.

```
public static int method0204(int n)
{
    int k1 = 2;
    int k2 = 3;
    int k3 = 4;
    for (int p = 1; p <= n; p++)
    {
        k1 = k2;
        k2 = k3;
        k3 = k1 + k2;
    }
    return k3;
}
```

What value is returned as a result of the call method0204(5) ?

(A) 23
(B) 35
(C) 47
(D) 62
(E) 71

05. Consider the following code segment and method.

```
int x = 5;
x = method0205(x);
System.out.println(x);

public static int method0205(int n)
{
    for (int k = n; k <= 10; k++)
        n += k;
    return n;
}
```

What is printed as a result of executing the code segment?

(A) 50
(B) 40
(C) 31
(D) 23
(E) 16

06. Consider the following code segment and method.

```
int x = 10;
int y = 20;
swap(x,y);
System.out.println(x + " " + y);

public static void swap(int p, int q)
{
    int t = p;
    p = q;
    q = t;
}
```

What is printed as a result of executing the code segment?

(A) 20 10
(B) 10 20
(C) 10 10
(D) 20 20
(E) 0 0

07. Consider the following two methods.

```java
/** Precondition:  n1 > 0
 *                 n2 > 0
 */
public static int method0207a(int n1, int n2)
{
    int temp = method0207b(n1,n2);
    return n1 / temp * n2;
}


/** Precondition:  p > 0
 *                 q > 0
 */
public static int method0207b(int p, int q)
{
    int rem = 1;
    int k = 0;
    while (rem != 0)
    {
        rem = p % q;
        if (rem == 0)
        {
            k = q;
        }
        else
        {
            p = q;
            q = rem;
        }
    }
    return k;
}
```

What value is returned as a result of the call method0207a(30,45) ?

(A) 30
(B) 45
(C) 90
(D) 150
(E) 450

08. Consider the following code segment and class.

```
Widget w1 = new Widget(66);
Widget w2 = new Widget(77);
System.out.println(w2.getWidgets() + "   " + w1.getWidgets());
System.out.println(w2 + "   " + w1);


class Widget
{
    private int numWidgets;

    public Widget(int nW)
    {
        numWidgets = nW;
    }

    public int getWidgets()
    {
        return numWidgets;
    }
}
```

What is printed as a result of executing the code segment?
Note: Memory reference values will fluctuate with different executions.

(A) 66   77
     Widget@2e81632f   Widget@addbf152

(B) 77   66
     77   66

(C) 77   66
     Widget@addbf152   Widget@2e81632f

(D) 66   77
     66   77

(E) 0   0
     0   0

09. Consider the following code segment and class.

```
Widget w1 = new Widget(66);
Widget w2 = new Widget(77);
System.out.println(w1.getWidgets() + "   " + w2.getWidgets());
System.out.println(w1 + "   " + w2);

class Widget
{
    private int numWidgets;
    public Widget(int numWidgets)    { numWidgets = numWidgets; }
    public int getWidgets()          { return numWidgets; }
}
```

What is printed as a result of executing the code segment?
Note: Memory reference values will fluctuate with different executions.

(A) 66   77
     Widget@2e81632f Widget@ addbf152

(B) 66   77
     66   77

(C) 77   66
     Widget@ addbf152 Widget@2e81632f

(D) 0   0
     Widget@ addbf152 Widget@2e81632f

(E) 0   0
     0   0

10. Consider the following program.

```
public class DS0210
{
    public static void main(String args[])   { samba(65.0); }
    public static void samba(int k)           { System.out.println(k); }
    public static void samba(double k)        { System.out.println(k); }
    public static void samba(char k)          { System.out.println(k); }
    public static void samba(String k)        { System.out.println(k); }
}
```

What is printed as a result of executing the program?

(A) 65
(B) 65.0
(C) k
(D) A
(E) A Duplicate method compile error message

11. Consider the following method.

```
public static int method0211 (int n)
{
    int temp = 1;
    for (int k = n; k > 1; k--)
        temp *= k;
    return temp;
}
```

What value is returned as a result of the call `method0211(5)` ?

(A) 2
(B) 6
(C) 24
(D) 120
(E) 720

12. Consider the following program.

```
public class DS0212
{
    public static void main(String args[])
    {
        waltz("Hello",100,Math.PI);
    }
    public static void waltz(String n)
    {
        System.out.println(n);
    }
    public static void waltz(String p, int q)
    {
        System.out.println(p + "   " + q);
    }
    public static void waltz(String x, int y, double z)
    {
        System.out.println(x + "   " + y + "   " + z);
    }
    public static void waltz(String a, int b, double c, int d)
    {
        System.out.println(a + "   " + b + "   " + c + "   " + d);
    }
}
```

What is printed as a result of executing the program?

(A) `Hello`
(B) `Hello   100`
(C) `Hello   100   3.141592653589793`
(D) An Unknown symbol compile error message
(E) A Duplicate method compile error message

Chapter 3 Review
Boolean Algebra

The review for the Boolean Algebra chapter will be longer than the other chapters. There are two reasons for this approach. First, most computer science text books do not include a Boolean Algebra chapter. Second, statistics performed on AP Computer Science results have demonstrated that students who perform poorly on Boolean Algebra questions are more likely to perform poorly on the test as a whole. The logic explained by Boolean Algebra is used regularly in program segments that involve control structures with compound conditions.

APCS Examination Alert

The APCS Examination includes a variety of Boolean logic questions. Many questions require indirect knowledge of Boolean logic, and other questions are directly focused on testing a student's understanding of Boolean concepts.

Test results have shown that many students score quite poorly on this part of the APCS Examination.

Statistical Analysis of these test results have also shown that the students who perform poorly on Boolean logic questions, perform poorly on the AP Exam as a whole; and the students who perform well on the Boolean Logic questions, perform well on the AP Exam as a whole.

A good starting point is to look at a variety of English sentences and determine if these sentences are Boolean statements or not. So, what are the criteria for a Boolean statement? The sentence, statement, condition, whatever, must be **true** or **false**. Questions, ambiguities, opinions and arguments are not Boolean statements. You can see why this branch of mathematics has a major impact on computer science. The basis of processing data in a computer is the binary system of **on** and **off**, which is identical to the Boolean **true** and **false**. Each of the following five English statements is a Boolean statement.

> *A mile is longer than a kilometer.*
> *July and August both have the same number of days.*
> *A pound of feathers is lighter than a pound of lead.*
> *The Moon is larger than the Sun.*
> *New York City has more people than Baltimore.*

Boolean Operators

The arithmetic operators (+ - * /) *addition*, *subtraction*, *multiplication* and *division* are performed according to the rules for each operator. There are also a set of Boolean operators with their own set of rules. The APCS Exam tests three different Boolean operators. The rules of Boolean operators can be conveniently displayed in a **truth table**. This is a table, which shows the possible combinations of a Boolean statement and indicates the value (**true** or **false**) of each Boolean expression.

In the truth tables that follow, a single letter indicates a single, simple Boolean condition. Such a condition is either **true** or **false**. Boolean statement **A** is true or false. Likewise Boolean statement **B** is true or false. The truth tables will show the results of Boolean statements that use both **A** and **B** with a variety of Boolean operators. Employment requirements will be used to explain the logic of each truth table. In each case, imagine that an accountant needs to be hired. Condition **A** determines if the applicant has a **Degree** and condition **B** determines if the applicant has at least five years of work experience.

Boolean *or* Operator

The or Operator		
A	B	A or B
T	T	T
T	F	T
F	T	T
F	F	F

Notice that two conditions have four possible combinations. It is important that you know the result for each type of combination.

In this case the employment analogy requires a **Degree or Experience**. This requirement is quite relaxed. You only have a Degree, fine. You only have Experience, that's also fine. You have both, definitely fine. You have neither, now that's a problem.

Boolean *and* Operator

The **and** Operator		
A	B	A **and** B
T	T	T
T	F	F
F	T	F
F	F	F

Now employment requires a **Degree and Experience**. This requirement is much more demanding than the **or** operator. You have a Degree, that may be fine, provided you also have Experience. If you have only one qualification, that is not good enough. If you have neither qualification, forget showing up.

Boolean *not*

The **not** Operator	
A	**not** A
T	F
F	T

The **not** operator is quite simple. Any statement is negated. Be careful not to assume that **not** implies **false**. The statement **not** A equals **true** whenever **A** equals **false**. It is the concept of the double negative that is discouraged by teachers. A statement like *I don't know nothing* logically means that the person *knows something*.

Truth Tables

Truth tables provide a convenient way to decide when a Boolean expression is **true**, and if an expression is equivalent to another Boolean expression. The last section introduced simple truth tables to explain the Boolean operators. Now we are going to look at more complex Boolean statements with the help of more complex truth tables. The Boolean statements will not only be more complex, they will also include a larger number of different conditions.

Consider the Boolean expression (A **and** B) **or** B, shown in Truth Table #1

Truth Table #1			
A	B	A **and** B	(A **and** B) **or** B
T	T	T	T
T	F	F	F
F	T	F	T
F	F	F	F

What can be learned from this first truth table? There may be many **T**s and **F**s, but something very significant is demonstrated. The compound Boolean statement of (A **and** B) **or** B has the same truth table as **B**. The value of A is irrelevant. If **B is true** the entire expression is **true**.

The expression (A **and** B) **or** C) is similar to the previous problem, but now a third Boolean operand is introduced. This third operand suddenly changes the truth table considerably. With two operands (A and B) there are four possible combinations to consider. Now that there are three operands (A, B and C), Truth Table #2 will need to consider eight different possibilities.

Truth Table #2				
A	B	C	A **or** B	(A **or** B) **and** C
T	T	T	T	T
T	T	F	T	F
T	F	T	T	T
T	F	F	T	F
F	T	T	T	T
F	T	F	T	F
F	F	T	F	F
F	F	F	F	F

Does Truth Table #2 demonstrate anything interesting? Notice that **C** must be true, otherwise the entire statement cannot be true. Perhaps this makes sense or maybe it seems very bizarre. So what exactly is the point of these truth tables? The point is somewhat obscure. There are Boolean rules that most people would not expect. In fact, a lot of people find some of the rules of Boolean Algebra pretty weird and do not believe them. Boolean Algebra is not very intuitive at the first introduction. Some Boolean Algebra rules seem to contradict well established regular high school Algebra facts. With the use of truth tables these rules can be proven. How? Because the truth tables of **equivalent** Boolean expressions are identical.

Truth Table Fact
The truth tables of **equivalent** Boolean expressions are identical.

Boolean expressions that use the **not** operator often create the most confusion and mistakes in computer science. In Boolean Algebra the **tilde** (~) is used for the **not** operator. Consider the following expression:

$$\sim (A \textbf{ or } B)$$

For reasons unknown it may be interesting to remove the parentheses and still maintain a Boolean expression with the same value. Armed with high school Algebra, the clever use of the *distributive property* will create the following:

$$\sim A \textbf{ or } \sim B$$

It may seem quite logical to use the *distributive property* to make the decision that the Boolean expression ~ (A **or** B) is equivalent to ~A **or** ~B. This type of logic is correct in high school **Algebra**. Will this same law also apply to **Boolean Algebra**? In this situation the trusty truth tables come to the rescue. Truth Table #3 creates a table for each one of the expressions and then compares the column values.

Truth Table #3						
A	B	A **or** B	~(A **or** B)	~A	~B	~A **or** ~B
T	T	T	F	F	F	F
T	F	T	F	F	T	T
F	T	T	F	T	F	T
F	F	F	T	T	T	T

Truth Table #3 shows that the *distributive property* logic of regular Algebra does not apply. The truth tables of the two expressions are not equivalent. The final truth tables have been highlighted with arrows. The table {F F F T} is quite different from the table {F T T T}.

The truth table demonstrated that the distributive property does not work with Boolean Algebra. So what does exactly happen the parentheses are removed? Regular Algebra is no help, the truth tables confirmed that. How about considering if the Expression ~ (A **or** B) is equivalent to ~A **and** ~B with Truth Table #4.

Truth Table #4						
A	B	A **or** B	~(A **or** B)	~A	~B	~A **and** ~B
T	T	T	F	F	F	F
T	F	T	F	F	T	F
F	T	T	F	T	F	F
F	F	F	T	T	T	T

Now the two expressions are equivalent. This is entirely too weird, but the facts are staring you straight in the face. Perhaps you can appreciate now why this chapter is needed. Armed with only the rudimentary truth tables of the previous section, you would not simply conclude what was just proven. Lack of this knowledge has negative consequences on your programs and it does not help your AP Examination score much either.

In Truth Table #5 a similar problem is presented. It is a matter of altering the Boolean operands and checking to see if the expression ~ (A **and** B) is equivalent to ~A **or** ~B.

Truth Table #5						
A	B	A **and** B	~(A **and** B)	~A	~B	~A **or** ~B
T	T	T	F	F	F	F
T	F	F	T	F	T	T
F	T	F	T	T	F	T
F	F	F	T	T	T	T

Once again, the expressions are equivalent to each other. You have actually been observing one of the most important laws of Boolean Algebra. There are actually many laws in Boolean Algebra which have names. This review book is not the place to list all these named laws. The APCS Exam will not require that type of detailed knowledge. However, you do need to know *DeMorgan's Law*, which has been demonstrated by the last two truth tables.

Venn Diagrams and Boolean Algebra

Venn diagrams are useful tools for teaching *Set Theory*. With a rectangle to represent the *universal set* and a group of circles, representing individual sets inside the rectangle, it is possible to visually demonstrate many Set Theory concepts. You probably learned about Venn diagrams in one or more mathematics classes. Boolean Algebra would not have been mentioned in any of these classes and you learned terms like *union* and *intersection*. The relationship between Boolean Algebra and Set Theory is very close, and the same visual benefits of Venn diagrams can apply to Boolean Algebra, as well as Set Theory.

Set Intersection behaves like the logical and

The Boolean Algebra logical **and (*)** can be demonstrated with Venn Diagrams, using **intersection**.

Venn Diagram 1 shows the intersection sets A and B. Consider one of the Boolean examples of the past. You have an employment requirement that applicants must have a college degree and they must also have five years of work experience. Now imagine that **Set A** represents people with a college degree, and **Set B** represents people with at least five years of work experience. In this case the shaded section is the result of saying **A and B** in Boolean Algebra or the *intersection* of **Set A** and **Set B** in Set Theory.

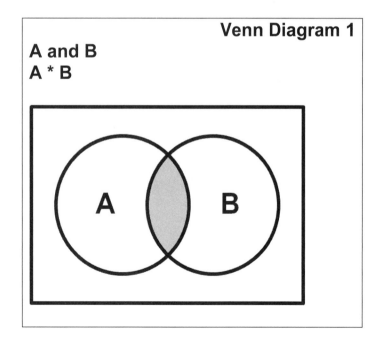

Venn Diagram 1

A and B
A * B

A   B

This time our business will hire people that have either a college degree or at least five years of experience. With the logical **or** there are now many more people qualified to apply for the job. We now can accept everybody in **Set A**, which are the college degree people as well as everybody in **Set B**, which are the experience people. In Boolean Algebra this is stated with the expression **A or B**. In set theory this is called the *union* of **Set A** and **Set B**, which is illustrated with Venn Diagram 2.

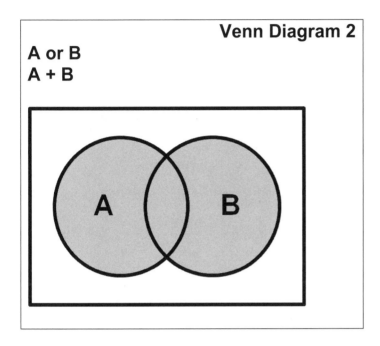

Venn Diagram 2

A or B
A + B

The reason for using Venn diagrams is to help illustrate Boolean Algebra concepts. With small expressions like **A and B** and **A or B** you may not see much need for using Venn diagrams.

However, more complex expressions can be assisted with the help of set theory. Venn diagrams are particularly helpful to demonstrate that two different expressions are equivalent. You have seen truth tables used for proving equivalent expressions. You can now do the same with the aid of Set Theory and Venn diagrams.

Additional Venn diagram examples will be shown. A few examples will be given that come from the laws of Boolean Algebra, but not every law is going to be illustrated with Set Theory.

Venn diagrams 3 and 4 illustrate the **not** operator, which is identical in Boolean Algebra, as well as in Set Theory. Expressions **not(A)** and **not(B)** are shown in the next two diagrams.

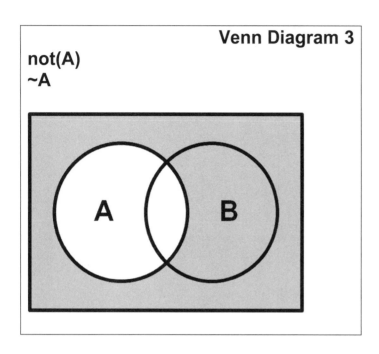

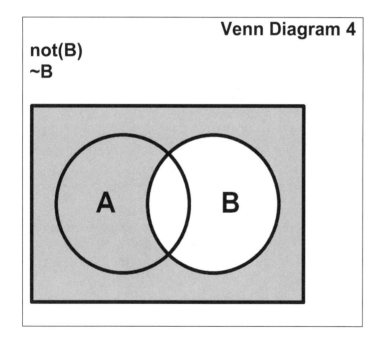

The remaining Venn diagrams will show a variety of compound Boolean expressions. Venn diagram 5 illustrates the negation of the *intersection* of **A** and **B**, which is **not(A and B)** in Boolean Algebra.

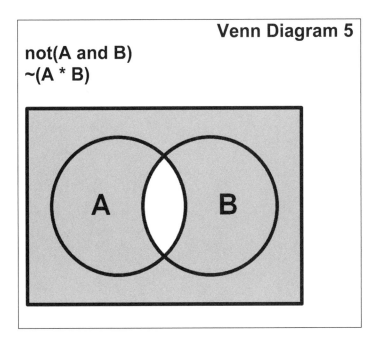

Venn diagram 6 is very similar to the previous example, but this illustrates the negation of the *union* of **Set A** and **Set B**. You can compare diagrams 5 and 6 with the earlier diagrams 1 and 2 to notice the pattern of negation.

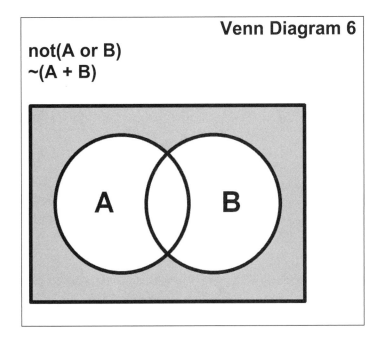

One of the most important Boolean Algebra Laws for computer science is called *DeMorgan's Law*, which was demonstrated earlier with truth tables. This law states that the Boolean expression **not(A or B)** is equivalent to the Boolean expression **not(A) and not(B)**. The correctness of this law was proven earlier with truth tables. DeMorgan's Law can also be illustrated with Venn diagrams. Note that Venn diagram 6 shows **not(A or B)** and Venn diagram 7 shows **not(A) and not(B)**. Most importantly, note that both Venn diagrams 6 and 7 illustrate the exact same result.

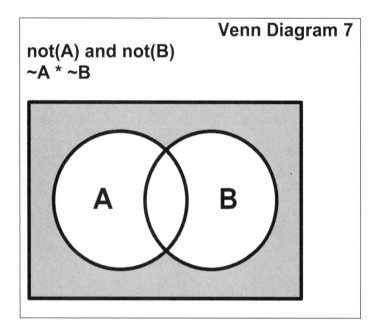

The second part of *DeMorgan's Law* states that Boolean expression **not(A and B)** is equivalent to Boolean expression **not(A) or not(B)**. This law is proven by Venn diagrams 5 and 8.

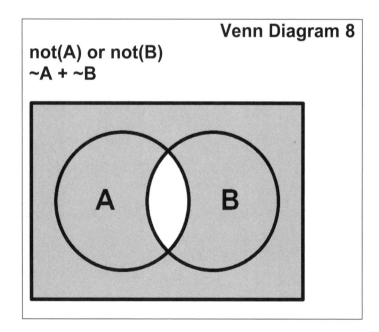

Boolean Algebra Pitfalls

The pitfalls with Boolean Algebra are usually caused by a lack of understanding of the rules of Boolean Algebra. A keen understanding of logic in general will solve many problems and truth tables, while tedious, assist in determining equivalent expressions. Seven Sample Problems follow that show a variety of Boolean Algebra questions with an explanation of their answer.

Sample Problem 1. Answer: (D)

The Boolean expression

    not(A **and** B **and** C)

is equivalent to which of the following expressions?

(A) A != B != C
(B) A **and** B **and** C
(C) A **or** B **or** C
(D) **not** A **or** **not** B **or** **not** C
(E) **not** A **and** **not** B **and** **not** C

Problem #1 checks to see if you can apply *DeMorgan's Law* to an expression with three operands. The same logic and the same rules apply. The Boolean operator is changed from **and** to **or**. The use of three operands does not alter the logic of DeMorgan's Law.

Sample Problem 2. Answer: (A)

The Boolean expression

    (A **and** B) **and** **not**(A **and** B)

evaluates to

(A) false in all cases.
(B) true in all cases.
(C) true whenever only A is true or only B is true.
(D) true whenever both A is true and B is true.
(E) false only when both A is false and B is false.

In problem #2 the Boolean expression **(A and B)** can only be true or false. Using **not** in front of the expression will change true to false or false to true. It is not possible for the Boolean expression **(A and B)** and the Boolean expression **not(A and B)** to have the same value. Two expressions that are always different with an **and** operator will always evaluate to **false**.

Sample Problem 3. Answer: (C)

The Boolean expression

not((A < B) **and** (C > D))

is equivalent to which of the following expressions?

(A) (A < B) **or** (C > D)
(B) (A >= B) **and** (C <= D)
(C) (A >= B) **or** (C <= D)
(D) (A > B) **and** (C < D)
(E) (A > B) **or** (C < D)

Problem #3 requires two steps and it may help to use some substitution. Consider the expression **not(X and Y)**. Removal of the parentheses in that expression, using *DeMorgan's Law*, results in **not X or not Y**. In problem #3 substitute (A < B) with X and (C > D) with Y.

With that substitution the results is **not(A < B) or not (C > D)**. After removal of the **not** operator you simply the expression to **(A >= B) or (C <= D)**.

Sample Problem 4. Answer: (E)

The Boolean expression

(A > B) **or** (A <= B)

can be simplified to which of the following expressions?

(A) A **or** B
(B) A **and** B
(C) A **and not** B
(D) **false**
(E) **true**

It is important to realize that **true** and **false** are Boolean expressions. This means that the Boolean expression **not(A > B)** equals (A <= B). It then follows that **true** or **false** always becomes **true**.

Sample Problem 5. Answer: (B)

The Boolean expression

(A **and** B) **and** (**not** A **or not** B)

evaluates to

(A) true in all cases.
(B) false in all cases.
(C) true only whenever both A is true and B is true.
(D) false only whenever both A is false and B is false.
(E) true only whenever A is true or B is true.

This problem may benefit from using DeMorgan's Law in reverse. The second Boolean expression (**not** A **or not** B) is equivalent to **not**(A **and** B). Now the entire expression with a substitution of x equals (A **and** B) results in (x **and not** x), which is always **false**. Perhaps the "logical" approach to deduce the correct answer is obscure. Anytime a Boolean problem is difficult to determine, truth tables can always be used. Truth table #6, below, handles the same problem and demonstrates in the final column that the expression is always false.

Truth Table #6

A	B	A **and** B	~A	~B	~A **or** ~B	(A **and** B) **and** (~A **or** ~B)
T	T	T	F	F	F	F
T	F	F	F	T	T	F
F	T	F	T	F	T	F
F	F	F	T	T	T	F

Sample Problem 6. Answer: (E)

If **a equals false**, what is the value of the following expression?

a and ((b or c) and (a or c) or (a and b) and (not b and not c))

(A) The expression cannot be evaluated without the values of **b** and **c**.
(B) The expression is **false**, if both **b** and **c** are **false**, and **true** otherwise.
(C) The expression is **true**, if both **b** and **c** are **true**, and **false** otherwise.
(D) **true**
(E) **false**

This problem looks much tougher than it is. The expression looks complex with many Boolean operands and lots of parentheses. The reality is that the very first **a** operand is immediately followed by an **and** operator. Boolean logic dictates that one **false** operand followed by an **and** operator makes the entire expression **false**. It is not necessary to create an involved truth table or logically digest the large expression following the first **and**. With **a** equals to **false**, the entire expression is **false**. This concept is called *short circuiting*.

Sample Problem 7. Answer: (D)

If **a equals true**, what is the value of the following expression?

a or ((b or c) and (a or c) or (a and b) and (not b and not c))

(A)   The expression cannot be evaluated without the values of **b** and **c**.
(B)   The expression is **false**, if both **b** and **c** are **false**, and **true** otherwise.
(C)   The expression is **true**, if both **b** and **c** are **true**, and **false** otherwise.
(D)   **true**
(E)   **false**

This problem is another example of *short circuiting*. Boolean logic dictates that one **true** operand followed by an **or** operator makes the entire expression **true**. Just like the previous problem, it is not necessary to create an involved truth table or logically digest the large expression following the first **or**. With **a** equals to **true**, the entire expression is **true**.

Solving Boolean Logic Programs

There are four ways to solve Boolean Logic problems:

1. Use known Boolean Algebra laws, like DeMorgan's law.

2. Use logical steps, such as shown by the previous problems.

3. Create truth tables to determine the results.

4. Use short circuiting where applicable.

Note: Java uses short circuiting with compound conditions.

Chapter 3 Questions
Boolean Algebra

01. The Boolean expression

    `(A || B) && A`

    is `true`

    (A) in all cases.
    (B) whenever A is `true`.
    (C) whenever B is `true`.
    (C) whenever either A is `true` or B is `true`.
    (E) whenever both A is `true` and B is `true`.

02. The Boolean expression

    `(A && B) || B`

    is `true`

    (A) in all cases.
    (B) whenever A is `true`.
    (C) whenever B is `true`.
    (C) whenever either A is `true` or B is `true`.
    (E) whenever both A is `true` and B is `true`.

03. The Boolean expression

    `(A && B) || (A && B)`

    is `true`

    (A) in all cases.
    (B) whenever A is `true`.
    (C) whenever B is `true`.
    (C) whenever either A is `true` or B is `true`.
    (E) whenever both A is `true` and B is `true`.

04. The Boolean expression

```
(A || B) || A
```

is

(A) `false` whenever A is `true`.
(B) `true` whenever B is `false`.
(C) `true` whenever either A is `true` or B is `true`.
(D) `true` whenever both A is `false` and B is `false`.
(E) never `true`.

05. Which Boolean law is demonstrates by

```
!(A || B) is equivalent to !A && !B
```

(A) Distributive property
(B) Commutative property
(C) DeMorgan's Law
(D) Descartes' Law
(E) Euclid's Law

06. Which Boolean law is demonstrates by

```
!(A && B) is equivalent to !A || !B
```

(A) Distributive property
(B) Commutative property
(C) DeMorgan's Law
(D) Descartes' Law
(E) Euclid's Law

07. The Boolean expression

    `(A || B) || !(A || B)`

    evaluates to

    (A) `false` in all cases.
    (B) `true` whenever only A is `true` or only B is `true`.
    (C) `true` whenever A is `true` or B is `true`.
    (D) `true` whenever both A is `true` and B is `true`.
    (E) `true` in all cases.

08. The Boolean expression

    `!(A || B)`

    evaluates to

    (A) `false` in all cases.
    (B) `true` in all cases.
    (C) `true` whenever only A is `true` or only B is `true`.
    (D) `true` whenever A is `true` or B is `true`.
    (E) `true` whenever both A is `false` and B is `false`.

09. The Boolean expression

    `!((A < B) || ( C > D))`

    is equivalent to which of the following expressions?

    (A) `(A < B) && (C > D)`
    (B) `(A >= B) || (C <= D)`
    (C) `(A > B) && (C < D)`
    (D) `(A > B) || (C < D)`
    (E) `(A >= B) && (C <= D)`

10. The Boolean expression

```
(A || B) && (!A && !B)
```

evaluates to

(A) `false` in all cases.
(B) `true` in all cases.
(C) `true` whenever only A is `true` or only B is `true`.
(D) `true` whenever A is true or B is `true`.
(E) `true` whenever both A is `false` and B is `false`.

11. Consider the following program segment.

```
int p = <some integer greater than zero>
int q = <some integer greater than zero>
while (p != 0 || q != 0)
{
    p--;
    q--;
    niftyMethod();
}
```

For which values of p and q will the loop structure condition short-circuit?

(A) Whenever p does not equal 0
(B) Whenever q does not equal 0
(C) Only whenever both p equals 0 and q equals 0
(D) Only whenever p equals 0 or q equals 0
(E) The structure will never short-circuit.

12. The Boolean expression

```
(A || B) && (!A || !B)
```

evaluates to

(A) `false` in all cases.
(B) `true` in all cases.
(C) `true` whenever only A is `true` or only B is `true`.
(D) `true` whenever A is `true` or B is `true`.
(E) `true` whenever both A is `true` and B is `true`.

Chapter 4 Review
Focus on OOP, Encapsulation

Object Oriented Programming (**OOP**) and Object Oriented Design (**OOD**) exist for the primary purpose of reliability. Programs can look attractive. Programs can execute rapidly. Programs may do many amazing things, but every fancy feature is irrelevant if the program does not perform in a reliable manner. How is this reliability achieved? This is no easy question. A thorough answer can be written in an entire text book, and this is only a brief review prior to a short set of questions. Perhaps the definition of OOP, shown below, tells the story.

> Object Oriented Programming (**OOP**) is
> a style of programming that incorporates
> the three features of **encapsulation**,
> **class interaction** and **polymorphism**.

If you are a stranger to *encapsulation*, *class interaction* and *polymorphism*, then it is time to get some serious help. Hopefully, the APCS Exam is not any time soon. This section concerns itself with *encapsulation*. There will be three additional chapters that will cover *inheritance*, *composition* and *polymorphism*. *Class interaction* is divided into *inheritance* and *composition*.

Encapsulation implies that something is placed inside a capsule or container. In computer science this means that the data and the methods, which process the data, are placed in the same container. Furthermore, only local methods that are in the same container may access the data.

Consider a typical airport. You arrive and check in your luggage for a flight to Rome. The suit cases are placed on a conveyer belt. The next person needs to go to Seattle and his suitcases go on the same conveyer belt. There may easily be 50 to 100 different destinations used by that same check-in counter and all the luggage goes on the same conveyer belt. This is a terrific example of a process that is the opposite of encapsulation. Data - *the passengers and luggage* - are handled by processes that are not dedicated to one mission. The same conveyer belt and the same check-in agent handle many totally different missions.

Now imagine an airport build with OOP features, such as *encapsulation*. You arrive and find an entrance for Rome. You enter a corridor without intersections. Other passengers for different destinations can be seen through glass walls but cannot be reached. You arrive at a check-in counter. The agent and the conveyer belt are exclusively used for passengers flying to Rome. The conveyer belt has a single purpose and all its luggage goes to the Rome gate. You continue and after security you arrive at a single gate with a plane waiting to fly you to Rome. This is encapsulation. You have arrived at a `Plane` class and and entered the `Rome` object where all the `Rome` methods are dedicated to getting the data - *passengers and luggage* - to Rome.

Object Oriented Programming Feature Encapsulation

Encapsulation places the data, called *attributes*, and the processes, called *methods*, which access the attributes, in the same container.

Encapsulation, when isolated away from inheritance and composition does not provide many complications. The 9th edition intentionally wants a strong focus on Object Oriented Programming and that starts with questions that isolate encapsulation problems.

Class interaction follows encapsulation in understanding Object Oriented Programming. It is great to design a class in such a manner that all the data and all the methods that access the data are contained in one class. It is also great that the data is protected from unwanted access and this is provided by declaring class attributes as `private`.

Now consider the following: if you have done a fine job with encapsulation and you have done this fine job to perhaps five or more classes then these classes exist in isolation. A class by itself has very limited capabilities. It is precisely the interaction with other classes, with either inheritance or composition or both, that makes a program functional.

In other words, in this first *Focus on OOP* chapter, the complete encapsulation story is not finished. It is hardly started. In the second focus chapter inheritance is added and then it really becomes a situation of combining encapsulation with inheritance. The third OOP unit adds composition in the mix and now three OOP features are combined. Finally, in the fourth OOP unit, Polymorphism rounds out the main OOP features and utilizes the functionality of the prior three Object Oriented topics.

OOP, Encapsulation Pitfalls

The program in **Example 4.1** compiles and it also executes. In this simple program there appears to be no problem. The reality is that the intention of encapsulation is severely violated. The attribute `numWidgets` is accessed twice by another class. The value of `numWidgets` is altered and then the value of `numWidgets` is displayed.

This is precisely what occurred in the days prior to Object Oriented Programming. Data could be accessed by pretty much any program segment from anywhere. This style of programming resulted in very serious *side-effects*. No bank allows a customer, regardless of bank balance, to step behind the teller counter and remove cash from the teller drawer. Even a very honest customer can unintentionally take too much or too little money.

Example 4.1

```
public class Example41
{
    public static void main(String args[])
    {
        Widget widget = new Widget(10);
        widget.numWidgets = 25;
        System.out.println("Widget Count: " + widget.numWidgets);

    }
}

class Widget
{
    int numWidgets;

    public Widget(int n)
    {
        numWidgets = n;
    }
}
```

Encapsulation Warning

The intention of *encapsulation* is to allow data access only by local methods, which should be designed to prevent improper data manipulation.

The problem shown in **Example 4.1** is solved by declaring the `numWidgets` attribute `private`. **Example 4.2** shows the improved `Widget` class. Reserved word `private` is now used to declare the `numWidgets` attribute. Any attempt to access the private attribute from outside the `Widget` class will generate a compile error.

Example 4.2

```
class Widget
{
    private int numWidgets;

    public Widget(int n)
    {
        numWidgets = n;
    }
}
```

In **Example 4.3** a subtle mistake is shown. The program compiles without problems. The program also executes, but the output displays a `Widget` count of `0`. What is happening? The arrow shows the problem statement. The constructor parameter, `numWidgets`, has the same identifier as the attribute being initialized. Java treats both `numWidgets` variables in the `Widget` constructor as the same local variable. The result is that `numWidgets`, which already was storing a default value of `0`, is now assigned to itself. It will still store a default `0`, not the `10` we wanted.

Example 4.3

```
public class Example43
{
    public static void main(String args[])
    {
        Widget widget = new Widget(10);
        System.out.println("Widget Count: " + widget.getWidgets());
    }
}

class Widget
{
    private int numWidgets;

    public Widget(int numWidgets)
    {
        numWidgets = numWidgets;    ⟵
    }

    public int getWidgets()
    {
        return numWidgets;
    }
}
```

Example 4.4 and **Example 4.5** each show a solution to this problem.

Example 4.4

```
public Widget(int n)
{
    numWidgets = n;   <-----
}
```

Example 4.5

```
public Widget(int numWidgets)
{
    this.numWidgets = numWidgets;   <-----
}
```

APCS Examination Alert

There are examples when attributes are **public**, like **PI** and **E** of the **Math** class. This is not commonly done, and when it is done such public attributes are declared **final**.

There are also examples when methods are **private**. Such methods are called *helper methods* and are meant only to be used by other local methods. One example might be a **public** sort method, which calls a local, **private** swap method.

When students write free response solutions on the
AP Computer Science Examination, they should declare
all attributes **private** and all methods **public**.

Chapter 4 Questions
Focus on OOP, Encapsulation

01. Consider the following code segment and class.

```
Student kathy = new Student();
System.out.println(kathy.getAge());

class Student
{
    private int age;
    public int getAge()   { return age; }
}
```

What is printed as a result of executing the code segment?

(A) a random number in the int range
(B) a memory reference value
(C) 0
(D) a compile error message
(E) an Exception error message

02. Consider the following code segment and class.

```
Student kathy = new Student(10);
System.out.println(kathy.getAge());

class Student
{
    private int age;
    public Student(int a)    { age = a; }
    public int getAge()      { return age; }
}
```

What is printed as a result of executing the code segment?

(A) 10
(B) a memory reference value
(C) 0
(D) a compile error message
(E) an Exception error message

03. Consider the following code segment and class.

```
Student kathy = new Student(10);
System.out.println(kathy.getAge());

class Student
{
    private int age;
    public Student(int age)   { age = age; }
    public int getAge()       { return age; }
}
```

What is printed as a result of executing the code segment?

(A) 10
(B) a memory reference value
(C) 0
(D) a compile error message
(E) an Exception error message

04. Consider the following code segment and class.

```
Student kathy = new Student(10);
System.out.println(kathy.getAge());

class Student
{
    private int age;
    public Student(int age)   { this.age = age; }
    public int getAge()       { return age; }
}
```

What is printed as a result of executing the code segment?

(A) 10
(B) a memory reference value
(C) 0
(D) a compile error message
(E) an Exception error message

05. Consider the following code segment and class.

```
Student kathy = new Student(10);
System.out.println(kathy.getAge());

class Student
{
    private int age;

    public Student(int age)
    {
        this.age = age;
    }

    public int getAge()
    {
        int age;
        return age;
    }
}
```

What is printed as a result of executing the code segment?

(A) 10
(B) a memory reference value
(C) 0
(D) a compile error message
(E) an Exception error message

06. Consider the following code segment and class.

```
Student kathy = new Student();
System.out.println(kathy.age);

class Student
{
    int age;

    public Student()
    {
        age = 10;
    }
}
```

What is wrong with this program?

(A) It does not compile, because age cannot be accessed directly.
(B) The intent of encapsulation is violated, because age can be accessed directly.
(C) The constructor has no parameter.
(D) There is no value assigned to the age instance variable.
(E) There is nothing wrong with the program.

07. Consider the following code segment and class.

```
Bank tom = new Bank(500.0);
tom.makeDeposit(300.0);
tom.makeDeposit(175.0);
tom.makeWithdrawal(1000.0);
tom.makeDeposit(100.0);
System.out.println(tom.getBalance());


class Bank
{
    private double balance;

    public Bank(double amount)
    {
        balance = amount;
    }

    public double getBalance()
    {
        return balance;
    }

    public void makeDeposit(double amount)
    {
        balance += amount;
    }

    public void makeWithdrawal(double amount)
    {
        if (amount > balance)
            balance -= 35.0;
        else
            balance -= amount;
    }
}
```

What is printed as a result of executing the code segment?

(A) 40.0
(B) 75.0
(C) 1040.0
(D) -40.0
(E) -75.0

08. Consider the following code segment and class.

```
Bank tom = new Bank(500.0);
Bank sue = new Bank(500.0);
sue.makeDeposit(225.0);
tom.makeWithdrawal(100.0);
System.out.println(tom.getBalance() + "    " + sue.getBalance());


class Bank
{
    private double balance;

    public Bank(double amount)
    {
        this.balance = amount;
    }

    public double getBalance()
    {
        return this.balance;
    }

    public void makeDeposit(double amount)
    {
        this.balance += amount;
    }

    public void makeWithdrawal(double amount)
    {
        this.balance -= amount;
    }
}
```

What is printed as a result of executing the code segment?

(A) 625.0   625.0
(B) 400.0   725.0
(C) 725.0   400.0
(D) 400.0   400.0
(E) 725.0   725.0

09. Consider the following code segment and class.

```
Bank tom = new Bank(500.0);
Bank sue = tom;
sue.makeDeposit(225.0);
tom.makeWithdrawal(100.0);
System.out.println(tom.getBalance() + "   " + sue.getBalance());


class Bank
{
    private double balance;

    public Bank(double amount)
    {
        balance = amount;
    }

    public double getBalance()
    {
        return balance;
    }

    public void makeDeposit(double amount)
    {
        balance += amount;
    }

    public void makeWithdrawal(double amount)
    {
        balance -= amount;
    }
}
```

What is printed as a result of executing the code segment?

(A) 625.0   625.0
(B) 400.0   725.0
(C) 725.0   400.0
(D) 400.0   400.0
(E) 725.0   725.0

10. Consider the following code segment and class.

```
Bank tom = new Bank(500.0);
Bank sue = new Bank(tom);
sue.makeDeposit(225.0);
tom.makeWithdrawal(100.0);
System.out.println(tom.getBalance() + "    " + sue.getBalance());


class Bank
{
    private double balance;

    public Bank(double amount)
    {
        balance = amount;
    }

    public Bank(Bank obj)
    {
        balance = obj.balance;
    }

    public double getBalance()
    {
        return balance;
    }

    public void makeDeposit(double amount)
    {
        balance += amount;
    }

    public void makeWithdrawal(double amount)
    {
        balance -= amount;
    }
}
```

What is printed as a result of executing the code segment?

(A) 625.0   625.0
(B) 400.0   725.0
(C) 725.0   400.0
(D) 400.0   400.0
(E) 725.0   725.0

11. Consider the following code segment and class.

```
Game game = new Game();
game.play();
System.out.println(game.getScore());


class Game
{
    private int score;

    public void play()
    {
        score = (int) (Math.random() * 10000);
    }

    public int getScore()
    {
        return score;
    }
}
```

What is printed by the code segment?

(A) 0
(B) a compile error message
(C) an `IllegalCastingException` error message
(D) an integer value x, such that $0 <= x < 10000$
(E) an integer value x, such that $0 < x <= 10000$

12. Consider the following code segment and class.

```
Game game1 = new Game(5);
game1.play();
System.out.println(game1.getScore());
Game game2 = new Game();
game2.play();
System.out.println(game2.getScore());


class Game
{
    private int score;
    private int level;

    public Game(int lev)
    {
        score = 0;
        level = lev;
    }

    public void play()
    {
        score = (int) (Math.random() * 10000);
        score = score / level;
    }

    public int getScore()
    {
        return score;
    }
}
```

What is printed as a result of executing the code segment?

(A) 0
(B) a compile error message
(C) an `IllegalCastingException` error message
(D) an integer value x, such that $0 <= x < 10000$
(E) an integer value x, such that $0 < x <= 10000$

Chapter 5 Review
Focus on OOP, Inheritance

Object Oriented Programming exists for the primary purpose of reliability. This was stated in the last chapter and it will become a common refrain. One of the most important aspects of Object Oriented Design is the use of proper class interaction. Classes interact with two OOP features, called *inheritance* and *composition*. Inheritance uses an **is-a** class relationship. A Student **is-a** Person and a Car **is-a** Vehicle. Composition uses a **has-a** relationship. A Car **has-an** Engine and a School **has-a** Principal. Right now we will focus on inheritance.

Inheritance helps tremendously with reliability. Consider some practical class, called `Dance`, which has been thoroughly tested. The bugs are cleaned up and the class performs as expected. You wish to create a new type-of-dance class, which is more specialized, called `Tango`. It is certainly possible to create a brand-new class, but then your new class needs to be tested from scratch. You have the `Dance` class ready to go and by making your `Tango` class a subclass of the `Dance` class, many established methods are available. You only create the new features.

Consider that you want to build camper vans. It is certainly possible to start from scratch and build the entire vehicle. You can also save lots of time by starting with a van that has proven quality. Now that you have obtained this excellent van, you put in special seats, a small bathroom and kitchen and create special fold-out beds. With surprising little effort you have a high quality camper van, without all the effort to start with all the basic details of van building.

Object Oriented Programming Feature Inheritance

Inheritance allows new classes, called subclasses, to use the attributes and methods of established classes, called superclasses.

Reliability is increased when programs are created with proven classes. Suppose that a new class is needed that includes 15 methods. It may well be that 12 methods already exist in a class that is ready to go. Use that class, do not touch it and benefit from the tested program code that was created in the past. In other words *do not re-invent the wheel*. When you make a new class, the only business is to **re-define** existing methods and **newly-define** methods that do not yet exist. Inheritance is not just a matter of greater reliability, it also saves programming time.

Composition will be handled later, but like inheritance it increases reliability by using one or more existing classes. This should help to explain the sequence. You start with a single class and insure proper data access using correct encapsulation. Test the new class thoroughly and you can then combine it in a program with other classes using inheritance.

Inheritance Pitfalls

The Java syntax required for inheritance class interaction is not complicated. With the class heading **public class Student extends Person** Java now understands that a new class is created, called `Student` that will be a subclass of the superclass `Person`. In other words, the new `Student` class will use the available features that exist in the `Person` class and then proceed to create new methods that are unique to the `Student` class.

You must be careful. Inheritance can be tricky when the time comes to pass information from a subclass constructor to a superclass constructor. Java is very picky and demands a strict approach. The program in **Example 5.1** looks innocent enough. There is a superclass, called `Morf`, and there is a subclass, called `Dorf`. A `Dorf` object is constructed with parameter **25**. This program will not compile. The problem is that all inheritance cases start by calling the constructor of the superclass, followed by the constructor of the subclass. This mistake is easily made, because the `main` method is only concerned with an object of the `Dorf` class. Parameter information is provided for the constructor of `Dorf`. The `Morf` constructor receives no value and complains loudly with compile error messages.

Example 5.1

```
public class Example51
{
    public static void main(String args[])
    {
        Dorf dorf = new Dorf(25);
        System.out.println("Dorf Count: " + dorf.getDorfs());
    }
}

class Morf
{
    private int numMorfs;
    public Morf(int m) { numMorfs = m; }
}

class Dorf extends Morf
{
    private int numDorfs;
    public Dorf(int d)     { numDorfs = d; }
    public int getDorfs() { return numDorfs; }
}
```

Inheritance requires considering the needs of the superclass as well as the subclass. When an object of the subclass, `Dorf` in this case, is constructed, information must be passed for all the classes that are used. You must remember that the superclass is involved whether you actually use the superclass name or not.

Consider the example of making a camper van. A camper van **is-a** van. The van is used for conversion to a camper van. The client who wants a camper van will have requests about the camper features. At the same time there must be information provided for the initial van. Is the engine a V-8 or a V-6? Is all-wheel drive required and what about the color? Surely you can think of many other requirements.

In Java, this is handled with the keyword **super**, which is placed at the start of the subclass constructor. The parameter in the **super** call is used to construct the superclass object. In **Example 5.2** you will see the correct way to provide information for both classes.

Example 5.2

```
public class Example52
{
    public static void main(String args[])
    {
        Dorf dorf = new Dorf(10,25);
        System.out.println("Morf Count: " + dorf.getMorfs());
        System.out.println("Dorf Count: " + dorf.getDorfs());


    }
}

class Morf
{
    private int numMorfs;

    public Morf(int m)
    {
        numMorfs = m;
    }

    public int getMorfs()
    {
        return numMorfs;
    }
}

class Dorf extends Morf
{
    private int numDorfs;

    public Dorf(int m, int d)
    {
        super(m);
        numDorfs = d;
    }

    public int getDorfs()
    {
        return numDorfs;
    }
}
```

Chapter 5 Questions
Focus on OOP, Inheritance

01. Consider the following code segment and two classes.

```
Mambo m = new Mambo();
Rumba r = new Rumba();


class Rumba
{
    public Rumba()
    {
        System.out.println("Executing the Rumba constructor");
    }
}

class Mambo
{
    public Mambo()
    {
        System.out.println("Executing the Mambo constructor");
    }
}
```

What is the relationship between class Rumba and class Mambo?

(A) inheritance only
(B) composition only
(C) both inheritance and composition
(D) polymorphism
(E) There is no class relationship between Rumba and Mambo.

02. Consider the following code segment and two classes.

```
Mambo m = new Mambo();
Rumba r = new Rumba();


class Rumba
{
    public Rumba()
    {
        System.out.println("Executing the Rumba constructor");
    }
}

class Mambo extends Rumba
{
    public Mambo()
    {
        /* missing code */
    }
}
```

The program output is expected to display the following:

```
Executing the Rumba constructor
Executing the Mambo constructor
Executing the Rumba constructor
```

Which of the following can be used to replace the /* **missing code** */
in constructor Mambo so that the desired output is achieved?

I.   ```
     Rumba.super();
     System.out.println("Executing the Mambo constructor");
     ```

II.  ```
     System.out.println("Executing the Mambo constructor");
     ```

III. ```
     super();
     System.out.println("Executing the Mambo constructor");
     ```

(A) I only
(B) II only
(C) III only
(D) I and II
(E) II and III
     ```

Questions 03-08 refer to the following `CircusPerformer` class declaration.

```
class CircusPerformer
{
    private String performerName;
    private String actName;

    public CircusPerformer(String pN, String aN)
    {
        performerName = pN;
        actName = aN;
    }

    public String getPerformer()
    {
        return performerName;
    }

    public String getAct()
    {
        return actName;
    }

    public void act()
    {
        entrance();
        performance();
        exit();
    }

    public void entrance()
    {
        System.out.println("Starts in ring center");
    }

    public void performance()
    {
        System.out.println("Runs in circles");
    }

    public void exit()
    {
        System.out.println("Exits from ring center");
    }
}
```

03. Consider the following code segment and incomplete `Equestrian` class.

```
Equestrian sue = new Equestrian("Sue","Amazing Ponies");
sue.act();

class Equestrian extends CircusPerformer
{
}
```

An `Equestrian` object is a `CircusPerformer` who rides ponies over obstacles.
Which of the following methods must be defined in the `Equestrian` class?

I.   `CircusPerformer` constructor
II.   `act`
III. `entrance`
IV. `performance`
V.   `exit`

(A) I only
(B) II only
(C) III, IV and V
(D) I and II
(E) I and IV

04. An `Equestrian` is a `CircusPerformer` who rides ponies over obstacles.
Consider the following incomplete `Equestrian` constructor.

```
public Equestrian(String pN, String aN)
{
    /* missing code */
}
```

Which of the following implementations can be used to replace /* **missing code** */ in constructor
`Equestrian` so that the `CircusPerformer` instance variables are properly initialized?

I.   `super();`
    `performerName = pN;`
    `actName = aN;`

II. `super(pN,aN);`

III. `super(performerName,actName);`

(A) I only
(B) II only
(C) III only
(D) I and II only
(E) I and III only

05. Consider the following code segment and class.

A `TightRopeWalker` is a `CircusPerformer` who walks and flips on a tight rope.

```
TightRopeWalker joe = new TightRopeWalker("Joe","Feats of Daring");
joe.act();


class TightRopeWalker extends CircusPerformer
{
    public void entrance()
    {
        System.out.println("Starts from tight rope platform");
    }

    public void performance()
    {
        System.out.println("Walks and flips on the tight rope");
    }

    public void exit()
    {
        System.out.println("Exits from tight rope platform");
    }
}
```

What is printed as a result of executing the code segment?

(A) ```
    Starts from tight rope platform
    Walks and flips on the tight rope
    Exits from tight rope platform
    ```

(B) ```
    Starts in ring center
    Walks and flips on the tight rope
    Exits from ring center
    ```

(C) ```
    Walks and flips on the tight rope
    ```

(D) Compile error message indicating that there is a problem with the constructor

(E) Compile error message indicating that there is a problem with the `act` method
    ```

06. Consider the following code segment and class.

A `TightRopeWalker` is a `CircusPerformer` who walks and flips on a tight rope.

```
TightRopeWalker joe = new TightRopeWalker("Joe","Feats of Daring");
joe.act();
```

```
class TightRopeWalker extends CircusPerformer
{
    public TightRopeWalker(String pN, String aN)
    {
        super(pN,aN);
    }

    public void entrance()
    {
        System.out.println("Starts from tight rope platform");
    }

    public void performance()
    {
        System.out.println("Walks and flips on the tight rope");
    }

    public void exit()
    {
        System.out.println("Exits from tight rope platform");
    }
}
```

What is printed as a result of executing the code segment?

(A) Starts from tight rope platform
    Walks and flips on the tight rope
    Exits from tight rope platform

(B) Starts in ring center
    Walks and flips on the tight rope
    Exits from ring center

(C) Walks and flips on the tight rope

(D) Compile error message indicating that there is a problem with the constructor

(E) Compile error message indicating that there is a problem with the `act` method

07. Consider the following code segment and class.

A `HighWireJuggler` is a `TightRopeWalker` who juggles as he walks and flips on a tight rope.

```
HighWireJuggler kathy = new HighWireJuggler("Kathy","High Wire Juggling");
kathy.act();

class TightRopeWalker extends CircusPerformer
{
    public TightRopeWalker(String pN, String aN)
    {
        super(pN,aN);
    }

    public void entrance()
    {
        System.out.println("Starts from tight rope platform");
    }

    public void performance()
    {
        System.out.println("Walks and flips on the tight rope");
    }

    public void exit()
    {
        System.out.println("Exits from tight rope platform");
    }
}

class HighWireJuggler extends TightRopeWalker
{
    public HighWireJuggler(String pN, String aN)
    {
        super(pN,aN);
    }
}
```

What is printed as a result of executing the code segment?

(A) ```
    Starts from tight rope platform
    Walks and flips on the tight rope
    Exits from tight rope platform
    ```

(B) ```
    Starts in ring center
    Walks and flips on the tight rope
    Exits from ring center
    ```

(C) ```
    Starts from tight rope platform
    Juggles while walking and flipping on the rope
    Exits from tight rope platform
    ```

(D) Compile error message indicating that there is a problem with the constructor

(E) Compile error message indicating that there is a problem with the act method.
    ```

08. Consider the following code segment and class.

A `HighWireJuggler` is a `TightRopeWalker` who juggles as he walks and flips on a tight rope.

```
HighWireJuggler kathy = new HighWireJuggler("Kathy","High Wire Juggling");
kathy.act();

class TightRopeWalker extends CircusPerformer
{
    public TightRopeWalker(String pN, String aN)   {   super(pN,aN);   }

    public void entrance()
    {
        System.out.println("Starts from tight rope platform");
    }
    public void performance()
    {
        System.out.println("Walks and flips on the tight rope");
    }
    public void exit()
    {
        System.out.println("Exits from tight rope platform");
    }
}

class HighWireJuggler extends TightRopeWalker
{
    public HighWireJuggler(String pN, String aN)
    {
        super(pN,aN);
    }
    public void performance()
    {
        System.out.println("Jugggles while walking and flipping a tight rope");
    }
}
```

What is printed as a result of executing the program?

(A) Starts from tight rope platform
    Walks and flips on the tight rope
    Exits from tight rope platform

(B) Starts in ring center
    Walks and flips on the tight rope
    Exits from ring center

(C) Starts from tight rope platform
    Juggles while walking and flipping on the rope
    Exits from tight rope platform

(D) Compile error message indicating that there is a problem with the constructor

(E) Compile error message indicating that there is a problem with the act method.

09. Consider the following code segment and two classes.

```
Aardvark andy = new Aardvark();
System.out.println(andy.getAnimalType());

class Animal
{
    private String animalType;

    public Animal()
    {
        animalType = "Unknown";
    }

    public String getAnimalType()
    {
        return animalType;
    }
}

class Aardvark extends Animal
{

}
```

Which of the following are true statements about the Aardvark class?

I.   Aardvark is a superclass of Animal.
II. Aardvark will have the exact same features and behaviors as the Animal class.
III. Aardvark objects have no access to any methods since the class declaration is empty.

(A) I only
(B) II only
(C) III only
(D) I and II
(E) I and III

10. Consider the following code segment and two classes.

```
Student tom = new Student(12);
Person sue = new Person();
tom.showData();

class Person
{
    public int age;

    public Person()
    {
        System.out.println("Person Constructor");
        age = 17;
    }

    public int getAge()        { return age; }
}

class Student extends Person
{
    public int grade;

    public Student(int g)
    {
        grade = g;
        System.out.println("Student Constructor");
    }

    public int getGrade()      { return grade; }

    public void showData()
    {
        System.out.println("Student's Grade is " + grade);
        System.out.println("Student's Age is " + age);
    }
}
```

What are the first 2 lines of output?

(A) Person Constructor
    Student Constructor

(B) Student Constructor
    Person Constructor

(C) Person Constructor
    Person Constructor

(D) Student Constructor
    Student Constructor

(E) No Output.
    This program does not compile.

11. Consider the following code segment and two classes.

```
Student tom = new Student(12);
Person sue = new Person();
tom.showData();

class Person
{
    public int age;

    public Person()
    {
        System.out.println("Person Constructor");
        age = 17;
    }

    public int getAge()        { return age; }
}

class Student extends Person
{
    public int grade;

    public Student(int g)
    {
        grade = g;
        System.out.println("Student Constructor");
    }

    public int getGrade()     { return grade; }

    public void showData()
    {
        System.out.println("Student's Grade is " + grade);
        System.out.println("Student's Age is " + age);
    }
}
```

What are the last 2 lines of output?

(A) `Student's Grade is 12`
    `Student's Age is 17`

(B) `Student's Age is 12`
    `Student's Grade is 17`

(C) `Student's Age is 17`
    `Student's Grade is 12`

(D) `Student Constructor`
    `Student's Age is 17`

(E) `Student Constructor`
    `Student's Grade is 12`

12. Consider the following code segment and two classes.

```
Person sue = new Person(32);
Student tom = new Student(12,25);
sue.showData();
tom.showData();

class Person
{
    private int age;

    public Person(int a)
    {
        System.out.println("Person Constructor");
        age = a;
    }

    public int getAge()
    {
        return age;
    }

    public void showData()
    {
        System.out.println("Student's Age is " + age);
    }
}
```

```
class Student extends Person
{
    private int grade;

    public Student(int g, int a)
    {
        super(a);
        grade = g;
        System.out.println("Student Constructor");
    }

    public int getGrade()
    {
        return grade;
    }

    public void showData()
    {
        super.showData();
        System.out.println("Student's Grade is " + grade);
    }
}
```

What are the last 2 lines of output?

(A) Student's Age is 32
    Student's Age is 25

(B) Student's Age is 25
    Student's Age is 32

(C) Student's Grade is 12
    Student's Age is 25

(D) Student's Age is 25
    Student's Grade is 12

(E) No Output.
    This program does not compile.

Chapter 6 Review
Static One-Dimensional Arrays

Java has two types of arrays. First, there is the static array, which is the traditional array using index brackets and no methods. Static arrays, as the name implies, cannot be resized during program execution. Second, there is the `ArrayList` class, which is a dynamic array with many methods for data access and processing. This array can be resized during program execution.

At first view, it may seem strange to include an older, and supposedly not-very-useful-anymore, array implementation. The static array cannot be resized. The static array does not offer the OOP type access with methods. Why do we even bother to keep such an array? There are several reasons why the static array is still being used. The most important reason is that static arrays allow creating multi-dimension array objects very easily. Objects of the newer `ArrayList` class can be used with multiple dimensions, but it is more complicated. Static arrays also can store primitive data types. `ArrayList` can only store objects. Finally, static arrays provide very convenient initializer lists. Additional details about the `ArrayList` class will be handled in a separate chapter.

APCS Examination Alert

Both **static** Java arrays and dynamic **ArrayList** arrays are tested on the APCS Exam.

The statements in **Example 6.1** demonstrate the declarations of three types of one-dimensional arrays. It also shows how to use three initializer lists during the declarations. It is not necessary to provide the size of the array with initializer lists. The number of elements in the lists indicates the size of the array object. Java accepts two styles of static array declarations. The two segments in **Example 6.1** are identical and demonstrate the two declaration styles.

Example 6.1

```
int list1[] = {11,22,33,44,55};
char list2[] = {'A','B','C','D','E'};
String list3[] = {"AAA","BBB","CCC","DDD","EEE"};
```

```
int[] list1 = {11,22,33,44,55};
char[] list2 = {'A','B','C','D','E'};
String[] list3  = {"AAA","BBB","CCC","DDD","EEE"};
```

The program in **Example 6.2** declares a one-dimensional array with 20 `int` elements. The `list` elements are displayed by a loop that uses the `length` field of static arrays. Make sure not to use `length()`. `length` is a field, when used with static arrays, and not a method.

Example 6.2

```
public class Example62
{
    public static void main(String args[])
    {
        int[] list = new int[20];
        for (int k = 0; k < 20; k++)
            list[k] = (int) (Math.random() * 900 + 100);

        for (int k = 0; k < list.length; k++)
            System.out.println(list[k]);
    }
}
```

The program in **Example 6.3** declares the same `list` array as **Example 6.2**. This time note that the enhanced `for` loop, introduced with Java 5.0, is used. The new `for` loop is a clean, concise control structure that can be used with many data structures.

Example 6.3

```
public class Example63
{
    public static void main(String args[])
    {
        int[] list = new int[20];
        for (int k = 0; k < 20; k++)
            list[k] = (int) (Math.random() * 900 + 100);

        for (int number: list)
            System.out.println(number);
    }
}
```

APCS Examination Alert

Expect the **"for..each"** loop structure, introduced with Java 5.0, to be used frequently in the APCS Exam.

Static Java Array Pitfalls

Java static arrays are quite straight forward and there are few subtle features that cause problems. The primary concern is using an index that is outside the index range. Each array has `length` array elements, but the largest index of the array is `length-1`. The program in **Example 6.4** compiles without difficulties, but generates an `ArrayIndexOutOfBoundsException` error message during program execution.

Example 6.4

```
public class Example64
{
    public static void main(String args[])
    {
        int[] list = new int[10];
        for (int k = 0; k < 10; k++)
            list[k] = (int) (Math.random() * 900 + 100);

        for (int k = 0; k <= list.length; k++)
            System.out.print(list[k] +"  ");
    }
}
```

Program Output

```
209  403  369  604  783  252  779  290  569  163  Exception in
thread "main" java.lang.ArrayIndexOutOfBoundsException:
10 at Example57.main(Example57.java:10)
```

Java Static Arrays Alert

An array declared in the following manner:

```
int[] list = new int[max]
```

has **max** elements, but the index range is **[0..max-1]**.

Any attempt to access an index outside the proper range will result in an **ArrayIndexOutOfBoundsException** error during program execution.

Chapter 6 Questions
Static One-Dimensional Arrays

01. Consider the following method.

```
/** Precondition: n >= 2
 */
public static int method0601(int n)
{
    int[] temp = new int[n];
    temp[0] = 4;
    temp[1] = 7;
    for (int k = 2; k < n; k++)
        temp[k] = temp[k-1] + temp[k-2];
    return temp[n];
}
```

What value is returned by the call `method0601(8)`?

(A) 47
(B) 76
(C) 123
(D) 199
(E) No value is returned due to an `ArrayIndexOutOfBoundsException` error

02. Consider the following method.

```
/** Precondition: list is a non-empty array.
 */
public static void method0602(int[] list)
{
    int max = list.length-1;
    for (int k = 0; k < max; k++)
        if (list[k] < list[k+1])
        {
            int temp = list[k];
            list[k] = list[k+1];
            list[k+1] = temp;
        }
}
```

Which of the following correctly decribes the result of calling method `method0602`?

(A) The smallest number is located in `list[max]`.
(B) The smallest number is located in `list[max-1]`.
(C) The largest number is located in `list[max]`.
(D) The largest number is located in `list[max-1]`.
(E) The elements in the `list` array are reversed.

03. Consider the following incomplete `getMean` method.

```
/**
 *  Precondition:  list is a non-empty array.
 *  Postcondition: getMean returns the mean of the list array values.
 */
public static double getMean(int[] list)
{
    /* missing code */
}
```

Which of the following implementations of /* **missing code** */ will make method `getMean` work as intended?

Implementation I
```
double temp = 0.0;
for (int k = 0; k < list.length; k++)
    temp += list[k];
return (temp / list.length);
```

Implementation II
```
int temp = 0;
for (int k = 0; k < list.length; k++)
    temp += list[k];
return (temp / list.length);
```

Implementation III
```
int temp = 0;
for (int k = 0; k < list.length; k++)
    temp += list[k];
return ((double) temp / list.length);
```

(A) I only
(B) II only
(C) III only
(D) I and II
(E) I and III

04. Consider the following method.

```java
/** Precondition: list is a non-empty array.
 */
public static void method0604(int[] list)
{
    for (int p = 0; p < list.length; p++)
    {
        int max = list.length - 1;
        int temp = list[p];
        list[p] = list[max-p];
        list[max-p] = temp;
    }
}
```

Which of the following correctly decribes the result of calling method0604?

(A) The elements in the list array are in random order.
(B) The list array is sorted in descending order.
(C) The list array is sorted in ascending order.
(D) The elements in the list array are in reverse order.
(E) The elements in the list array appear unchanged.

05. Consider the following method.

```java
/** Precondition: list is a non-empty array.
 */
public static void method0605(int[] list)
{
    for (int p = 0; p < list.length/2; p++)
    {
        int max = list.length - 1;
        int temp = list[p];
        list[p] = list[max-p];
        list[max-p] = temp;
    }
}
```

Which of the following correctly describes the result of calling method0605?

(A) The elements in the list array are in random order.
(B) The list array is sorted in descending order.
(C) The list array is sorted in ascending order.
(D) The elements in the list array are in reverse order.
(E) The elements in the list array appear unchanged.

06. Consider the following code segment.

```
int[] list = {5,10,15,20,25,20,15,10,5};
int max = list.length-1;
for (int k = max; k > 0; k--)
    list[k] = list[k] / list[max];
for (int k = 0; k < list.length; k++)
    System.out.print(list[k] + "   ");
```

What will be printed as a result of executing the code segment?

(A) 5   10   15   20   25   1   10   15   20
(B) 1   2   3   4   5   4   3   2   1
(C) 5   10   15   20   25   20   15   10   1
(D) 1   1   1   1   1   1   1   1   1
(E) 5   5   5   5   5   5   5   5   5

07. Consider the following code segment.

```
int[] list = {2,4,8,16,32,64,128,256};
for (int k = 1; k < list.length ; k++)
    list[k] = list[k] / list[k-1];
for (int k = 0; k < list.length; k++)
    System.out.print(list[k] + "   ");
```

What will be printed as a result of executing the code segment?

(A) 1   1   1   1   1   1   1   1
(B) 2   4   8   16   32   64   128   256
(C) 1   2   4   8   16   32   64   128
(D) 2   2   2   2   2   2   2   2
(E) 2   2   4   4   8   8   16   16

08. Consider the following code segment.

```
int[] list1 = {2,4,8,16,32,64,128,256};
int[] list2 = list1;
int max = list1.length - 1;
for (int k = 0; k < list1.length ; k++)
    list2[k] = list1[max-k];
for (int k = 0; k < list1.length; k++)
    System.out.print(list1[k] + "   ");
```

What will be printed as a result of executing the code segment?

(A) 256   128   64   32   32   64   128   256
(B) 256   128   64   32   16   8   4   2
(C) 256   256   256   256   256   256   256   256
(D) 2   2   2   2   2   2   2   2
(E) 4   8   16   32   64   128   256   512

09. Consider the following code segment and method.

```
int[] list = {56,23,78,54,11,95,60,17,64};
list = mystery(list);
for (int item: list)
    System.out.print(item + "   ");

/** Precondition: x is a non-empty array.
 */
public static int[] mystery(int[] x)
{
    int[] temp = new int[x.length];
    int q = temp.length - 1;
    for (int p = 0; p < x.length; p++)
    {
        temp[q] = x[p];
        q--;
    }
    return temp;
}
```

What will be printed as a result of executing the code segment?

(A) 56   23   78   54   11   95   60   17   64
(B) 11   17   23   54   56   60   64   78   95
(C) 95   78   64   60   56   54   23   17   11
(D) 64   17   60   95   11   54   78   23   56
(E) An ArrayIndexOutOfBoundsException error message

10. Consider the following code segment.

```
int[] list = {56,23,78,54,11,95,60,17,64};
for (int item: list)
{
    item = 99;
    System.out.print(item + "  ");
}
```

What will be printed as a result of executing the code segment?

(A) 56 23 78 54 11 95 60 17 64
(B) 64 17 60 95 11 54 78 23 56
(C) 99 23 78 54 11 95 60 17 64
(D) 56 23 78 54 11 95 60 17 99
(E) 99 99 99 99 99 99 99 99 99

11. Consider the following code segment.

```
int[] list = {56,23,78,54,11,95,60,17,64};
for (int item: list)
    item = 99;
for (int item: list)
    System.out.print(item + "  ");
```

What will be printed as a result of executing the code segment?

(A) 56 23 78 54 11 95 60 17 64
(B) 64 17 60 95 11 54 78 23 56
(C) 99 23 78 54 11 95 60 17 64
(D) 56 23 78 54 11 95 60 17 99
(E) 99 99 99 99 99 99 99 99 99

12. Consider the following code segment and method.

```
int[] list1 = {56,23,78,54,11,95,60,17,64};
int[] list2 = {32,44,87,11,90,56};
swap(list1,list2);
for (int item1: list1)
    System.out.print(item1 + "  ");
System.out.println();
for (int item2: list2)
    System.out.print(item2 + "  ");

public static void swap(int[] l1, int[] l2)
{
    int[] l3 = l1;
    l1 = l2;
    l2 = l3;
}
```

What will be printed as a result of executing the code segment?

(A) 56 23 78 54 11 95 60 17 64
    32 44 87 11 90 56

(B) 32 44 87 11 90 56
    56 23 78 54 11 95 60 17 64

(C) 56 23 78 54 11 95 60 17 64
    56 23 78 54 11 95 60 17 64

(D) 32 44 87 11 90 56
    32 44 87 11 90 56

(E) An `ArrayIndexOutOfBoundsException` error message

Chapter 7 Review
Static Two-Dimensional Arrays

Chapter 7 continues the *static array* topic started in chapter 6. The code segment in **Example 7.1** demonstrates how to declare a two-dimensional array using an initializer list. It is not required that the initializer list is written in a two-dimensional matrix format. However, this is the common convention and it adds readability to a program.

Example 7.1

```
private int matrix[][] = { {1,2,3},
                           {4,5,6},
                           {7,8,9}}
```

The program in **Example 7.2** declares a two-dimensional array of 7 rows and 5 columns. It also shows how to use the `length` field with a two-dimensional array. With two dimensions, `length` indicates the number of rows in an array. A two-dimensional array is, in fact, *an array of arrays*. This means that each row in the `matrix` array is a one-dimensional array. Accessing the size of the array in a row is done with `matrix[0].length`.

Example 7.2

```
public class Example72
{
    public static void main(String args[])
    {
        int k = 1;
        int matrix[][] = new int[7][5];
        for (int r = 0; r < matrix.length; r++)
            for (int c = 0; c < matrix[0].length; c++)
            {
                matrix[r][c] = k;
                k++;
            }

        for (int r = 0; r < matrix.length; r++)
        {
            for (int c = 0; c < matrix[0].length; c++)
                System.out.print(matrix[r][c]) + "  ");
            System.out.println();
        }
    }
}
```

Consider the following statement:

```
int matrix[][] = new int[5][4];
```

The value of **matrix.length** is 5, which is the number of rows.

The value of **matrix[0].length** is 4, which is the number of columns

A Java static two-dimensional array can be created a piece at a time. It is possible to first declare only the number of the rows and later declare the length of each individual row. In the case of **Example 7.3**, each row has a different length. This type of array is not rectangular, as the output shows. This is called a *ragged array*.

Example 7.3

```
public class Example73
{
    public static void main(String args[])
    {
        int x[][] = new int[5][];
        x[0] = new int[1];
        x[1] = new int[2];
        x[2] = new int[3];
        x[3] = new int[4];
        x[4] = new int[5];

        for (int r = 0; r < x.length; r++)
        {
            for (int c = 0; c < x[r].length; c++)
                System.out.print(x[r][c] + "  ");
            System.out.println();
        }
    }
}
```

```
                         Program Output
0
0  0
0  0  0
0  0  0  0
0  0  0  0  0
```

The warning stated in the previous chapter is repeated here. Index issues are the biggest problem when working with arrays. Each array has `length` array elements, but the largest index of the array is `length-1`. The program in **Example 7.4** compiles without difficulties, but generates an `ArrayIndexOutOfBoundsException` error during program execution.

Example 7.4

```
public class Example57
{
    public static void main(String args[])
    {
        int list[] = new int[10];
        for (int k = 0; k < 10; k++)
            list[k] = (int) (Math.random() * 900 + 100);

        for (int k = 0; k <= list.length; k++)
            System.out.print(list[k] +"  ");
    }
}
```

Program Output

```
209  403  369  604  783  252  779  290  569  163  Exception in
thread "main" java.lang.ArrayIndexOutOfBoundsException:
10 at Example57.main(Example57.java:10)
```

Java Static 2D Arrays Alert

A 2D array declared in the following manner:

```
int[][] list = new int[maxr][maxc]
```

has **maxr** rows and **maxc** columns and **maxr * maxc** total elements, but the index range is **[0,0..maxr-1,maxc-1]**.

Any attempt to access an index outside the proper range will result in an **ArrayIndexOutOfBoundsException** error during program execution.

Chapter 7 Questions
Static Two-Dimensional Arrays

01. Consider the following code segment.

```
int row = 4;
int col = 5;
double[][] matrix = new double[row][col];
System.out.println(matrix.length);
System.out.println(matrix[0].length);
System.out.println(matrix[row].length);
System.out.println(matrix[col].length);
```

Which of the following statements stores the number of rows in `matrix`?

(A) `matrix.length`
(B) `matrix.rowLength`
(C) `matrix[row].length`
(D) `matrix[col].length`
(E) `matrix[0].length`

02. Consider the following code segment.

```
int row = 4;
int col = 5;
double[][] matrix = new double[row][col];
System.out.println(matrix.length);
System.out.println(matrix[0].length);
System.out.println(matrix[row].length);
System.out.println(matrix[col].length);
```

Which of the following statements stores the column length of `matrix`?

(A) `matrix.length`
(B) `matrix.rowLength`
(C) `matrix[row].length`
(D) `matrix[col].length`
(E) `matrix[0].length`

03. Consider the following incomplete `convertTo1D` method.

```
/** Precondition:  m is a non-empty two-dimensional array of int values.
 *  Postcondition: convertTo1D returns a one-dimensional array,
 *                 which stores the values of m.
 */
public static int[] convertTo1D(int[][] m)
{
    int size = m.length * m[0].length;
    int[] temp = new int[size];

    /* missing code */

    return temp;
}
```

Which of the following implementations of /* **missing code** */ will make method `convertTo1D` work as intended?

Implementation I	Implementation II

`int index = 0;`
`for (int row = 0; row < m.length; row++)`
`    for (int col = 0; col < m[0].length; col++)`
`    {`
`        temp[index] = m[row][col];`
`        index++;`
`    }`
	`int row = 0;`
	`int col = 0;`
	`for (int index = 0; index < size; index++)`
	`{`
	`    temp[index] = m[row][col];`
	`    col++;`
	`    if (col > m[0].length-1)`
	`    {`
	`        row++;`
	`        col = 0;`
	`    }`
	`}`

Implementation III
 	
`int index = 0;`
`int row = 0;`
`while (row < m.length)`
`{`
`    int col = 0;`
`    while (col < m[0].length)`
`    {`
`        temp[index] = m[row][col];`
`        index++;`
`        col++;`
`    }`
`    row++;`
`}`
	(A) Implementation I only
	(B) Implementation II only
	(C) Implementations I and II only
	(D) Implementations I and III only
	(E) Implementations I, II and III

04. Consider the following code segment and method.

```java
int[] list = {1,2,3,4,5,6,7,8,9,1,2,3};
int rowSize = 3;
int colSize = 5;
int[][] matrix = convertTo2D(list,rowSize,colSize);
for (int row = 0; row < matrix.length; row++)
{
    for (int col = 0; col < matrix[0].length; col++)
        System.out.print(matrix[row][col] + "  ");
    System.out.println();
}

public static int[][] convertTo2D(int[] x, int rowSize, int colSize)
{
    int[][] temp = new int[rowSize][colSize];
    int index = 0;
    int row = 0;
    int col = 0;
    while (index <= x.length-1)
    {
        temp[row][col] = x[index];
        index++;
        col++;
        if (col > colSize-1)
        {
            row++;
            col = 0;
        }
    }
    return temp;
}
```

What is printed as a result of executing the code segment?

(A) 1 2 3 4 5 6 7 8 9 1 2 3 0 0 0

(B) 1 2 3 4 5
     6 7 8 9 1
     2 3 0 0 0

(C) 1 2 3 4 5
     6 7 8 9 1
     2 3

(D) 1 2 3 4 5
     6 7 8 9 1

(E) An ArrayIndexOutOfBoundsException error message

05. Consider the following code segment.

```
int[][] matrix = {{11,22,33},{44,55,66},{77,88,99}};
int n = matrix.length;
for (int row = 1; row < n; row++)
    matrix[row][0] = matrix[row-1][0];
```

Which of the following describes the values stored in matrix after the code segment executes?

(A) All the values in the top row are zero.
(B) All the values in the entire matrix are zero.
(C) All the values in the entire matrix are the same.
(D) All the values in the left column are the same.
(E) All the values in the entire matrix are the same.

06. Consider the following code segment.

```
int[][] matrix = {{11,22,33},{44,55,66},{77,88,99}};

for (int row = 1; row < 3; row++)
    for (int col = 0; col < 3; col++)
        matrix[row][col] = matrix[row-1][col];
```

Which of the following describes which values, stored in matrix, are left unchanged after the code segment executes?

(A) All the values in the matrix are the same.
(B) All the values in the matrix are changed.
(C) Every row in the matrix is the same.
(D) Every column in the matrix is the same.
(E) Both diagonals in the matrix are the same.

07. Consider the following code segment.

```
int[][] matrix = {{11,22,33},
                  {44,55,66},
                  {77,88,99}};
```

Display I
```
for (int row = 0; row < 3; row++)
{
    for (int col = 0; col < 3; col++)
        System.out.print(matrix[row][col] + "   ");
    System.out.println();
}
System.out.println("\n\n");
```

Display II
```
for (int[] row: matrix)
{
    for (int number: row)
        System.out.print(number + "   ");
    System.out.println();
}
System.out.println("\n\n");
```

Display III
```
System.out.println(matrix);
```

There are three output displays of the matrix object.
The intention of the output code is to display a square matrix like

```
11   22   33
44   55   66
77   88   99
```

Which of the three **Display** segments prints the matrix correctly?

(A) Display I only
(B) Display II only
(C) Display III only
(D) Display I and II only
(E) Display I, II and III

08. Consider the following method.

```
/** Postcondition: m is displayed in a rectangular matrix like:
 *                          1  2  3  4
 *                          5  6  7  8
 */
public static void displayMatrix(int[][] m)
{
    for (int r = 0; r < m.length; r++)
    {
        for (int c = 0; c < m.length; c++)
            System.out.print(m[r][c] + "  ");
        System.out.println();
    }
}
```

Will method displayMatrix satisfy its postcondition?

(A) No, all the numbers will display in one row.
(B) No, all the numbers will display in one column.
(C) Yes, all the numbers will display in a correct rectangular display.
(D) Yes, but only if the row-size and col-size are identical.
(E) No, because the code will generate an IndexArrayOutOfBoundsException error.

09. Consider the following code segment.

```
int[] list = {1,2,3,4,5,6};
int n = list.length/2;
int[][] matrix = new int[n][n];
int r = 0;
int c = 0;
for (int index = 0; index < list.length; index++)
{
    if (r < n)
    {
        if (c < n)
        {
            matrix[r][c] = list[index];
            c++;
        }
        r++;
        c = 0;
    }
}
```

What values are stored in matrix after the code segment executes?

(A)			(B)			(C)			(D)			(E)		
1	0	0	1	2	3	1	4	0	0	0	0	1	2	3
2	0	0	4	5	6	2	5	0	1	2	3	0	0	0
3	0	0	0	0	0	3	6	0	4	5	6	0	0	0

10. Consider the following code segment.

```
int[] list = {1,2,3,4,5,6};
int n = list.length/2;
int[][] matrix = new int[n][n-1];
int count = 0;
for (int p = 0; p < n; p++)
    for (int q = 0; q < n-1; q++)
    {
        matrix[p][q] = list[count];
        count++;
    }
```

What values are stored in matrix after the code segment executes?

(A) 1 2 3
     4 5 6

(B) 1 2
     3 4
     5 6

(C) 1 3 5
     2 4 6

(D) 1 4
     2 5
     3 6

(E) The program will have an ArrayIndexOutOfBoundsException error message.

11. Consider the following code segment.

```
int[][] matrix = new int[3][4];
int[][] matrix = {{1,1,1,1},{2,2,2,2},{3,3,3,3}};

for (int[] row: matrix)
{
    for (int number: row)
        System.out.print(number + "  ");
    System.out.println();
}
```

What is printed as a result of executing the code segment?

(A) A compile error message

(B) An `ArrayOutOfBoundsException` error message

(C) 1 1 1 1 2 2 2 2 3 3 3 3

(D) 1, 1, 1, 1, 2, 2, 2, 2, 3, 3, 3, 3

(E) 1 1 1 1
   2 2 2 2
   3 3 3 3

12. Consider the following code segment.

```
int[][] matrix = {{1,1,1,1},{2,2,2,2},{3,3,3,3}};

for (int[] row: matrix)
{
    for (int number: row)
        System.out.print(number + "  ");
    System.out.println();
}
```

What is printed as a result of executing the code segment?

(A) A compile error message

(B) An `ArrayIndexOutOfBoundsException` error message

(C) 1 1 1 1 2 2 2 2 3 3 3 3

(D) 1, 1, 1, 1, 2, 2, 2, 2, 3, 3, 3, 3

(E) 1 1 1 1
   2 2 2 2
   3 3 3 3

Chapter 8 Review
String Methods

Java uses the `String` class and the `StringBuffer` class to manipulate strings of characters. Only the `String` class and its methods will be tested on the APCS Exam. String processing is important in many areas of data processing. Word processing programs are the most common applications that utilize string manipulation features.

APCS Examination Alert

There are two string manipulation classes in Java, which are the `String` class and the `StringBuffer` class.

Only the `String` class is tested on the APCS Exam.

The primary challenge with the Java `String` class is to know the available methods and understand the required parameters for correct string processing. The program in **Example 8.1** starts with a demonstration of the **length()** method. It is easy to get confused here. The Java static array has a **length** field, the dynamic `ArrayList` has a `size` method and the `String` class has a `length` method. **Example 8.1** also shows that the plus (+) operator performs *concatenation* with `String` objects.

Example 8.1

```
public class Example81
{
    public static void main (String args[])
    {
        String s1 = "Argentine";
        String s2 = "Tango";
        String s3 = s1 + " " + s2;
        System.out.println("s1 length: " + s1.length());
        System.out.println("s2 length: " + s2.length());
        System.out.println("s3 length: " + s3.length());
        System.out.println();
    }
}
```

```
                         Program Output
s1 length:  9
s2 length:  5
s3 length:  15
```

String Class Method length

The `String` class uses the `length()` method to return the number of characters in a `String` object.

Note that the Java static array uses a `length` field, the Java `String` class uses a `length()` method and the `ArrayList` class uses a `size()` method.

The `String` class has two `substring` methods. The more common version is shown in program **Example 8.2**, which uses two parameters. The first parameter is the index of the first character of the returned substring. The second parameter is the upper boundary of the substring. It is not the last character of the substring, but the next character. Look at the program output and check the substrings, which are returned with each iteration through the loop.

Example 8.2

```
public class Example82
{
    public static void main (String args[])
    {
        String str = "Racecar";
        int n = str.length();
        for  (int k = 1; k <= n; k++)
            System.out.println(str.substring(0,k));
        System.out.println();
        for (int k = 0; k <= n-3; k++)
            System.out.println(str.substring(k,k+3));
    }
}
```

```
                          Program Output
R
Ra
Rac
Race
Racec
Raceca
Racecar

Rac
ace
cec
eca
car
```

The `substring` method is overloaded. There also is a version with a single parameter. This single parameter is the starting index of the substring. There is no information required for the end index, since this method always goes from start-index to the end of the `String` object. The program in **Example 8.3** has a loop starting at `0` and ending at `n-1`. The result is a substring, which starts as the entire string and ends as a single character.

Example 8.3

```
public class Example83
{
    public static void main (String args[])
    {
        String str = "ABCDEFGH";
        int n = str.length();
        for  (int k = 0; k < n; k++)
            System.out.println(str.substring(k));
    }
}
```

Program Output
ABCDEFGH
BCDEFGH
CDEFGH
DEFGH
EFGH
FGH
GH
H

String Class substring Methods

The `substring` method is overloaded.

`String substring(int a, int b)`
    returns a substring starting at index `a` and ending at index `b-1`

`String substring(int a)`
    returns a substring starting at index `a` and ending
    at index `length()-1`

The next `String` method to be considered is `indexOf`, which is a practical method to find the first occurrence of one string as a substring in a second string. The program in **Example 8.4** demonstrates how the index value is returned if a substring is found and how −1 is returned if the substring does not exist.

Example 8.4

```
public class Example84
{
    public static void main (String args[])
    {
        String s1 = "racecar";
        String s2 = "car";
        String s3 = "qwerty";
        int index1 = s1.indexOf(s2);
        int index2 = s1.indexOf(s3);
        System.out.println(s2 + " starts at " + index1 + " in " + s1);
        System.out.println(s3 + " starts at " + index2 + " in " + s1);

    }
}
```

Program Output

```
car starts at 4 in racecar
qwerty starts at -1 in racecar
```

String Class Method indexOf

```
int indexOf(String str)
```
returns the index of the first occurrence of `str`.
returns −1 if `str` is not found.

The last `String` method to be considered is `compareTo`, which compares two strings alphabetically. The program in **Example 8.5** makes four comparisons. Characters have code values, such as *A has value 65, B has value 66, C has value 67*, etc. When **"Aardvark"** is compared to **"Zebra"** the difference between the string code values is 25. It matters which string is the parameter. Note that the same strings are compared twice. If the parameter string has the larger value, a negative number is returned. If the strings are, the same 0 is returned and if the parameter has a smaller value, a positive number is returned.

Example 8.5

```
public class Example85
{
    public static void main (String[] args)
    {
        String s1 = "AARDVARK";
        String s2 = "ZEBRA";
        String s3 = "AARDVARK";
        String s4 = "BART";

        int value1 = s1.compareTo(s2);
        int value2 = s1.compareTo(s3);
        int value3 = s2.compareTo(s1);
        int value4 = s1.compareTo(s4);

        System.out.println("value1:   " +  value1);
        System.out.println("value2:   " +  value2);
        System.out.println("value3:   " +  value3);
        System.out.println("value4:   " +  value4);
        System.out.println();
    }
}
```

Program Output

```
value1:  -25
value2:  0
value3:  25
value4:  -1
```

String compareTo method

int distance = s1.compareTo(s2);

Method **compareTo** returns **0** if **s1** equals **s2**, otherwise an integer is returned based on the difference between **s1** and **s2**.

If the returned value is negative, it means that **s1** goes <u>before</u> **s2**.
If the returned value is positive, it means that **s1** goes <u>after</u> **s2**.

String Class Pitfalls

A common `String` pitfall was addressed earlier in this chapter. It is very easy to use the `substring` method - with two parameters - incorrectly. Students frequently think that a method call statement like...

$$str.substring(a,b)$$

...will return a substring that starts at index `a` and ends at index `b`. Remember that the second parameter is a boundary. This means that a substring is returned that starts at index `a` and ends at index `b-1`.

`String` objects do have a subtle problem that can cause logic errors. Consider the program in **Example 8.6**. `String` objects `s1` and `s2` are compared for equality. The program output states that the objects are not equal. This seems counter to what many students might expect with two objects, both storing `Foxtrot`, staring them in the face.

Example 8.6

```
public class Example86
{
    public static void main (String args[])
    {
        String s1 = new String("Foxtrot");
        String s2 = new String("Foxtrot");

        if (s1 == s2)
        System.out.println(s1 + " equals " + s2);
        else
            System.out.println(s1 + " does not equal " + s2);
    }
}
```

Program Output
`Foxtrot does not equal Foxtrot`

The problem is that s1 and s2 are objects of a class and not variables of a primitive type, like int. Only variables of primitive types can be compared using the == operator. What happens in **Example 8.6** is that the immediate (shallow) value of s1 is a memory reference and the same is true of s2. Both objects are instantiated with a different memory reference. It is true that the values at the memory reference, Foxtrot and Foxtrot, are identical. The comparison made with the == operator does not check the deeper values.

The program in **Example 8.7** solves the comparison problem. Equality can be tested with String objects, but it must be done with the equals method, which is re-defined from the Object class, for the String class.

Example 8.7

```
public class Example86
{
    public static void main (String args[])
    {
        String s1 = new String("Foxtrot");
        String s2 = new String("Foxtrot");

        if (s1.equals(s2))
            System.out.println(s1 + " equals " + s2);
        else
            System.out.println(s1 + " does not equal " + s2);
    }
}
```

Program Output

```
Foxtrot equals Foxtrot
```

String objects equality

The == operator can only be used with primitive data types like **int**, **double**, **char** and **boolean**.

The **equals** method is required with **String** objects when testing equality using the program statement like:

if (s1.equals(s2))

Chapter 8 Questions
String Methods

01. Consider the following code segment.

```
String s1 = "Computer Science";
String s2 = "Computer";
String s3 = "Science";
System.out.print(s1.indexOf(s2));
System.out.print("   ");
System.out.println(s1.indexOf(s3));
```

What will be output when the code segment executes?

(A) 0   8
(B) 0   9
(C) 1   7
(D) 1   8
(E) 1   9

02. Consider the following code segment.

```
String s1 = "Queen Mary";
String s2 = "1936 Queen Mary";
String s3 = "Queen Elizabeth";
System.out.print(s2.indexOf(s1) + "   ");
System.out.println(s3.indexOf(s1));
```

What will be output when the code segment executes?

(A) 5   5
(B) 6   0
(C) 5   0
(D) 6   -1
(E) 5   -1

03. Consider the following code segment.

```
String s1 = "Djakarta";
String s2 = s1.substring(3,7);
String s3 = s1.substring(3);
System.out.println(s2);
System.out.println(s3);
```

What will be output when the code segment executes?

(A) kart
    karta

(B) jakarta
    akarta

(C) karta
    karta

(D) kart
    karta

(E) akart
    akarta

04. Consider the following code segment.

```
String s1 = "MADAM";
String s2 = "";
for (int k = 1; k <= s1.length(); k++)
{
    s2 += s1.substring(0,k);
    s2 += " ";
}
System.out.println(s2);
```

What will be output when the code segment executes?

(A) MADAM
(B) M A D A M
(C) M MA MAD MADA MADAM
(D) MA MAD MADAM MADAM
(E) An StringOutOfBoundsException error message

05. Consider the following code segment.

```
String s1 = "MADAM";
String s2 = "";
for (int k = 0; k < s1.length(); k++)
{
    s2 += s1.substring(k);
    s2 += " ";
}
System.out.println(s2);
```

What will be output when the code segment executes?

(A) M A D A M
(B) MAD ADA DAM
(C) ADAM ADAM DAM AM M
(D) MADAM ADAM DAM AM M
(E) An `StringOutOfBoundsException` error message

06. Consider the following method.

```
/** Precondition: s != null
 */
public static String method06(String s)
{
    String t = "";
    for (int k = s.length()-1; k >= 0; k--)
        t += s.substring(k,k+1);
    return t;
}
```

What string value is returned by the call `method06("A NUT FOR A JAR OF TUNA")` ?

(A) TUNA OF JAR A FOR NUT A
(B) A NUT FOR A JAR OF TUNA ANUT FO RAJ A ROF TUN A
(C) A NUT FOR A JAR OF TUNA
(D) ANUTFORAJAROFTUNA
(E) ANUT FO RAJ A ROF TUN A

07. Consider the following method.

```
/** Precondition: s != null
 */
public static String method07(String s)
{
    String temp = "";
    for (int k = s.length()-1; k >= 0; k--)
        temp = s.substring(k);
    return temp;
}
```

What string value is returned by the call `method07("A NUT FOR A JAR OF TUNA")` ?

(A) `TUNA OF JAR A FOR NUT A`
(B) `A NUT FOR A JAR OF TUNA ANUT FO RAJ A ROF TUN A`
(C) `A NUT FOR A JAR OF TUNA`
(D) `ANUTFORAJAROFTUNA`
(E) `ANUT FO RAJ A ROF TUN A`

08. Consider the following method.

```
/** Precondition: s is a non-empty string.
 */
public static boolean method08(String s)
{
    boolean temp = true;
    int k = 1;
    int n = s.length();
    while (temp && k < n)
    {
        String s1 = s.substring(k-1,k);
        System.out.print(s1 + "   ");
        String s2 = s.substring(n-k,n-k+1);
        System.out.println(s2);
        if (!s1.equals(s2))
            temp = false;
        k++;
    }
    return temp;
}
```

For which values of s does method `method08` returns `true` ?

(A) Any string with only lower-case letters
(B) Any string with only upper-case letters
(C) For all string values of `s`
(D) For no string values of `s`
(E) For all string values of `s` that are "palindromes" (a string that reads the same backwards)

09. Consider the following two methods.

```
/** Precondition: s != null
 *                n < s.length()
 */
public static String method09a(int n, String s)
{
    return s.substring(n);
}


/** Precondition: s != null
 *                n < s.length
 */
public static String method09b(int n, String s)
{
    return s.substring(n,s.length());
}
```

For which values of s is the same value returned by both methods?

(A) Whenever s is a string with one character
(B) For all string values of s
(C) Whenever s has an odd number of characters
(D) For no string values of s
(E) For all string values of s that are "palindromes" (a string that reads the same backwards)

10. Consider the following code segment.

```
String s1 = "A";
String s2 = "H";
System.out.print(s1.compareTo("B"));
System.out.print("   ");
System.out.println(s2.compareTo("B"));
```

What is printed as a result of executing the code segment?

(A) 1   6
(B) 6   1
(C) -1   6
(D) 6   -1
(E) -1   -6

11. Consider the following code segment and method.

```
String s1 = new String("AARD");
String s2 = new String("AARDVARK");
String s3 = new String("ZULU");
System.out.println(method11(s1,s2));
System.out.println(method11(s2,s2));
System.out.println(method11(s3,s2));


/** Precondition: s1 != null and s2 != null
 */
public static String method11(String s1, String s2)
{
    String message = "";
    int n = s1.compareTo(s2);
    if (n < 0)
        message = s1 + " is less than " + s2;
    else if (n == 0)
        message = s1 + " is equal to " + s2;
    else
        message = s1 + " is greater than " + s2;
    return message;
}
```

What is printed as a result of executing the code segment?

(A) AARD is less than AARDVARK
    AARDVARK is less than AARDVARK
    ZULU is greater than TIGER

(B) AARD is less than AARDVARK
    AARDVARK is equal to AARDVARK
    ZULU is greater AARDVARK

(C) AARD is greater than AARDVARK
    AARDVARK is greater to AARDVARK
    ZULU is less than AARDVARK

(D) AARDVARK is equal to AARDVARK
    ZULU is greater than AARDVARK
    AARD is less than AARDVARK
    ZULU is less than TIGER

(E) StringIndexOutOfBoundsException error message

12. Consider Java's two overloaded `substring` methods.

```
String substring(int from, int to)
String substring(int from)
```

Given a string s, when returns `s.substring(p,q)` the same `String` value as `s.substring(p)` ?

(A) Anytime, as long as `p >= 0`
(B) Anytime, as long as `q == s.length()`
(C) Only, whenever `p == 0` and `s.length == 1`
(D) Only, whenever `p == 0`
(E) Only whenever every character in s is the same, like `"QQQQQQQQ"`

Chapter 9 Review
Dynamic Arrays with the ArrayList Class

Java static arrays were shown in Chapters 06 and 07. Static arrays cannot be resized during program execution, and there are no methods available to manipulate static array objects. On the other hand, the biggest reason for using static arrays is the multi-dimension capability. The `ArrayList` class in this chapter handles arrays of one dimension easily. Multiple dimensions are harder with the `ArrayList` class.

The square index brackets used by static arrays for array element access will be replaced with parentheses that contain parameters for various methods. `ArrayList` objects can be resized during program execution. Resizing may increase or decrease the number of elements.

The program in **Example 9.1** uses the `add` method to add additional members to the `list` object. It also shows the `size` method. Unfortunately, you now have a third keyword for handling data size. Static arrays use a `length` field. `String` objects use a `length` method. `ArrayList` objects use a `size` method.

Data Structure Size Alert

Java static arrays use the **length** field.

The **String** class uses the **length()** method.

The **ArrayList** class uses the **size()** method.

Example 9.1

```
public class Example91
{
    public static void main(String args[])
    {
        ArrayList names = new ArrayList();
        names.add("Isolde");
        names.add("John");
        names.add("Greg");
        System.out.println(names);
        System.out.println("There are " + names.size() + " names.");
    }
}
```

| Program Output |
```
[Isolde, John, Greg]
There are 3 names.
```

The add method is overloaded. With a single parameter, the new array element is added to the end of the ArrayList object. It is also possible to add a new element at a specified index location. The program, in **Example 9.2** adds a fourth name at index 1. The former element at index 1, Sue in this case, is moved up one index value.

Example 9.2

```
public class Example92
{
    public static void main(String args[])
    {
        ArrayList names = new ArrayList();
        names.add("Bob");
        names.add("Sue");
        names.add("Tom");
        System.out.println(names);
        names.add(1,"Meg");
        System.out.println(names);
    }
}
```

Program Output

```
[Bob, Sue, Tom]
[Bob, Meg, Sue, Tom]
```

ArrayList Class Methods add and size

int size()
> returns the number of elements in an **ArrayList** object

boolean add(E obj)
> adds object to the end of the **ArrayList** object
> **E** is the class of the Elements in the **ArrayList** object

boolean add(int index, E obj)
> replaces the element at position **index** with **obj**
> all elements with starting position index are shifted one index higher
> index value outside the index range generates an OutOfBounds error

ArrayList Class Pitfalls

The methods of the `ArrayList` class are not difficult to use, but there are a variety of problems that must be recognized. For starters the `ArrayList` shares the `IndexOutOfBoundsException` runtime error with the static array. Static or dynamic ... it does not matter ... you can only use index values of actual array elements. This error can occur with any method that accesses any array element by index number. The `ArrayList` class has several methods that access element by index values. The `get` method, which returns the object at the specified location, is one of the methods that is vulnerable to out-of-bounds errors.

Example 9.3 demonstrates how to use the `get` method. In this example the program will not compile, as the output cell indicates. The goal is to copy the elements of one array into another array. The `get` method returns an object when a `String` is needed. This is a problem of the Java versions prior to the release of Java 5.0. It is also a problem when you fail to specify the element class that will be stored in the `ArrayList` object.

Example 9.3

```
public class Example93
{
    public static void main(String args[])
    {
        ArrayList names1 = new ArrayList();
        ArrayList names2 = new ArrayList();
        names1.add("Bob");
        names1.add("Sue");
        names1.add("Tom");
        for (int k = 0; k < names1.size(); k++)
        {
            String temp = names1.get(k);
            names2.add(temp);
        }
    }
}
```

```
                          Program Output

C:\ExpoJava2012\ExpoJavaA08152012\ChapterProgsA2012\Progs20\Example93.java:21:
incompatible types
found   : java.lang.Object
required: java.lang.String
          String temp = names1.get(k);
                                  ^
```

Java programs prior to the release of Java 5.0 handled the problem of **Example 9.3** by casting the class, `(String)` in this case, to prevent Java confusion. We now have a simpler approach. The `ArrayList` class is one of the *generic* classes and the type to be used can be specified when an `ArrayList` object is declared. The new approach is shown in **Example 9.4**. The next program example also shows how to use the newer (since Java 5.0) `for..each` loop with an `ArrayList` object.

Example 9.4

```
public class Example94
{
    public static void main(String args[])
    {
        ArrayList<String> names1 = new ArrayList<String>();
        ArrayList<String> names2 = new ArrayList<String>();
        names1.add("Bob");
        names1.add("Sue");
        names1.add("Tom");
        for (int k = 0; k < names1.size(); k++)
        {
            String temp = names1.get(k);
            names2.add(temp);
        }
        for (String name: names2)
            System.out.println(name);
    }
}
```

Program Output

```
Bob
Sue
Tom
```

APCS Examination Alert

Generics is tested on APCS Exam.

You can expect multiple choice questions and free response questions that assume a knowledge of generic classes.

Generic classes eliminate the need for *class casting*, but *wrapper classes* are still used since *autoboxing* is not be part of APCS Exam.

ArrayList Class Method get

E get(int index)
    returns the element at position index
    E is the declared type of the **ArrayList** elements

Program **Example 9.5** shows two additional methods, `set` and `remove`. Both methods are used in the same program. The `set` method replaces an existing element at the specified index with a new parameter object. There is a catch, because method `set` is a return method and it returns the element that formerly occupied the position. Look carefully at the output and you will see that `300`, the former element at index 2, is displayed. Method `remove` deletes an element at the specified index. The pitfall here is that students forget that other elements are now shifted to a lower index.

Example 9.5

```
public class Example95
{
    public static void main(String args[])
    {
        ArrayList<Integer> numbers = new ArrayList<Integer>();
        for (int k = 100; k < 500; k+= 100)
            numbers.add(new Integer(k));
        System.out.println(numbers);
        System.out.println(numbers.set(2,new Integer(999)));
        System.out.println(numbers);
        numbers.remove(1) ;
        System.out.println(numbers);
    }
}
```

Program Output

```
[100, 200, 300, 400]
300
[100, 200, 999, 400]
[100, 999, 400]
```

ArrayList Class Methods set and remove

E set (int index, E obj)
    replaces the element at position **index** with **obj**
    returns the element that was formerly at the specified position

E remove(int index)
    removes and returns the element at position **index**
    shifts array element at position **index+1** and higher to the left

Chapter 9 Questions
Dynamic Arrays with the ArrayList Class

01. Consider the following code segment.

```
ArrayList<String> towns = new ArrayList<String>();
towns.add("Baltimore");
towns.add("Bethesda");
towns.add("Wheaton");
towns.add("Greenbelt");
towns.add("Rockville");
for (int k = 1; k < towns.size(); k++)
    System.out.print(towns.get(k) + "   ");
```

What is printed as a result of executing the code segment?

(A) `IndexOutOfBoundsException` message
(B) `Baltimore   Bethesda   Wheaton   Greenbelt   Rockville`
(C) `Baltimore   Bethesda   Wheaton   Greenbelt`
(D) `Bethesda   Wheaton   Greenbelt   Rockville`
(E) `Bethesda`
    `Wheaton`
    `Greenbelt`
    `Rockville`

02. Consider the following code segment.

```
ArrayList<String> towns = new ArrayList<String>();
towns.add("Baltimore");
towns.add("Bethesda");
towns.add("Wheaton");
towns.add("Greenbelt");
towns.add("Rockville");
for (int k = 0; k <= towns.size(); k++)
    towns.set(k,"Aardvark");
System.out.println(towns);
```

What is printed as a result of executing the code segment?

(A) Compile error message
(B) An `IndexOutOfBoundsException` message
(C) `Baltimore   Bethesda   Wheaton   Greenbelt   Rockville`
(D) `Aardvark   Aardvark   Aardvark   Aardvak   Aardvark`
(E) `Baltimore   Bethesda   Wheaton   Greenbelt   Rockville`
    `Aardvark   Aardvark   Aardvark   Aardvak   Aardvark`

03. Consider the following code segment.

```
ArrayList<String> towns = new ArrayList<String>();
towns.add("Baltimore");
towns.add("Bethesda");
towns.add("Wheaton");
towns.add("Greenbelt");
towns.add("Rockville");
for (String town: towns)
    System.out.print(town + ", ");
System.out.println();
System.out.println(towns);
```

What is printed as a result of executing the code segment?

(A) IndexOutOfBoundsException message

(B) Baltimore, Bethesda, Wheaton, Greenbelt, Rockville
    Memory reference address

(C) Baltimore, Bethesda, Wheaton, Greenbelt, Rockville
    Baltimore, Bethesda, Wheaton, Greenbelt, Rockville

(D) [Baltimore, Bethesda, Wheaton, Greenbelt, Rockville]
    [Baltimore, Bethesda, Wheaton, Greenbelt, Rockville]

(E) Baltimore, Bethesda, Wheaton, Greenbelt, Rockville,
    [Baltimore, Bethesda, Wheaton, Greenbelt, Rockville]

04. Consider the following code segment.

```
ArrayList<String> towns = new ArrayList<String>();
towns.add("Baltimore");
towns.add("Bethesda");
towns.add("Wheaton");
towns.add("Greenbelt");
towns.add("Rockville");
for (String town: towns)
    town = "Dallas";
System.out.println(towns);
```

What is printed as a result of executing the code segment?

(A) Compile error message
(B) Memory reference address
(C) Baltimore, Bethesda, Wheaton, Greenbelt, Rockville
(D) [Baltimore, Bethesda, Wheaton, Greenbelt, Rockville]
(E) [Dallas, Dallas, Dallas, Dallas, Dallas]

05. Consider the following code segment.

```
ArrayList<String> towns = new ArrayList<String>();
towns.add("Dallas");
towns.add("Austin");
towns.add("Houston");
towns.add("Plano");
towns.set(2,towns.get(1));
towns.set(1,towns.get(2));
System.out.println(towns);
```

What is printed as a result of executing the code segment?

(A) [Dallas, Austin, Austin, Plano]
(B) [Dallas, Houston, Austin, Plano]
(C) [Houston, Dallas, Austin, Plano]
(D) [Houston, Houston, Austin, Plano]
(E) [Dallas, Dallas, Austin, Plano]

06. Consider the following code segment.

```
ArrayList<String> towns = new ArrayList<String>();
towns.add("Dallas");
towns.add("Austin");
towns.add("Houston");
towns.add("Plano");
int n = towns.size();

for (int k = 1; k <= n; k++)
    towns.set(k-1,towns.get(k % n));
System.out.println(towns);
```

What is printed as a result of executing the code segment?

(A) [Austin, Austin, Austin, Austin]
(B) [Plano, Houston, Austin, Dallas]
(C) [Plano, Dallas, Austin, Houston]
(D) [Austin, Houston, Plano, Dallas]
(E) [Austin, Houston, Plano, Austin]

07. Consider the following code segment.

```
ArrayList<Integer> list1 = new ArrayList<Integer>();
ArrayList<Integer> list2 = new ArrayList<Integer>();
for (int k = 10; k < 20; k++)
    list1.add(k);
for (int number: list1)
    list2.add(0,number);
System.out.println(list2);
```

What is printed as a result of executing the code segment?

(A) [10, 11, 12, 13, 14, 15, 16, 17, 18, 19]
(B) [0, 0, 0, 0, 0, 0, 0, 0, 0, 0]
(C) [19, 18, 17, 16, 15, 14, 13, 12, 11, 10]
(D) [0, 10, 0, 11, 0, 12, 0, 13, 0, 14, 0, 15, 0, 16, 0, 17, 0, 18, 0, 19]
(E) An IndexOutOfBoundsException message

08. Consider the following code segment and method `reduce`.

```
int[] numbers = {56,34,76,89,32,18,37,75,99,55};
ArrayList<Integer> temp = new ArrayList<Integer>();
for (int nr: numbers)
    temp.add(nr);
reduce(temp);
System.out.println(temp);

public static ArrayList<Integer> reduce(ArrayList<Integer> temp)
{
    for (int k = 0; k < temp.size(); k++)
        if (k % 2 == 0)
            temp.remove(k);
    return temp;
}
```

What is printed as a result of executing the code segment?

(A) [34, 76, 32, 18, 75, 99]
(B) [34, 89, 18, 75, 55]
(C) [56, 76, 32, 37, 99]
(D) [89, 37, 75, 99, 55]
(E) An `IndexOutOfBoundsException` message

09. Consider the following code segment and method `mystery`.

```
int[] numbers1 = {56,34,76,89,32,18,37,75,99,55};
ArrayList<Integer> numbers2 = mystery(numbers1);
System.out.println(numbers2);

public static ArrayList<Integer> mystery(int[] x)
{
    ArrayList<Integer> temp = new ArrayList<Integer>();
    for (int nr: x)
        temp.add(0,nr);
    return temp;
}
```

What is printed as a result of executing the code segment?

(A) [55, 99, 75, 37, 18, 32, 89, 76, 34, 56]
(B) [56, 34, 76, 89, 32, 18, 37, 75, 99, 55]
(C) [18, 32, 34, 37, 55, 56, 75, 76, 89, 99]
(D) [99, 89, 76, 75, 56, 55, 37, 34, 32, 18]
(E) [56, 34, 76, 89, 32, 32, 89, 76, 34, 56]

10. Consider the following code segment and method reduce.

```java
int[] numbers = {56,34,76,89,32,18,37,75,99,55};
ArrayList<Integer> temp = new ArrayList<Integer>();
for (int nr: numbers)
    temp.add(nr);
alter(temp);
System.out.println(temp);


public static void alter(ArrayList<Integer> temp)
{
    for (int k = 0; k < temp.size(); k++)
    {
        temp.add(temp.remove(k));
    }
}
```

What is printed as a result of executing the code segment?

(A) [56, 34, 76, 89, 32, 18, 37, 75, 99, 55]
(B) [18, 37, 75, 99, 55]
(C) [34, 89, 18, 75, 55]
(D) [ ]
(E) An IndexOutOfBoundsException message

11. Consider the following code segment.

```
ArrayList<String> cats = new ArrayList<String>();
cats.add("Lions");
cats.add("Tigers");

ArrayList<String> swimmers = new ArrayList<String>();
swimmers.add("Whales");
swimmers.add("Dolphins");

ArrayList<String> primates = new ArrayList<String>();
primates.add("Gorillas");
primates.add("Chimpanzees");

ArrayList<ArrayList<String>> mammals = new ArrayList<ArrayList<String>>();
mammals.add(cats);
mammals.add(swimmers);
mammals.add(primates);


for (ArrayList<String> mammal: mammals)
{
    for (String animal: mammal)
        System.out.println(animal);
    System.out.println();
}
```

Which of the following is true about the execution of this segment?

(A) This program will not compile.
(B) Two-dimensional arrays are not possible with the `ArrayList` class.
(C) This program will compile, but there is no output.
(D) The nested `for..each` loop used in this segment only functions with one-dimensional arrays.
(E) The program compiles and displays every element of the `mammals` object.

12. Consider the following code segment.

```
ArrayList<String> cats = new ArrayList<String>();
cats.add("Lions");
cats.add("Tigers");

ArrayList<String> swimmers = new ArrayList<String>();
swimmers.add("Whales");
swimmers.add("Dolphins");

ArrayList<String> primates = new ArrayList<String>();
primates.add("Gorillas");
primates.add("Chimpanzees");

ArrayList<ArrayList<String>> mammals = new ArrayList<ArrayList<String>>();
mammals.add(cats);
mammals.add(swimmers);
mammals.add(primates);

/* missing code */
```

Which of the following implementations of /* **missing code** */ will display every element of the mammals array?

Implementation I
```
for (ArrayList<String> mammal: mammals)
{
    for (String animal: mammal)
        System.out.println(animal);
    System.out.println();
}
```

Implementation II
```
System.out.println(mammals);
```

Implementation III
```
System.out.println(cats);
System.out.println(swimmers);
System.out.println(primates);
```

(A) I only
(B) II only
(C) III only
(D) I and II only
(E) I, II and III

Chapter 10 Review
Focus on OOP, Composition

One of the corner stones of Object Oriented Programming is *class interaction*, which is divided into two subtopics, *inheritance* and *composition*. The first subtopic, *inheritance*, was presented back in Chapter 5. Now we will continue and focus on the second subtopic, *composition*.

Composition, the **has-a** relationship, does not get the attention and recognition as *inheritance*. Inheritance is the big deal in OOP and composition is mentioned rather casually without much respect. It is not really fair to composition, because the *has-a* relationship is used in many programs. Furthermore, knowing how to use inheritance and knowing how to pass information to superclass constructors does not help with composition. The process is very different.

Most classes contain data. This has been true since the very first class you created. These data elements are also called *attributes* or *instance variables*. The majority of early data types you saw were simple or primitive data types like `int`, `double` and `char`. It should make sense that the attributes in a class can be objects of another class.

Regardless of using inheritance, composition or both in the same class, the primary goal of OOP is satisfied. In both cases reliability is achieved by using one or more classes that has already been tested.

There is a reason why this chapter did not follow the inheritance chapter immediately. Composition is very frequently used in a class, which has an array of objects. The previous chapters on static and dynamic arrays needed to be presented first before a proper review on composition was possible.

Class interaction requires that the existing class, which is being used either in an "is-a" relationship or a "has-a" relationship, receives proper information for its constructor. You are using an existing class and that is not possible without first constructing an object of the existing class. This general concept of dealing with the existing class first is the same for inheritance and composition. The actual implementation to pass information to the constructor of the existing class is quite different. With inheritance the `super` method was used to pass information to the superclass. Composition also needs to pass information to another class, but the approach will be very different.

Consider the program in **Example 10.1a**, which instantiates a `Car` class. However, a `Car` object cannot be constructed until an `Engine` object is available. An `Engine` object is an attribute in the `Car` class. A `Car` "has-an" `Engine`.

Now a good question comes to mind. How is information passed to the *attribute* constructor in composition? Think back to classes with only primitive data types. Each of the attributes is declared in the class. Inside the constructor are assignment statements to provide information for the data during the instantiation of a new object. This same approach is used when an object contains another object. Look at **Example 10.1a** and then continue to read additional details on the steps required to make composition work correctly. It may be a little trickier than inheritance, but it really follows the same process you have seen used in constructors for some time now.

Example 10.1a

```java
public class Example101
{
    public static void main(String args[])
    {
        Car car = new Car("Ford",350);
        car.showData();
    }
}

class Engine
{
    private int horsePower;

    public Engine(int hp)
    {
        System.out.println("Engine Constructor Called");
        horsePower = hp;
    }

    public int getHorsePower()
    {
        return horsePower;
    }
}

class Car
{
    private String type;
    private Engine engine;

    public Car(String t, int hp)
    {
        engine = new Engine(hp);
        System.out.println("Car Constructor Called");
        type = t;
    }

    public void showData()
    {
        System.out.println("Car Type:    " + type);
        System.out.println("Horse Power: " + engine.getHorsePower());
    }
}
```

Example 10.1b shows the output of the `Example101` program. It shows the logical sequence of constructing an `Engine` object before constructing a `Car` object. Do realize that Java knows little about cars and engines. Java requires that the `super` statement is used first in a subclass constructor when inheritance in used. With composition it is not required that the existing class is constructed as the first statement.

Example 10.1b

```
Engine Constructor Called
Car Constructor Called

Car Type:     Ford
Horse Power: 350
```

To see how the construction of two objects is possible, let us follow the information starting with the `Car car = new Car("Ford",350);` statement in the `main` method.

The two parameters arrive in the `Car` constructor. Inside the `Car` constructor a new `Engine` object is constructed and it is the `Car` constructor that assigns the proper information to the `Car` class attributes. Parameter `Ford` is assigned to the `Car type` and `350` is used in the `engine = new Engine(hp);` statement to construct a new `Engine` object.

This can be done with a greater degree of complexity. Multiple classes can be used with composition. Continuing with a `Car` class we can say that a `Car` has-a `Radio`; a `Car` has-a `Transmission`; a `Car` has four `Tires`, and many more. Such complexity does mean many additional statements in the `Car` constructor to instantiate every object. The logic is not more complex. It is a matter of more statements and more work.

It is another matter when there are multiple levels of composition, similar to multi-level inheritance. Consider that a `Country` has `States`, a `State` has `Counties` and finally a `County` has `Cities`. **Example 10.2** demonstrates a class with multiple levels of composition. Look carefully how the information passed. For clarity each of the arrays only constructs one object for the first element in the array. This is not practical, but it keeps the code simpler.

Example 10.2

```
class Country
{
    private State[] states;

    public Country(int stateSize)
    {
        states = new State[stateSize];
        states[0] = new State(50);
    }
}

class State
{
    private County[] counties;

    public State(int countySize)
    {
        counties = new County[countySize];
        counties[0] = new County(100);
    }
}

class County
{
    private City[] cities;

    public County(int citySize)
    {
        cities = new City[citySize];
        cities[0] = new City("Plano");
    }
}


class City
{
    private String cityName;

    public City(String cn)
    {
        cityName = cn;
    }
}
```

The key thing to observe is that there is a pattern at each level of composition. In particular, note where the objects are constructed. Follow the statements with new. Pay particular attention that one new operator is used to construct an array with a specified number of elements. Then each element in the array, which is an object, needs to be constructed. This continues deeper and deeper into the program.

There is a concern with composition that will result in an infinite loop that eventually crashes during runtime. **Example 10.3** first shows a `Student` class. This `Student` class is then contained inside the `School` class as a member of a `students` array. This is very typical composition where an object of one class is used as an array element inside another class. The classes in **Example 10.3** present no problem or concern.

Example 10.3

```
class Student
{
    private String name;
    private int age;

    public Student(String n, int a)
    {
        name = n;
        age = a;
    }
}

class School
{
    private int size;
    private Student[] students;

    public School(int s)
    {
        size = s;
        students = new Student[size];
        students[0] = new Student("Tom",16);
    }
}
```

Consider the following scenario which may be intentional or unintentional. What happens if class A has-a class B and then class B has-a class A. In other words with the two classes used in the last example, a `School` has-a `Student` and then a `Student` has-a `School`. Will this even compile? Such a program is shown in **Example 10.4.**

Example 10.4

```java
public class Example104
{
    public static void main(String[] args)
    {
        School plano = new School(2000);
    }
}

class Student
{
    private String name;
    private int age;
    private School school;

    public Student(String n, int a)
    {
        name = n;
        age = a;
        school = new School(100);
    }
}

class School
{
    private int size;
    private Student[] students;

    public School(int s)
    {
        size = s;
        students = new Student[size];
        students[0] = new Student("Tom",16);
    }
}
```

This `Example104` program does compile. Java finds no problem with the syntax. Now to be fair as you check each line of code there is not a syntax problem anywhere. The problem starts quickly at runtime. Here is the program sequence.

A new `School` object is instantiated.
This results in constructing a new `students` array.
This in turn instantiates a new `Student` object.
However, the `Student` constructor now wants to call the `School` constructor.

The program is caught in an infinite loop. Do not let this happen to you.

Chapter 10 Questions
Focus on OOP, Composition

01. Consider the following two classes.

```
class Rumba
{
    private Mambo mambo;

    public Rumba()
    {
        mambo = new Mambo();
        System.out.println("Executing the Rumba constructor");
    }
}

class Mambo
{
    public Mambo()
    {
        System.out.println("Executing the Mambo constructor");
    }
}
```

What is the relationship between class Rumba and class Mambo?

(A) inheritance only
(B) composition only
(C) both inheritance and composition
(D) polymorphism
(E) There is no relationship between Rumba and Mambo.

02. Consider the following code segment and two classes.

```
Mambo m = new Mambo();
Rumba r = new Rumba();

class Rumba
{
    private Mambo mambo;

    public Rumba()
    {
        mambo = new Mambo();
        System.out.println("Executing the Rumba constructor");
    }
}

class Mambo
{
    public Mambo()
    {
        System.out.println("Executing the Mambo constructor");
    }
}
```

What are the first two lines printed as the result of executing the code segment?

(A) Executing the Rumba constructor
     Executing the Rumba constructor

(B) Executing the Mambo constructor
     Executing the Mambo constructor

(C) Executing the Rumba constructor
     Executing the Mambo constructor

(D) Executing the Mambo constructor
     Executing the Rumba constructor

(E) Compile error message

03. Consider the following code segment and `List` class.

```
List list = new List();
list.showList();


class List
{
    private int[] list;

    public List()
    {
        list = new int[5];
    }

    public void showList()
    {
        for (int item: list)
            System.out.print(item + "   ");
    }
}
```

What is printed as a result of executing the code segment?

(A) 5   5   5   5   5
(B) No output since there are not any values assigned to `list`.
(C) 0   0   0   0   0
(D) Compile error message
(E) An `ArrayIndexOutOfBoundsException` error message

04. Consider the following code segment and `List` class.

```
List list = new List(8,5);
list.showList();


class List
{
    private int[] intArray;

    public List()
    {
        intArray = new int[5];
    }

    public List(int size, int value)
    {
        intArray = new int[size];
        for (int k = 0; k < intArray.length; k++)
        intArray[k] = value;
    }

    public void showList()
    {
        for (int k = 0; k < intArray.length; k++)
            System.out.print(intArray[k] + "   ");
    }
}
```

What is printed as a result of executing the code segment?

(A) 5   5   5   5   5   5   5   5
(B) 8   8   8   8   8
(C) 0   0   0   0   0   0   0   0
(D) Duplicate identifier compile error message
(E) An `ArrayIndexOutOfBoundsException` error message

05. Consider the following three classes.

```
class Engine
{
    public Engine()
    {
        System.out.println("Executing the Engine constructor");
    }
}


class Car
{
    private Engine engine;

    public Car()
    {
        System.out.println("Executing the Car constructor");
        engine = new Engine();
    }
}


class Hybrid extends Car
{
    public Hybrid()
    {
        System.out.println("Executing the Hybrid constructor");
    }
}
```

What relationships exist among the three classes?

(A) inheritance only
(B) composition only
(C) inheritance and composition only
(D) encapsulation and polymorphism only
(E) inheritance, composition and polymorphism

06. Consider the following code segment and three classes.

```java
Hybrid prius = new Hybrid();


class Engine
{
    public Engine()
    {
        System.out.println("Executing the Engine constructor");
    }
}


class Car
{
    private Engine engine;

    public Car()
    {
        System.out.println("Executing the Car constructor");
        engine = new Engine();
    }
}


class Hybrid extends Car
{
    public Hybrid()
    {
        System.out.println("Executing the Hybrid constructor");
    }
}
```

What is printed as a result of executing the code segment?

(A) Executing the Hybrid constructor

(B) Executing the Car constructor
    Executing the Hybrid constructor

(C) Executing the Car constructor
    Executing the Engine constructor
    Executing the Hybrid constructor

(D) Executing the Engine constructor
    Executing the Hybrid constructor

(E) An Exception error message

07. Consider the following code segment and two classes.

```
List list = new List();
list.showList();


class Person
{
    public Person()
    {
        System.out.println("New Person");
    }
}


class List
{
    private Person[] persons;

    public List()
    {
        persons = new Person[5];
    }

    public void showList()
    {
        for (Person person: persons)
            System.out.print(person + "   ");
    }
}
```

What is printed as a result of executing the code segment?

(A) five memory reference outputs like `Person@1cd2e5f`
(B) `null   null   null   null   null`
(C) `0   0   0   0   0`
(D) no output since individual `Person` objects are not constructed
(E) `New Person   New Person   New Person   New Person   New Person`

08. Consider the following code segment and two classes.

```
List list = new List();
list.showList();


class Person
{
    public Person()
    {
        System.out.println("New Person");
    }
}


class List
{
    private Person[] persons;

    public List()
    {
        persons = new Person[5];
    }

    public void showList()
    {
        for (Person person: persons)
            System.out.print(person + "   ");
    }
}
```

How many times is the new operator used as a result of executing the code segment?

(A) one time
(B) two times
(C) five times
(D) six times
(E) seven times

09. Consider the following code segment and two classes.

```
List list = new List();
list.showList();


class Person
{
    public Person()
    {
        System.out.print("New Person");
    }
}


class List
{
    private Person[] persons;

    public List()
    {
        persons = new Person[5];
        for (int k =0; k < persons.length; k++)
            persons[k] = new Person();
    }

    public void showList()
    {
        System.out.println();
        for (Person person: persons)
            System.out.print(person + "   ");
    }
}
```

What is printed as a result of executing the code segment?

(A) Five memory reference outputs like `Person@1cd2e5f4`

(B) `null   null   null   null   null`

(C) `0   0   0   0   0`

(D) `New PersonNew PersonNew PersonNew PersonNew Person`

(E) `New PersonNew PersonNew PersonNew PersonNew Person`
    Five memory reference outputs like `Person@1cd2e5f4`

10. Consider the following code segment and two classes.

```
List list = new List();
list.showList();


class Person
{
    public Person()
    {
        System.out.print("New Person");
    }
}


class List
{
    private Person[] persons;

    public List()
    {
        persons = new Person[5];
        for (int k =0; k < persons.length; k++)
            persons[k] = new Person();
    }

    public void showList()
    {
        System.out.println();
        for (Person person: persons)
            System.out.print(person + "   ");
    }
}
```

How many times is the new operator used as a result of executing the code segment?

(A) one time
(B) two times
(C) five times
(D) six times
(E) seven times

Questions 11-12 refer to the following three class declarations.

```java
class Person
{
    protected int age;

    public Person(int a)
    {
        age = a;
    }
}


class Student extends Person
{
    protected double gpa;

    public Student(int a, double g)
    {
        super(a);
        gpa = g;
    }

    public String toString()
    {
        return (age + "   " + gpa);
    }
}


class Course
{
    private Student[] students;

    public Course(int size, int a, double g)
    {
        /* Missing code 1 */
    }

    public void displayCourse()
    {
        /* missing code 2 */
    }
}
```

11. Consider the following code segment and the previously mentioned three classes.

```
int count = 6;        // number of students in the course
int age = 15;         // initial age for each student
double gpa = 3.875;   // initial gpa for each student
Course algebra = new Course(count,age,gpa);
algebra.displayCourse();
```

Which of the following implementations of /* **missing code 1** */ will
construct the Course object correctly?

Implementation I
```
students = new Student[size];
for (Student student: students)
    student = new Student(a,g);
```

Implementation II
```
students = new Student[size];
for (int k =0; k < students.length; k++)
    students[k] = new Student(a,g);
```

Implementation III
```
students = new Person[size];
for (int k =0; k < students.length; k++)
    students[k] = new Person(a,g);
```

(A) I only   (B) II only   (C) III only   (D) I and II   (E) II and III

12. Consider the following code segment and the previously mentioned three classes.

```
int count = 6;        // number of students in the course
int age = 15;         // initial age for each student
double gpa = 3.875;   // initial gpa for each student
Course algebra = new Course(count,age,gpa);
algebra.displayCourse();
```

Which of the following implementations of /* **missing code 2** */
will display the attribute values of each Student object?

Implementation I
```
for (int k =0; k < students.length; k++)
    System.out.println(students[k]);
```

Implementation II
```
for (Student student: students)
    System.out.println(student);
```

Implementation III
```
System.out.println(students);
```

(A) I only   (B) II only   (C) III only   (D) I and II   (E) II and III

Chapter 11 Review
Focus on OOP, Polymorphism

Polymorphism is the fourth, and final, feature of the *Focus on OOP*. It is also the feature of OOP that is the most elusive. The exotic name does not help, but with today's special effects, students know about morphing from one shape into another shape. Morph means shape or form and *polymorphism* means *many forms*. For starters, do be concerned with the technical vocabulary. You must know the vocabulary and be assured that it will show up on the APCS Exam. The key point is not to be intimidated by strange words. The strangeness is due to lack of familiarity.

We now have a feature in computer science in general and Java specifically that has many forms. You have seen some early examples in the form of the plus (+) operator. This operator performs arithmetic addition with numerical values. This same plus operator can also handle string concatenation. In this case the plus operator has many forms. When you first learned about this operator, you probably learned that the operator is overloaded.

Later in the course you learned about methods with identical identifiers and different heading signatures. This is common with constructors and also with some methods. The `substring` method is one example of an *overloaded* method. This too is polymorphism.

Now the examples you learned earlier in the course that were called *overloaded* is not at issue here. There are different varieties of polymorphism and this chapter assumes that the *overloaded* operators and methods are in good shape and shall remain with the term *overloaded*.

This chapter is concerned with the ability of a single method to behave in many different ways. This is not a case of different method signatures. Imagine that a method is called multiple times. Furthermore, this method is always called with the same method signature and somehow this single method has the amazing ability to behave differently, as appropriate.

Let's consider a high school theatre production. Students are getting ready to perform for the first time. The curtain is about to go up and the director gives last minute instructions. It is a production of *Beauty and the Beast* and each student has their own lines to perform. Right before the curtain raises the director tells the students to go out there and **act**. The director does not go down the line and tells each actor how to act. No simply **act**. Every student knows his or her job and "acts" accordingly. This is polymorphism. The verb act has many forms and the form is dictated to each character portrayed by the students.

It was mentioned earlier that the goal of OOP is reliability, and each of the four OOP features brings reliability to the table. How does *polymorphism* add reliability? Suppose that some outside code segment calls many different objects and tells these objects to behave. Each object is provided with behavior instructions appropriate to the object. That sounds good, but it is quite possible that the wrong instructions are passed on.

On the other hand, if each class is responsible for its own behavior, then such behavior is implemented with the creation of the class. In good program design, the behavior is also tested. Now it is only necessary to tell an actor to go ahead and act. This is somewhat like the play just mentioned. During rehearsals each actor is told what to say and what to do. The night of the performance, actors are told *to act*. Each actor now performs the job he/she is meant to do. This adds reliability.

The program in **Example 11.1** shows a complete program that demonstrates *polymorphism*. There are three classes, which implement the `Animal` interface. The abstract method of the `Animal` interface is implemented three different ways. When the same `getMove` method is called three times, three different outputs result with three objects of three different classes. The three classes are different, but all three classes implement the same `Animal` interface, which makes this process possible.

Example 11.1

```java
public class Example111
{
    public static void main (String args[])
    {
        Animal animal1 = new Mammal();
        Animal animal2 = new Bird();
        Animal animal3 = new Fish();
        ArrayList<Animal> animals = new ArrayList<Animal>();
        animals.add(animal1);
        animals.add(animal2);
        animals.add(animal3);

        for (Animal animal: animals)
            System.out.println(animal.getMove());

        System.out.println();
    }
}


abstract interface Animal
{
    abstract String getMove();
}

class Mammal implements Animal
{
    String animalType;
    public Mammal()                 { animalType = "Mammal"; }
    public String getMove()         { return animalType + " walks."; }
}

class Bird implements Animal
{
    String animalType;
    public Bird()                   { animalType = "Bird"; }
    public String getMove()         { return animalType +" flies."; }
}

class Fish implements Animal
{
    String animalType;
    public Fish()                   { animalType = "Fish"; }
    public String getMove()         { return animalType +" swims."; }
}
```

Example 11.1

```
                    Program Example 111 Output
A Mammal walks.
A Bird flies.
A Fish swims.
```

In the last example an interface was used to be the *umbrella* for the implementing class. The *polymorphic* method, `getMove`, is present in the *umbrella interface*. Let's look at another program example and this time an *umbrella class* will be used. This program will be presented in stages. In **Example11.2** four classes are presented. There is no class interaction visible. You do see that each class has a `greeting` method and every class is a subclass of `Language`. The method heading is identical, but the each method has a greeting unique to its own language.

Example 11.2

```java
class English extends Language
{
   public void greeting()
   {
      System.out.println("In English you say Good Day");
   }
}

class German extends Language
{
   public void greeting()
   {
      System.out.println("In German you say Guten Tag");
   }
}

class Dutch extends Language
{
   public void greeting()
   {
      System.out.println("In Dutch you say Goeden Dag");
   }
}

class French extends Language
{
   public void greeting()
   {
      System.out.println("In French you say Bonjour");
   }
}
```

Polymorphism requires an *umbrella*. This *umbrella* is an interface or a class that becomes an umbrella for implementing classes or subclasses. In English we have many umbrella nouns, such as *students, athletes, and teachers.* In high school the 9th graders, 10th graders, 11th graders and 12th graders all fall under the umbrella of High School Students.

In **Example11.3** you now see the superclass `Language`. Note that the `greeting` method is defined in the superclass or the *umbrella* class `Language`. In each subclass, method `greeting` is then re-defined.

Example 11.3

```
class Language
{
   public void greeting()
   {
      System.out.println("All languages have a greeting");
   }
}
```

We now have an umbrella, `Language`. We also have four subclasses and each subclass re-defines the polymorphic method `greeting`. Now in **Example11.4** array object `countries` stores objects of each language. The array is an array of `Language` objects. This is necessary. We need an umbrella that allows objects with different method definitions to be grouped together. After each `Language` object is added to the `countries` object there is a loop that cycles through each object and calls the `greeting` method. Of great importance is to realize that no effort is made to identify the object so as to execute the correct method. Each object greets according to its own definition just like each student acts according to its own character during a theatre performance. This is polymorphism.

Example 11.4

```
public class Example114
{
   public static void main (String[] args)
   {
      ArrayList<Language> countries = new ArrayList<Language>();
      countries.add(new English());
      countries.add(new German());
      countries.add(new Dutch());
      countries.add(new French());

      for (Language country: countries)
         country.greeting();
      System.out.println("\n\n");
   }
}
```

Example 11.4

```
                         Program Output

In English you say Good Day
In German you say Guten Tag
In Dutch you Goeden Dag
In French you say Bonjour
```

Polymorphism Pitfalls

Polymorphism requires some "umbrella" interface or "umbrella" superclass. The program in
Example 11.5 appears to have an interface. It seems like `Animal` is the umbrella, but there are
three separate classes without any interface to implement or a superclass to extend. Forget this
detail and the program does not compile. It recognizes that an `Animal` interface exists, but sees
no relationship and then creates compile errors. In **Example116** you do see the `Animal`
interface and it does have the `getMove` polymorphic method that is defined in classes `Mammal`,
`Bird` and `Fish`. All of that is fine, but without any class interaction it will not even compile.
You will be rewarded with an ample amount of error message stuff.

The program will work just fine when each one of the classes implements `Animal`, like ...

```
class Mammal implements Animal
```

Example 11.5

```java
public class Example115
{
    public static void main (String args[])
    {
        Mammal animal1 = new Mammal();
        Bird animal2 = new Bird();
        Fish animal3 = new Fish();
        ArrayList<Animal> animals = new ArrayList<Animal>();
        animals.add(animal1);
        animals.add(animal2);
        animals.add(animal3);
        for (Animal animal: animals)
            System.out.println(animal.getMove());
    }
}
```

Example 11.6

```
interface Animal
{
    public String getMove();
}

class Mammal
{
    String animalType;
    public Mammal()            { animalType = "Mammal"; }
    public String getMove()    { return animalType + " walks."; }
}

class Bird
{
    String animalType;
    public Bird()              { animalType = "Bird"; }
    public String getMove()    { return animalType +" flies."; }
}

class Fish
{
    String animalType;
    public Fish()              { animalType = "Fish"; }
    public String getMove()    { return animalType +" swims."; }
}
```

```
Example115.java:11: error: no suitable method found for add(Mammal)
                animals.add(animal1);
                           ^
    method Collection.add(Animal) is not applicable
      (argument mismatch; Mammal cannot be converted to Animal)
    method List.add(Animal) is not applicable
      (argument mismatch; Mammal cannot be converted to Animal)
    method AbstractCollection.add(Animal) is not applicable
      (argument mismatch; Mammal cannot be converted to Animal)
    method AbstractList.add(Animal) is not applicable
      (argument mismatch; Mammal cannot be converted to Animal)
    method ArrayList.add(Animal) is not applicable
      (argument mismatch; Mammal cannot be converted to Animal)
Example115.java:12: error: no suitable method found for add(Bird)
                animals.add(animal2);
                           ^
    method Collection.add(Animal) is not applicable
      (argument mismatch; Bird cannot be converted to Animal)
    method List.add(Animal) is not applicable
      (argument mismatch; Bird cannot be converted to Animal)
    method AbstractCollection.add(Animal) is not applicable
      (argument mismatch; Bird cannot be converted to Animal)
    method AbstractList.add(Animal) is not applicable
      (argument mismatch; Bird cannot be converted to Animal)
    method ArrayList.add(Animal) is not applicable
      (argument mismatch; Bird cannot be converted to Animal)
Example115.java:13: error: no suitable method found for add(Fish)
                animals.add(animal3);
                           ^
    method Collection.add(Animal) is not applicable
      (argument mismatch; Fish cannot be converted to Animal)
    method List.add(Animal) is not applicable
      (argument mismatch; Fish cannot be converted to Animal)
    method AbstractCollection.add(Animal) is not applicable
      (argument mismatch; Fish cannot be converted to Animal)
    method AbstractList.add(Animal) is not applicable
      (argument mismatch; Fish cannot be converted to Animal)
    method ArrayList.add(Animal) is not applicable
      (argument mismatch; Fish cannot be converted to Animal)
Note: Some messages have been simplified; recompile with -Xdiags:verbose to
3 errors
```

Chapter 11 Questions
Focus on OOP, Polymorphism

Questions 01-02 refer to the following two classes.

```
class Equestrian
{
    private String name;
    private String actName;

    public Equestrian(String n, String aN)
    {
        name = n;
        actName = aN;
    }

    public void act()
    {
        System.out.println("Runs in circles");
    }
}


class TightRopeWalker
{
    private String name;
    private String actName;

    public TightRopeWalker(String n, String aN)
    {
        name = n;
        actName = aN;
    }

    public void act()
    {
        System.out.println("Walks and flips on the tight rope");
    }
}
```

01. Consider the following code segment and the previously mentioned two classes.

```
Equestrian olga = new Equestrian("Olga","Amazing Ponies");
TightRopeWalker ivan = new TightRopeWalker("Ivan","Feats of Daring");
ivan.act();
olga.act();
```

What is printed as a result of executing the code segment?

(A) A compile error message, because the two classes do not implement an interface.

(B) A compile error message, because the two classes do not extend a superclass.

(C) ```
Runs in circles
Walks and flips on the tight rope
```

(D)  ```
Walks and flips on the tight rope
Runs in circles
```

(E) ```
Olga Amazing Ponies
Runs in circles
Ivan Feats of Daring
Walks and flips on the tight rope
```

02.  Consider the following code segment and the previously mentioned two classes.

```
Equestrian olga = new Equestrian("Olga","Amazing Ponies");
TightRopeWalker ivan = new TightRopeWalker("Ivan","Feats of Daring");
ivan.act();
olga.act();
```

What is true about the two `act` methods?

(A) They are examples of overloaded methods.
(B) They are examples of abstract methods.
(C) They demonstrate the use of polymorphism.
(D) They demonstrate inheritance and composition.
(E) None of the above
```

03. Consider the following code segment and two sets of declarations.

```
CircusPerformer olga = new Equestrian();
CircusPerformer ivan = new TightRopeWalker();
ivan.act();
olga.act();
```

DECLARATION I
```
class CircusPerformer
{
    public void act(){ System.out.println("Walks in the entrance parade"); }
}

class Equestrian extends CircusPerformer
{
    public void act(){ System.out.println("Runs in circles"); }
}

class TightRopeWalker extends CircusPerformer
{
    public void act(){ System.out.println("Walks and flips on the tight rope"); }
}
```

DECLARATION II

```
interface CircusPerformer
{
    public void act();
}

class Equestrian implements CircusPerformer
{
    public void act(){ System.out.println("Runs in circles"); }
}

class TightRopeWalker implements CircusPerformer
{
    public void act(){ System.out.println("Walks and flips on the tight rope"); }
}
```

There are two separate declarations that can be used by the code segment.
If it is not known which declaration group is used, what will be printed by executing the code segment?

(A) The two outputs will be identical.

(B) The two outputs will be different.

(C) The code will not compile with either declaration.

(D) There is only one output with **DECLARATION I**.
Using **DECLARATION II** will generate a compile error message.

(E) There is only one output with **DECLARATION II**.
Using **DECLARATION I** will generate a compile error message.

04. Consider the following code segment, interface and implementing classes.

```
CircusPerformer olga = new Equestrian("Olga");
CircusPerformer lizzy = new Equestrian("Lizzy");
CircusPerformer saskia = new Equestrian("Saskia");
CircusPerformer ivan = new TightRopeWalker("Ivan");
CircusPerformer bert = new TightRopeWalker("Bert");
ArrayList<CircusPerformer> performers = new ArrayList<CircusPerformer>();
performers.add(olga);
performers.add(lizzy);
performers.add(saskia);
performers.add(ivan);
performers.add(bert);
for (CircusPerformer performer: performers)
    performer.act();


interface CircusPerformer
{
    public void act();
}

class Equestrian implements CircusPerformer
{
    private String name;

    public Equestrian(String n)
    {
        name = n;
    }
    public void act(){ System.out.println(name + " runs in circles."); }
}

class TightRopeWalker implements CircusPerformer
{
    private String name;

    public TightRopeWalker(String n)
    {
        name = n;
    }
    public void act(){ System.out.println(name + " walks and flips on the tight rope.");
}
```

What is printed as a result of executing the code segment?

(A)	(B)	(C)
Olga runs in circles. Lizzy runs in circles. Saskia runs in circles. Ivan walks and flips on the tight rope. Bert walks and flips on the tight rope.	walks and flips on the tight rope. walks and flips on the tight rope. runs in circles. runs in circles. runs in circles.	runs in circles. runs in circles. runs in circles. walks and flips on the tight rope. walks and flips on the tight rope.

(D)	A compile error message, indicating improper polymorphic definition

(E)	An `Exception` error message indicating that polymorphism is not allowed with an interface

05. Consider the following code segment and three classes.

```
CircusPerformer olga = new Equestrian("Olga");
CircusPerformer lizzy = new Equestrian("Lizzy");
CircusPerformer saskia = new Equestrian("Saskia");
CircusPerformer ivan = new TightRopeWalker("Ivan");
CircusPerformer bert = new TightRopeWalker("Bert");
ArrayList<CircusPerformer> performers = new ArrayList<CircusPerformer>();
performers.add(olga);   performers.add(lizzy);   performers.add(saskia);
performers.add(ivan);   performers.add(bert);
for (CircusPerformer performer: performers)
    performer.act();


class CircusPerformer
{
    public void act(){ System.out.println("Circus performer enters in the parade."); }
}

class Equestrian extends CircusPerformer
{
    private String name;

    public Equestrian(String n)
    {
        name = n;
    }
    public void act(){ System.out.println(name + " runs in circles.");    }
}

class TightRopeWalker extends CircusPerformer
{
    private String name;

    public TightRopeWalker(String n)
    {
        name = n;
    }
    public void act(){ System.out.println(name + " walks and flips on the tight rope.");}
}
```

What is printed as a result of executing the code segment.

(A)	(B)
Olga runs in circles. Lizzy runs in circles. Saskia runs in circles. Ivan walks and flips on the tight rope. Bert walks and flips on the tight rope.	runs in circles. runs in circles. runs in circles. walks and flips on the tight rope. walks and flips on the tight rope.

(C)
Circus performer enters in the parade runs in circles. Circus performer enters in the parade runs in circles. Circus performer enters in the parade runs in circles. Circus performer enters in the parade walks and flips on the tight rope. Circus performer enters in the parade walks and flips on the tight rope.

(D)   A compile error message, indicating improper polymorphic definition

(E)   An Exception error indicating that polymorphism is not allowed without an interface

06. Consider the following code segment, interface and two classes.

```
Equestrian olga = new Equestrian("Olga");
Equestrian lizzy = new Equestrian("Lizzy");
Equestrian saskia = new Equestrian("Saskia");
TightRopeWalker ivan = new TightRopeWalker("Ivan");
TightRopeWalker bert = new TightRopeWalker("Bert");
olga.act();  lizzy.act();  saskia.act();  ivan.act();   bert.act();


interface CircusPerformer
{
    public void act();
}

class Equestrian implements CircusPerformer
{
    private String name;

    public Equestrian(String n)
    {
        name = n;
    }
    public void act(){ System.out.println(name + " runs in circles."); }
}

class TightRopeWalker implements CircusPerformer
{
    private String name;

    public TightRopeWalker(String n)
    {
        name = n;
    }
    public void act(){System.out.println(name + " walks and flips on the tight rope.");}
}
```

What is printed as a result of executing the code segment.

(A) ```
Olga
Lizzy
Saskia
Ivan
Bert
```

(B) ```
Olga runs in circles.
Lizzy runs in circles.
Saskia runs in circles.
Ivan walks and flips on the tight rope.
Bert walks and flips on the tight rope.
```

(C) ```
runs in circles.
runs in circles.
runs in circles.
walks and flips on the tight rope.
walks and flips on the tight rope.
```

(D) A compile error message, indicating improper polymorphic method definition

(E) An Exception error indicating that polymorphism is not allowed without a superclass.
```

07. This question involves a comparison of question 05 and question 06.

Both questions are used in a polymorphism review chapter.
Question 05 uses a superclass with inheritance.
Question 06 uses an abstract interface with implementing classes.

For the `Circus` program, which one demonstrates polymorphism better?

(A) Question 05, because polymorphism only works with a superclass.
(B) Question 06, because polymorphism only works with an abstract interface.
(C) Both approaches work equally well.
(D) Neither approach is appropriate for a polymorphic example.
(E) Question 05, because it uses polymorphism. Question 06 does not use polymorphism properly.

08. Consider the following code segment, interface and classes.

```
German german = new German();
Dutch dutch = new Dutch();
French french = new French();
german.greeting();
dutch.greeting();
french.greeting();

interface Language
{
    public void greeting();
}

class German implements Language
{
    public void greeting()  { System.out.println("In German you say Guten Tag"); }
}

class Dutch implements Language
{
    public void greeting()  { System.out.println("In Dutch you say Goeden Dag"); }
}

class French implements Language
{
    public void greeting()  { System.out.println("In French you say Bonjour"); }
}
```

The program code is meant to demonstrate polymorphism. What is true about this demonstration?

(A) There is an umbrella interface `Language`.
(B) There is a polymorphic method `greeting`.
(C) The program output is generated without using polymorphism.
(D) All the classes implement the interface.
(E) All of the above

Questions 09-10 refer to the following interface and three classes.

```java
interface Shape
{
    public void drawShape();
}

class Circle implements Shape
{
    private Graphics g;

    public Circle(Graphics g)
    {
        this.g = g;
    }

    public void drawShape()
    {
        g.fillOval(20,20,50,50);
    }
}

class Square implements Shape
{
    private Graphics g;

    public Square(Graphics g)
    {
        this.g = g;
    }

    public void drawShape()
    {
        g.fillRect(100,150,100,100);
    }
}

class Triangle implements Shape
{
    private Graphics g;

    public Triangle(Graphics g)
    {
        this.g = g;
    }

    public void drawShape()
    {
        Polygon triangle = new Polygon();
        triangle.addPoint(300,300);
        triangle.addPoint(350,400);
        triangle.addPoint(250,400);
        g.fillPolygon(triangle);
    }
}
```

09. Consider the following code segment and the previously mentioned declarations.

```
Shape shape1 = new Circle(g);
Shape shape2 = new Square(g);
Shape shape3 = new Triangle(g);
```

Which of the following windows is displayed as a result of executing the code segment?

(A) An empty applet window
(B) An applet window with three different shapes
(C) An applet window with three circles
(D) An Exception error message stating that polymorphism is not allowed in graphics displays.
(E) An Exception error message stating that an interface is not allowed for polymorphism.

10. Consider the following code segment and the previously mentioned declarations.

```
ArrayList<Shape> shapes = new ArrayList<Shape>();
shapes.add(new Circle(g));
shapes.add(new Square(g));
shapes.add(new Triangle(g));
for (Shape shape : shapes)
    shape.drawShape();
```

Which of the following windows is displayed as a result of executing the code segment?

(A) An empty applet window
(B) An applet window with three different shapes
(C) An applet window with three circles
(D) An Exception error message stating that polymorphism is not allowed in graphics displays.
(E) An Exception error message stating that an interface is not allowed for polymorphism.

Questions 11-12 refer to the following four classes.

```
class Shape
{
    private Graphics g;
    public Shape(Graphics g)       { this.g = g; }
    public void drawTitle(String t, int x, int y)  { g.drawString(t,x,y); }
    public void drawShape()        { }
}

class Circle extends Shape
{
    private Graphics g;
    public Circle(Graphics g)      { super(g); this.g = g; }
    public void drawShape()
    {
        drawTitle("CIRCLE",20,15);
        g.fillOval(20,20,50,50);
    }
}

class Square extends Shape
{
    private Graphics g;
    public Square(Graphics g)      { super(g); this.g = g; }
    public void drawShape()
    {
        drawTitle("SQUARE",130,145);
        g.fillRect(100,150,100,100);
    }
}

class Triangle extends Shape
{
    private Graphics g;
    public Triangle(Graphics g)  { super(g); this.g = g; }
    public void drawShape()
    {
        drawTitle("TRIANGLE",275,295);
        Polygon triangle = new Polygon();
        triangle.addPoint(300,300);
        triangle.addPoint(350,400);
        triangle.addPoint(250,400);
        g.fillPolygon(triangle);
    }
}
```

11. Consider the following code segment and the previously mentioned declarations.

```
ArrayList<Shape> shapes = new ArrayList<Shape>();
shapes.add(new Circle(g));
shapes.add(new Square(g));
shapes.add(new Triangle(g));
for (Shape shape: shapes)
    shape.drawShape();
```

Which of the following windows is displayed as a result of executing the code segment?

(A) An empty applet window
(B) An applet window with three different shapes
(C) An applet window with three shapes and titles on top
(D) An applet window with three titles only
(E) An `Exception` error message stating that an interface is not allowed for polymorphism.

12. Consider the following code segment and the previously mentioned declarations.

```
ArrayList<Shape> shapes = new ArrayList<Shape>();
shapes.add(new Circle(g));
shapes.add(new Square(g));
shapes.add(new Triangle(g));
for (Shape shape: shapes)
    shape.drawShape();
```

Which of the following methods are used polymorphically?

I.   Method `drawTitle`
II.   Constructor methods
III. Method `drawShape`

(A) I only
(B) II only
(C) III only
(D) I and II only
(E) II and III only

Chapter 12 Review
Interfaces and Abstract Classes

Interfaces were used in the polymorphism chapter. You can use an umbrella superclass or an umbrella interface to set up polymorphism. This chapter will continue and present additional information about interfaces as well as abstract classes. An interface by itself does nothing. You cannot instantiate an interface and the methods lack information necessary for execution. It will always be necessary that a concrete class exists, which implements the abstract methods in the abstract interface. **Example 12.1** shows a `Bank` interface with a second `MyBank` class to implement the interface.

Example 12.1

```
interface Bank
{
    public double getCheckingBalance();
    public void makeCheckingDeposit(double amount);
    public void makeCheckingWithdrawal(double amount);
}


class MyBank implements Bank
{
    private double checking;

    public MyBank(double c)
    {
        checking = c;
    }

    public double getCheckingBalance()
    {
        return checking;
    }

    public void makeCheckingDeposit(double amount)
    {
        checking += amount;
    }

    public void makeCheckingWithdrawal(double amount)
    {
        checking -= amount;
    }
}
```

An interface is abstract and all the methods in an interface declaration are also abstract. There exists an `abstract` reserved word, which explicitly states that an interface, class or method is `abstract`. This `abstract` reserved word is optional with an `interface` declaration. **Example 12.2** displays the `Bank` interface again with the optional `abstract` reserved word added with the interface and the methods.

Example 12.2

```
abstract interface Bank
{
    public abstract double getCheckingBalance();

    public abstract void makeCheckingDeposit(double amount);

    public abstract void makeCheckingWithdrawal(double amount);
}
```

Implementation Rule

A **class**, which **implements** an **interface**, must implement <u>every method</u> declared in the **interface**.

Java also has an abstract class, which adds to the collection of different program containers. The first class students learned was the *concrete* class. It is rarely called *concrete*. In such a class every method is fully functional and the class can be used in a program to instantiate an object. This is the most common type of class.

Later the interface was introduced and every method in the interface is abstract. It is not possible to create an object with an interface. An interface can be the "umbrella" of a group of implementing classes, each with a method that has the same identifier. This is one approach to set up polymorphism.

There is also an *abstract class*, which is a curious hybrid. An abstract class <u>may have both abstract methods and concrete methods,</u> but there must have at least one abstract method. At first, it seems that anything done in an abstract class could be done in an interface, but that is not necessarily true.

Some people uses the abstract class as an umbrella for polymorphism and that works just fine, but it has a special role that is used a lot in Java and that is as an intermediate step between the interface and the concrete class.

A **HighSchool** program will be used to help explain a good use for the abstract class. Start with **Example 12.3**, which is a small class to test the **HighSchool** program. It shows two objects, **tom** and **sue**, who both are being processed as new students and then go through a variety of procedures, such as:,

Enroll new student, get emergency information, compute student GPA, mail progress report, take attendance, register for courses, attend orientation and participate in fundraising.

The testing program below creates the two objects and then tests each one of the **High School** methods. The methods will not perform any practical functionality. Each method will display a message indicating that it was called.

Example 12.3

```
public class TestHighSchool
{
    public static void main(String[] args)
    {
        HighSchool tom = new Sophomore();
        HighSchool sue = new Senior();
        tom.enroll();
        tom.test();
        tom.emergency();
        tom.computeGPA();
        tom.progress();
        tom.attendance();
        tom.register();
        tom.orientation();
        tom.fundRaising();
        sue.enroll();
        sue.test();
        sue.emergency();
        sue.computeGPA();
        sue.progress();
        sue.attendance();
        sue.register();
        sue.orientation();
        sue.fundRaising();
    }
}
```

The testing program shows that the methods are called twice, once for each object. You also need to realize that the methods fall into two categories. First there are a group of methods that apply to all the students. This includes procedures like enrolling for school, providing emergency information and taking attendance. Second, there are procedures that are different based on school year. Registration for classes is different for 9th graders than it is for 12th graders. The same is true for orientation and fund raising. Keep this in mind as we move on. Our program starts with an interface of 9 abstract methods. All methods in an interface are abstract and the **abstract** reserved word is not required. An abstract method is a method heading only that ends with a semi-colon. There is no method body. **Example 12.4** shows the interface with its 9 methods.

Example 12.4

```
interface HighSchool
{
   public void enroll();
   public void test();
   public void emergency();
   public void computeGPA();
   public void progress();
   public void attendance();
   public void register();
   public void orientation();
   public void fundRaising();
}
```

Suppose you already know that there will be four concrete classes, one for each high school grade level, to implement all the methods. You may anticipate that each one of the 9 methods will need to be implemented in the four concrete classes.

Now stop for a moment. There are 9 methods, but some of these methods are 100% the same for every grade level. One example is taking attendance and there are many other examples. Imagine now that you have four implementing classes, which implement 9 methods. That is a total of 36 methods. What comes to the rescue is the *abstract class*. In **Example 12.5** you see the implementation of 6 methods. In other words we have identified 6 methods out of 9 that will be identical for each grade level. These six methods are implemented in the abstract class, called **HighSchoolAdapter**. This leaves 3 methods to be implemented later. The difference? Now you have 6 methods implemented plus 4 x 3 later for a total of 18 methods. That is a considerable savings in method writing.

Example 12.5

```
abstract class HighSchoolAdapter implements HighSchool
{
   public void enroll()    {System.out.println("Enroll-All");}
   public void test()      {System.out.println("Test-All");}
   public void emergency() {System.out.println("Emergency-All");}
   public void computeGPA(){System.out.println("GPA-All");}
   public void progress()  {System.out.println("Progress-All"); }
   public void attendance(){System.out.println("Attendance-All");}
}
```

You will note that each one of the methods in **HighSchoolAdapter** includes the word **All**. This indicates that the method works properly for all grade levels. In **Example 12.6** you will see the 4 individual concrete classes for each grade level. Each method is specific to its own grade level and for demonstration purposes it is done with the grade-level number. Why are the methods different? Take the example of registration. A 9th grade student registers for English I while a 12th grader registers for English IV. Each class receives an orientation, and each grade-level has a different orientation. Discussions about Senior Prom are exclusive to the 12th grade orientation, along with graduation. 11th grade orientation includes university admission policy that will start early in the 12th grade and military academy appointments which has a process that already starts in the 11th grade.

The abstract class serves a special role here. A concrete class is required to implement every abstract method of an interface. This can cause a tedious duplication of identical methods. There is an intermediate process, which by convention is usually called adapter that works perfectly with an abstract class. In the adapter-abstract class, only the common methods are implemented. Any remaining methods will be implemented in the subclasses of the adapter, abstract class.

Example 12.6

```
class Freshman extends HighSchoolAdapter
{
    public void register()    {System.out.println("Register - 9");}
    public void orientation() {System.out.println("Orient - 9");}
    public void fundRaising() {System.out.println("Fund - 9");}
}

class Sophomore extends HighSchoolAdapter
{
    public void register()    {System.out.println("Register - 10");}
    public void orientation() {System.out.println("Orient - 10");}
    public void fundRaising() {System.out.println("Fund - 10");}
}

class Junior extends HighSchoolAdapter
{
    public void register()    {System.out.println("Register - 11");}
    public void orientation() {System.out.println("Orient - 11");}
    public void fundRaising() {System.out.println("Fund - 11");}
}

class Senior extends HighSchoolAdapter
{
    public void register()    {System.out.println("Register - 12");}
    public void orientation() {System.out.println("Orient - 12");}
    public void fundRaising() {System.out.println("Fund - 12");}
}
```

The biggest concern with interfaces, abstract classes and concrete classes is to make sure that all the proper methods are implemented at the right place. This also means that some concrete classes may require some "dummy" method implementations when only a single method is actually needed.

The KeyList01 class in **Example 12.7** implements the KeyListener interface. The only method needed is the keyPressed method for the purpose of identifying which arrow key is pressed. Even if only the keyPressed method is required, the keyReleased method and the keyTyped method of the KeyListener interface must also be implemented. In this case they are "dummy" methods with empty method bodies to satisfy the implementation requirement.

Example 12.7

```
public class KeyList01 extends Applet implements KeyListener
{

    public void init()
    {
        addKeyListener(this);
    }

    public void keyPressed(KeyEvent evt)
    {
        int key = evt.getKeyCode();

        if (key == KeyEvent.VK_LEFT)
            System.out.println("Left Arrow Key Pressed");
        else if (key == KeyEvent.VK_RIGHT)
            System.out.println("Right Arrow Key Pressed");
        else if (key == KeyEvent.VK_UP)
            System.out.println("Up Arrow Key Pressed");
        else if (key == KeyEvent.VK_DOWN)
            System.out.println("DownArrow Key Pressed");
    }

    public void keyReleased(KeyEvent evt)   { }   // dummy method
    public void keyTyped(KeyEvent evt)      { }   // dummy method

}
```

Chapter 12 Questions
Interfaces and Abstract Classes

01. Consider the following abstract interface and abstract class.

```
abstract interface CircusShow
{
    abstract public void entrance();
    abstract public void act();
    abstract public void announcement();
    abstract public void performance();
    abstract public void exit();
}


abstract class CircusShow
{
    abstract public void entrance();
    abstract public void act();
    abstract public void announcement();
    abstract public void performance();
    abstract public void exit();
}
```

What is the difference between the use of abstract interface and the abstract class?

    (A)   They are used exactly in the same manner in a program. There is no difference.
    (B)   The interface allows polymorphism, while the class cannot be used for polymorphism.
    (C)   The class allows polymorphism, while the interface cannot be used for polymorphism.
    (D)   One uses the reserved word `interface` and the other uses the reserved word `class`.
    (E)   Using the interface requires `implements` and using the class requires `extends`.

02. Consider the following abstract interface and abstract class.

```
abstract interface CircusShow
{
    abstract public void entrance();
    abstract public void act();
    abstract public void announcement();
    abstract public void performance();
    abstract public void exit();
}


abstract class CircusPerformer
{
    abstract public void entrance()
    {
        System.out.println("Performer enters arena in parade.");
    }
    abstract public void act();
    abstract public void announcement();
    abstract public void performance();
    abstract public void exit();
}
```

What is true about the use of the reserved word `abstract`?

I. None of the `abstract` words are required in the interface declaration.
II. None of the `abstract` words are required in the class declaration.
III. The entrance method in `CircusPerformer` is not abstract.

(A) I only
(B) II only
(C) III only
(D) I and II only
(E) I and III

03. Consider the following program.

```
public class DS1203
{
    public static void main(String[] args)
    {
        CircusPerformer ivan = new CircusPerformer();
    }
}


interface CircusPerformer
{
    public String getPerformer();
    public void act();
    public void entrance();
    public void performance();
    public void exit();
}
```

Which of the following are reason(s) why the program does not compile?

I. CircusPerformer is abstract and cannot be used to instantiate an object.
II. The CircusPerformer interface is not implemented by the required classes.
III. There is no constructor defined in interface CircusPerformer.

(A) I only
(B) II only
(C) III only
(D) I and II only
(E) I, II and III

04. Consider the following code segment, interface and class.

```
Acrobat ivan = new Acrobat("Ivan");
ivan.act();

interface CircusPerformer
{
    public String getPerformer();
    public void act();
    public void entrance();
    public void performance();
    public void exit();
}

class Acrobat implements CircusPerformer
{
    private String performerName;
    public Acrobat(String pN) { performerName = pN; }
    public void act()
    {
        entrance();
        performance();
        exit();
    }
    public void entrance()
    {
        System.out.println("Parades with performers");
    }
    public void performance()
    {
        System.out.println("Flips forwards and backwards on trapeze");
    }
}
```

What is printed as a result of executing the code segment?

(A) Flips forwards and backwards on trapeze
     Parades with performers
     Lands in safety net

(B) Ivan Flips forwards and backwards on trapeze
     Ivan Parades with performers
     Ivan Lands in safety net

(C) Ivan
     Flips forwards and backwards on trapeze
     Parades with performers
     Lands in safety net

(D) A compile error message, due to implementing a method that was not declared in the interface.

(E) A compile error message, due to not implementing a method that was declared in the interface.

05. Consider the following code segment, interface and class.

```
Acrobat ivan = new Acrobat("Ivan");
ivan.act();


interface CircusPerformer
{
    private String name;
    public String getPerformer();
    public void act();
    public void entrance();
    public void performance();
    public void exit();
}


class Acrobat implements CircusPerformer
{
    private String name;
    public Acrobat(String n)     { name = n; }
    public void act()
    {
        entrance();
        performance();
        exit();
    }
    public String getPerformer() { return name; }
    public void entrance(){System.out.println(name + " parades with performers");}
    public void performance()
    {
        System.out.println(name + " flips forwards and backwards on trapeze");
    }
    public void exit(){ System.out.println(name + " lands in safety net"); }
}
```

What is printed as a result of executing the code segment?

(A) ```
    parades with performers
    flips forwards and backwards on trapeze
    lands in safety net
    ```

(B) ```
    Ivan parades with performers
    Ivan flips forwards and backwards on trapeze
    Ivan lands in safety net
    ```

(C) ```
    Ivan
    parades with performers
    flips forwards and backwards on trapeze
    lands in safety net
    ```

(D) A compile error message, due to improperly using an attribute in the interface.

(E) A compile error message, due to implementing a method that was not declared in the interface.
    ```

06. Consider the following code segment, interface and class.

```
Acrobat ivan = new Acrobat("Ivan");
ivan.act();

interface CircusPerformer
{
    public String preName = "The great ";
    public String getPerformer();
    public void act();
    public void entrance();
    public void performance();
    public void exit();
}

class Acrobat implements CircusPerformer
{
    private String name;
    public Acrobat(String n)     { name = preName + n;}
    public void act()
    {
        entrance();
        performance();
        exit();
    }
    public String getPerformer() { return name; }
    public void entrance()
    {
        System.out.println(name + " parades with performers");
    }
    public void performance()
    {
        System.out.println(name + " flips forwards and backwards on trapeze");
    }
    public void exit()
    {
        System.out.println(name + " lands in safety net");
    }
}
```

What is printed as a result of executing the code segment?

(A) ```
parades with performers
flips forwards and backwards on trapeze
lands in safety net
```

(B) ```
Ivan parades with performers
Ivan flips forwards and backwards on trapeze
Ivan lands in safety net
```

(C) ```
The great Ivan parades with performers
The great Ivan flips forwards and backwards on trapeze
The great Ivan lands in safety net
```

(D) A compile error message, due to improperly using an attribute in the interface.

(E) A compile error message, due to implementing a method that was not declared in the interface.
```

07. Consider the following code segment and `Dance` interface.

```
Waltz waltz = new Waltz("Moon River");
ChaCha chacha = new ChaCha();
Tango tango = new Tango();
waltz.playMusic();
chacha.danceBasic();
tango.makeRoutine();

interface Dance
{
    public void playMusic();
    public void danceBasic();
}
```

Which of the following classes correctly implements the `Dance` interface?

```
class Waltz implements Dance
{
    private String music;
    public Waltz(String m)    { music = m; }
    public void playMusic()   { System.out.println("Play " + music); }
    public void danceBasic()
    {
        System.out.println("Forward-side-close, back-side-close");
    }
}

class ChaCha implements Dance
{
    public void playMusic()   { System.out.println("Play music"); }
    public void danceBasic()
    {
        System.out.println("Rock-step, cha-cha-cha");
    }
}

class Tango implements Dance
{
    public void playMusic()   { System.out.println("Play music "); }
    public void danceBasic()
    {
        System.out.println("Forward, forward, forward-side-drag");
    }
    public void makeRoutine() { System.out.println("Make dance routine"); }
}
```

(A) `Waltz` only
(B) `ChaCha` only
(C) `Waltz` and `ChaCha` only
(D) `ChaCha` and `ChaCha` only
(E) `Waltz`, `ChaCha` and `Tango`

08. Consider the following abstract `Dance` class.

```
abstract class Dance
{
    private String music;
    public Dance(String m)              { music = m; }
    public String getMusic()            { return music; }
    public abstract void playMusic();
    public abstract void danceBasic();
}
```

Which of the following classes correctly declares a subclass of Dance?

Subclass-1
```
class Tango extends Dance
{
    public Tango(String m)     { super(m); }
    public void playMusic()    { System.out.println("Play " + getMusic()); }
    public void danceBasic()
    {
        System.out.println("Dance fwd, fwd, fwd-side-drag");
    }
}
```

Subclass-2
```
class Tango extends Dance
{
    public Tango()             { }
    public void playMusic()    { System.out.println("Play music"); }
    public void danceBasic()
    {
        System.out.println("Dance fwd, fwd, fwd-side-drag");
    }
}
```

Subclass-3
```
class Tango extends Dance
{
    public void playMusic()    { System.out.println("Play music "); }
    public void danceBasic()
    {
        System.out.println("Dance fwd, fwd, fwd-side-drag");
    }
    public void makeRoutine() { System.out.println("Make dance routine"); }
}
```

(A) Subclass-1 only
(B) Subclass-2 only
(C) Subclass-3 only
(D) Subclass-2 and Subclass-3 only
(E) Subclass-1, Subclass-2 and Subclass-3

Questions 09-12 refer to the following interface, abstract class and classes.

```
interface CircusShow
{
    public void entrance();
    public void act();
    public void announcement();
    public void performance();
    public void exit();
}

abstract class Performer implements CircusShow
{
    public void entrance()
    {
        System.out.println("Performer enters arena in parade.");
    }
    public void act()
    {
        entrance();
        announcement();
        performance ();
        exit();
    }
    public void announcement()
    {
        System.out.println("Ringmaster announces performer entering arena.");
    }
    public void exit()
    {
        System.out.println("Performer receives flowers and leaves arena.");
    }
}

class Juggler extends Performer
{
    public void performance()
    {
        System.out.println("Performer juggles 4 knives.");
    }
}

class Equestrian extends Performer
{
    public void performance()
    {
        System.out.println("Performer rides standing on two ponies.");
    }
}

class LionTamer extends Performer
{
    public void performance()
    {
        System.out.println("Performer manages five lions in a cage.");
    }
}
```

09. What is true about the design of the previously shown program code?

I. The `Juggler, Equestrian` and `LionTamer` classes could implement the `CircusShow` directly without the use of the abstract `Performer` class.

II. The `Performer` abstract class is used for greater program writing efficiency.

III. The `Performer` abstract class is necessary for using polymorphic methods.

(A) I only
(B) II only
(C) III only
(D) I and II only
(E) II and III only

10. Consider the following three code segments.

Segment-1
```
Juggler sue = new Juggler();
Equestrian tom = new Equestrian();
LionTamer tarzan = new LionTamer();
```

Segment-2
```
Performer sue = new Juggler();
Performer tom = new Equestrian();
Performer tarzan = new LionTamer();
```

Segment-3
```
CircusShow sue = new Juggler();
CircusShow tom = new Equestrian();
CircusShow tarzan = new LionTamer();
```

Which of the three segments properly instantiates three new objects?

(A) I only
(B) II only
(C) III only
(D) I and II only
(E) I, II and III

11. Consider the following code segment.

```
Performer sue = new Juggler();
Performer tom = new Equestrian();
Performer tarzan = new LionTamer();
ArrayList<Performer> performers = new ArrayList<Performer>();
performers.add(sue);
performers.add(tom);
performers.add(tarzan);
for (Performer performer: performers)
    performer.act();
```

Which of the following three programming concepts is used with this program?

I.   Implementing abstract interface
II. Extending abstract class
III. Polymorphism

(A) I only
(B) I and II only
(C) I and III only
(D) II and III only
(E) I, II and III

12. Consider the following code segment.

```
CircusShow sue = new Juggler();
CircusShow tom = new Equestrian();
CircusShow tarzan = new LionTamer();
ArrayList<CircusShow> performers = new ArrayList<CircusShow>();
performers.add(sue);
performers.add(tom);
performers.add(tarzan);
for (CircusShow performer: performers)
    performer.act();
```

What is printed as a result of executing the code segment?

(A) Performer enters arena in parade.
    Ringmaster announces performer entering arena.
    Performer juggles 4 knives.
    Performer receives flowers and leaves arena.
    Performer enters arena in parade.
    Ringmaster announces performer entering arena.
    Performer rides standing on two ponies.
    Performer receives flowers and leaves arena.
    Performer enters arena in parade.
    Ringmaster announces performer entering arena.
    Performer manages five lions in a cage.
    Performer receives flowers and leaves arena.

(B) Performer juggles 4 knives.
    Performer rides standing on two ponies.
    Performer manages five lions in a cage.

(C) An `ArrayIndexOutOfBoundsException` error message

(D) A compile error, indicating that objects are incorrectly instantiated

(E) A compile error, indicating that generic data structures cannot be used with polymorphism

Chapter 13 Review
Program Design

In a few short pages it is not possible to "review" program design properly. Program design does not have the concrete descriptions of computer science features that can be demonstrated with a program, like a binary search algorithm. A few fundamental comments will be made here, but please find a good text book that includes program design or do research on this topic. Especially, check on the College Board web site and read the information about program design that is included with the course description for AP Computer Science. Be especially concerned with *Object Oriented Design*. Today programs are more complicated. Object Oriented Programming was born to handle these huge complicated programs in a reliable manner. **Table 13.1** shows the four basic steps involved with program design based on Object Oriented Programming.

Table 13.1

Step #	Step Mission
1	Understand the Problem Description
2	Class Design
3	Method Design
4	Class Interaction

Object Oriented Design is great, but it cannot ignore some fundamental rules of program design that have existed for several decades before Object Oriented Programming came on the scene. The rules in **Table 13.2** serve any style of programming well.

Table 13.2

Fundamental Program Design Rules
• Write your program in a clear, consistent style.   • Use meaningful, self-documenting identifiers.   • Do not place all your code in one module.   • Use the *one task - one module* philosophy.   • Place common purpose modules in one file.

Your knowledge of program design is expected to be at an introductory level. What does that mean? Well for starters, you are expected to understand clearly how a program works. In other words, before you can design your own programs, you must be able to understand how somebody else's design works. You are also expected to design a single class.

Design is great, but at some point comes implementation and students in a first course must be able to write the method body of the method signature described in a class design. Additionally, you should also be able to write a class that implements an interface. **Table 13.3** specifies the individual design topics that students must understand.

Table 13.3

AP Examination Alert
Program design topics at the APCS "A" level: • Comprehend the design of a provided program • Understand a problem description, purpose and goals • Apply data abstraction and encapsulation • Understand class specifications • Understand "is-a" class relationships • Understand "has-a" class relationships • Understand and implement a given class hierarchy • Identify and use existing class libraries • Identify reusable code from existing code • Design a single class • Know implementation techniques
You can expect AP Computer Science Examination questions on the multiple choice segment and also on the free response segment about program design.

Program Design Pitfalls

Program design is the least objective topic on the APCS Examination. Many questions involve using program code and the free-response section requires writing program code. Program code is correct or is not correct. Program design is more elusive. It is a mistake to answer design questions based on your opinion of how programs should be created. You need to get an idea how the people creating the APCS Exam view program design. Their approach is to follow acceptable policies established at important universities by leaders in computer science. It is a good idea to go to the College Board web site and look at the course description for AP Computer Science. This includes valuable information about program design. The information presented in the course description will give you an accurate indication of the feelings about program design that will be reflected on the APCS Exam.

Chapter 13 Questions
Program Design

Questions 01-06 refer to the following hospital program design specifications.

A hospital needs a new patient administration program. The purpose of the program
is to track patients administratively for their entire stay in the hospital.
The program does not include any hospital non-patient functions, such as employee records,
employee payroll or staff scheduling.

The hospital patient program is neither concerned with diagnosing illnesses nor
determining any type of treatment. All such procedures are under the responsibility
of the patient's personal physicians.

Since all patients are treated administratively in the same manner, the program design does
not need to implement methods polymorphically, because methods will not be providing
different functionality for different situations.

01. You are at the first stage of program development. The hospital has given very
clear specifications that will not likely alter. Their main concern is complete
reliability in the manner that patients are tracked during their hospital stay.

Considering that different programs have different design priorities and requirements,
which of the following is the most logical first step in program development for this program?

(A) Design an umbrella interface with implementing classes for all of the functionalities of the program.

(B) Design an umbrella superclass that will include all the concrete functionalities of the program.

(C) Design a `Patient` unit class that will be responsible for all the individual patient information.

(D) Design a `Hospital` class that will store all the hospital administrative data and process methods.

(E) Create a `PatientData` class that will store data for all the patients so that other classes can
efficiently access any of the patient information.

Questions 02-06 refer to the following `Patient` unit class.

Be aware that a realistic class includes far more members, but is not practical in the limited space and limited time provided for questions.

```
class Patient
{
    private String patientName;
    private String doctorName;
    private String patientIllness;
    private String insuranceName;

    // additional attributes for storing patient information

    public Patient(String pN, String dN, String pI, String iN)
    {
        patientName = pN;
        doctorName = dN;
        patientIllness = pI;
        insuranceName = iN;
    }

    public String getPatient()              { return patientName; }
    public String getDoctor()               { return doctorName; }
    public String getIllness()              { return patientIllness; }
    public String getInsurance()            { return insuranceName; }

    public void setPatient(String pN)    { patientName = pN; }
    public void setDoctor(String dN)     { doctorName = dN; }
    public void setIllness(String pI)    { patientIllness = pI; }
    public void setInsurance(String iN)  { insuranceName = iN; }

    // additional methods to process administrative procedures for patients
}
```

02. The `Patient` class is responsible for storing all the administrative procedures of a single patient. After this first stage start, what is the next step in our hospital program?

(A) Create a data structure to store information about all the patients.

(B) Test the `Patient` unit class thoroughly to insure reliability, before any interaction with another class.

(C) Extend the `Patient` class with specific classes for each patient.

(D) Instantiate multiple objects of the `Patient` class to store in a larger container class.

(E) Re-define `Patient` methods in subclasses for specific functionality.

03. It is decided that the `Patient` unit class must be thoroughly tested before the class can interact with any other class in the hospital program. For example, the code segment below should display:

```
Tom Jones
Tulika Jain
Knee Surgery
Aetna
```

```
Patient tom;
tom = new Patient("Tom Jones","Tulika Jain","Knee Surgery","Aetna");
System.out.println(tom);
```

Method `toString` can be used to conveniently display the data attributes of a class.
Which one of the following re-definitions of method `toString` will test the `Patient` class as specified?

Re-definition I
```
public String toString()
{
    String temp = patientName + "\n";
    temp = temp + doctorName + "\n";
    temp = temp + patientIllness + "\n";
    temp = temp + insuranceName + "\n";
    return temp;
}
```

Re-definition II
```
public String toString()
{
    return patientName + "\n" + doctorName + "\n" + patientIllness +
            "\n" + insuranceName;
}
```

Re-definition III
```
public String toString()
{
    return patientName + " " + doctorName + " " + patientIllness +
            " " + insuranceName;
}
```

(A) I only
(B) II only
(C) III only
(D) I and II only
(E) II and III only

04. Consider the following `Hospital` class and the previous `Patient` class.

```
class Hospital
{
    private int patientCount;
    private ArrayList<Patient> patients;

    // additional attributes to store patient information

    public Hospital()
    {
        patientCount = 0;
        patients = new ArrayList<Patient>();
    }

    // Additional methods to enter, alter, display patient information
}
```

Assume that the `Patient` class has been tested and is ready for interaction with other classes.
What is the class interaction between the `Hospital` class and the `Patient` class?

I.   Inheritance
II. Composition
III. Polymorphism

(A) I only
(B) II only
(C) III only
(D) I and II only
(E) I, II and III

05. Consider the following `Hospital` class and the previous `Patient` class.

```
class Hospital
{
    private int patientCount;
    private ArrayList<Patient> patients;

    // additional attributes to store patient information

    public Hospital()
    {
        patientCount = 0;
        patients = new ArrayList<Patient>();
    }

    public void newPatient()
    {
        /* code that inputs the patient information for
             patient's name        pN
             doctor's name         dN
             patient's illness     pI
             insurance's name      iN
        */

        /* Missing Code */
    }
}
```

A `newPatient` method needs to be implemented, which is partially completed. Which of the following implementations of /* **Missing Code** */ will enter the information correctly in the `Hospital` class?

Implementation I
```
Patient temp = new Patient(pN,dN,pI,iN);
patients.add(temp);
```

Implementation II
```
Patient temp = new Patient(pN,dN,pI,iN);
patients.add(temp);
return temp;
```

Implementation III
```
patients.add(new Patient(pN,dN,pI,iN));
```

(A) I only
(B) II only
(C) III only
(D) I and II only
(E) I and III only

06. Consider the following `Hospital` class and the previous `Patient` class.

```
class Hospital
{
    private int patientCount;
    private ArrayList<Patient> patients;
    // additional attributes to store patient information

    public Hospital()
    {
        patientCount = 0;
        patients = new ArrayList<Patient>();
    }

    public void newPatient()
    {
        /* code that inputs the patient information for
            patient's name        pN
            doctor's name         dN
            patient's illness     pI
            insurance's name      iN
        */

        /* Missing Code */

    }

    public void showPatients()
    {
        /* Missing Code */
    }
}
```

A `showPatients` method needs to be implemented, which will display all the patient records. Which of the following implementations of /* **Missing Code** */ will display the `Hospital` data?

Implementation I
```
for (Patient p: patients)
    System.out.println(p);
```

Implementation II
```
for (patients p: Patient)
    System.out.println(p);
```

Implementation III
```
System.out.println(Patient);
```

(A) I only
(B) II only
(C) III only
(D) I and II only
(E) I and III only

Questions 07-12 refer to the following requirements for a complex administrative program.

You are the team program leader in charge of designing a reliable program that can
be easily debugged and enhanced by a team of programmers.

Circus Kroner needs a program to manage its performances. This is not a program to keep
track of employees pay and benefits. It is strictly a program for the current and future
performances of circus Kroner.

The program needs the flexibility to adds different types of circus performers in the future,
with minimal effort. Furthermore, the program needs to take advantage of the fact that many
performers engage in similar activities that should not be duplicated in the program.

It is expected that the program will take advantage of the reliability gained by proper class
interaction using inheritance and composition. Polymorphism will also be used, which works
especially well when the number of performers and the number of classes grow in the future.

It has been decided that the first consideration will be for the umbrella that will manage future
classes. Should this be a class or should it be an interface? Consider the two choices below and
keep in mind that a real program would have many more methods than are shown.

```
interface Circus                          class Circus
{                                         {
  public void costume();                    public void costume()      {/* code */}
  public void entrance();                   public void entrance()     {/* code */}
  public void announcement();               public void announcement() {/* code */}
  public void act();                        public void act()          {/* code */}
  public void performance();                public void performance()  {/* code */}
  public void exit();                       public void exit()         {/* code */}
}                                         }
```

07. Select the `interface` or the `class` to start designing the program.
     Which of the following is the most plausible argument for your selection?

   (A) The `class` approach is better, because it has immediate functional methods that can be tested
        and improved. It allows the programmers to get to work quicker.

   (B) The `class` approach is better, because polymorphism is part of the future program design as
        new acts are added to the show. Polymorphism is much easier with a `class` umbrella.

   (C) The `interface` approach is better, because polymorphism is part of the future program design as
        new acts are added to the show. Polymorphism is much easier with an `interface` umbrella.

   (D) The `interface` approach is better, because it allows maximum flexibility between the programming
        team and the client about the requirements without any concerns yet about implementations.

   (E) It simply does not matter. It is strictly a personal preference and both the `class` approach
        and the `interface` approach work equally well for program design.

08. The decision by the programming team is to start with writing an `interface`.
The `Circus interface` is shown below and will be the umbrella for the actions of the program.

```
interface Circus
{
    public void costume();
    public void entrance();
    public void announcement();
    public void act();
    public void performance();
    public void exit();
}
```

The next consideration is to decide whether to implement every abstract method of the interface in a concrete class directly or to use an intermediate abstract class first.

Select the immediate concrete class implementations or the abstract class intermediate approach. Which of the following is the most plausible argument for your selection?

(A) The intermediate abstract class approach is better, because it allows implementation of all the common methods that have identical actions first, and then the individual performing classes focus on the differences. It will also allow the addition of a new circus performer with minimal additional code.

(B) The intermediate abstract class approach is better, because polymorphism can already start at the abstract class level and does not need to wait for concrete class extensions.

(C) The immediate concrete class implementation is better, because it can specifically construct individual objects and get down to the business of testing a realistic program.

(D) The immediate concrete class implementation is better, because polymorphism is only possible with the implementation of methods at the concrete class level.

(E) A proper decision cannot be made until it is known how the program will change in the future.

09. The decision by the programming team is to design an intermediate abstract class, called `Performer`. It is also decided that the following actions are identical for all circus performers and can therefore be implemented in the abstract `Performer` class.

Method `entrance`, since all performers enter the arena in a parade at the start of the show.
Method `announcement`, since everybody is announced as they enter the arena.
Method `act`, since the sequence of performer actions is identical.
Method `exit`, since all performers take a bow, receive flowers and leave the arena.

The remainder of the methods will stay abstract, to be implemented in the individual concrete classes.

Method `costume`, since each performer has a specific costume for their show and their size.
Method `performance`, since each performer has a unique responsibility to dazzle the audience.

Which of the three `Performer` abstract classes below correctly implements `Circus`?

```
abstract class Performer1 implements Circus
{
    public void entrance()     {System.out.println("Performer enters arena in a parade."); }
    public void announcement() {System.out.println("Performer is announced.");    }
    public void act()          {entrance(); announcement(); performance(); exit(); }
    public void exit()         {System.out.println("Performer receives flowers."); }
}
```

```
abstract class Performer2 implements Circus
{
    public void entrance()     {System.out.println("Performer enters arena in a parade."); }
    public void announcement() {System.out.println("Performer is announced.");    }
    public void act()          {entrance(); announcement(); performance(); exit(); }
    public void exit()         {System.out.println("Performer receives flowers."); }
    public abstract void costume();
    public abstract void performance();
}
```

```
class Performer3 implements Circus
{
    public void entrance()     {System.out.println("Performer enters arena in a parade."); }
    public void announcement() {System.out.println("Performer is announced.");    }
    public void act()          {entrance(); announcement(); performance(); exit(); }
    public void exit()         {System.out.println("Performer receives flowers."); }
    public void costume();
    public void performance();
}
```

(A) `Performer1` only
(B) `Performer2` only
(C) `Performer3` only
(D) `Performer1` and `Performer2` only
(E) `Performer2` and `Performer3` only

```
interface Circus
{
    public void costume();
    public void entrance();
    public void announcement();
    public void act();
    public void performance();
    public void exit();
}
```

```
abstract class Performer implements Circus
{
    public void entrance()     { System.out.println("Performer enters arena in a parade."); }
    public void announcement() { System.out.println("Performer is announced."); }
    public void act()          { entrance(); announcement(); performance(); exit(); }
    public void exit()         { System.out.println("Performer receives flowers."); }
}
```

```
class Acrobat extends Performer
{
    public void costume()     { System.out.println("Wears white leotards"); }
    public void performance() { System.out.println("Flies and flips on the trapeze"); }
}
```

```
class Clown extends Performer
{
    public void costume()     { System.out.println("Wears funny outfits and clown make-up"); }
    public void performance() { System.out.println("Acts funny and makes audience laugh"); }
}
```

```
class LionTamer extends Performer
{
    public void costume()     { System.out.println("Wears Tarzan outfit"); }
    public void performance() { System.out.println("Manages lions and tigers in a cage"); }
}
```

10. The current program should have established the ability to use polymorphism with the `Circus` umbrella interface. Polymorphism is not yet actually used, but which of the methods can be used polymorphically?

    (A) All the abstract methods
    (B) All the implemented methods
    (C) Methods `costume` and `performance`
    (D) Method `act` only
    (E) Methods `entrance`, `announcement`, `act` and `exit`

11. Consider the following code segment and previously mentioned interface, abstract class and class extensions.

```
Circus olga = new Acrobat();
Circus paljasso = new Clown();
Circus igor = new LionTamer();

ArrayList<Circus> performers = new ArrayList<Circus>();
performers.add(olga);
performers.add(paljasso);
performers.add(igor);
for (Circus p: performers)
{
    p.costume();
    p.performance();
}
```

What is printed as a result of executing the code segment?

(A) Wears white leotards
     Flies and flips on the trapeze
     Wears funny outfits and clown make-up
     Acts funny and makes audience laugh
     Wears Tarzan outfit
     Manages lions and tigers in a cage

(B) olga Wears white leotards
     olga Flies and flips on the trapeze
     paljasso Wears funny outfits and clown make-up
     paljasso Acts funny and makes audience laugh
     igor Wears Tarzan outfit
     igor Manages lions and tigers in a cage

(C) olga
     Wears white leotards
     Flies and flips on the trapeze
     paljasso
     Wears funny outfits and clown make-up
     Acts funny and makes audience laugh
     igor
     Wears Tarzan outfit
     Manages lions and tigers in a cage

(D) An Exception error message indicating that polymorphism is not allowed in this manner

(E) A compile error message indicating that methods costume and performance must be declared
     abstract in the Performer class

12. Consider the following code segment and previously mentioned interface, abstract class and class extensions.

```
Circus olga = new Acrobat();
Circus paljasso = new Clown();
Circus igor = new LionTamer();

ArrayList<Circus> performers = new ArrayList<Circus>();
performers.add(olga);
performers.add(paljasso);
performers.add(igor);
for (Circus p: performers)
    p.act();
```

The output of this program displays the action sequence of each circus performer.
Is this proof that method `act` is a polymorphic method?

(A) Yes, because the method executions have many forms, each according to their own class definition.

(B) Yes, because method `act` is defined individually for each concrete class.

(C) No, because this code segment does not use polymorphism.

(D) No, because method `act` only has one form, and then calls methods `costume` and `performance`, both of which are polymorphic.

(E) No, because method `act` is an abstract method.

Chapter 14 Review
Re-defining toString and equals

There is more to method writing then starting with a method heading and filling in program statements between the opening brace and closing brace. A new method can be created in one of three ways. First, you can create a brand-new method. This method must be designed and written from scratch. Second, you can re-define an existing superclass method. Third, you can implement an abstract method from an interface or an abstract class. This chapter is concerned with re-defining methods, specifically the `toString` and `equals` methods.

Inheritance allows access to the public methods of a superclass. Inheritance also allows the re-definition of superclass methods. You might wonder why there is a need to use inheritance if superclass methods can be re-defined. The point of using inheritance is to increase program reliability by using existing classes that have been thoroughly tested and improved. Sooner or later the situation occurs where you wish to create a class that is similar to an existing class. It is possible to start from scratch, but the existing class contains a number of methods that are perfect for your needs. The existing class also contains several methods that must be rewritten. In such a situation your new class benefits by becoming a subclass of the existing class. You happily use the existing superclass methods that are perfect for your needs and you re-define the other methods. This approach gives greater reliability and less work.

This may seem a repeat of the inheritance chapter, but there is a point. There are two important Java methods that are used very frequently and they are constantly re-defined in different classes. They are methods `toString` and `equals`.

The highest level class, which is the superclass for all other classes, is the `Object` class. The `Object` class contains the original definition of methods `toString` and `equals`. This means that these two methods are always available in any class you create. It also means that you will always get the original definition of these methods, unless you re-define one or both of them. Before re-definition becomes an issue, you must realize the details of the original definitions in the `Object` class.

APCS Examination Alert

The **Object** class is the superclass of all other classes.

Methods **toString** and **equals** are defined in the **Object** class.

Methods **toString** and **equals** can be used by any class you create.

Methods **toString** and **equals** are tested on the APCS Exam.

Method `toString` works quietly in the background. Methods `print` and `println` display a string, which is returned by method `toString`. Even though it is not visible in the program code, each time `print` or `println` is used in any program statement, `toString` is also used to assist in the output display of the parameter information used by `print` and `println`. The original `toString` method returns the string representation of the *immediate* or *shallow* value of a variable. That means you will get practical values for primitive data types, but memory references for objects.

The Original toString Method

print and **println** request display instructions from the **toString** method.

The **toString** method, as defined by the **Object** class, returns the actual string representation values of all the primitive types like **int** and **double**.

toString returns the class name followed by the memory reference of any variable object.

Program **Example 14.1** declares a small `Student` class. Method `println` is used to display the value of the `int` variable `number` and the `student` object. The output shows the `100` value for `number`, but the output of `student` is the name of the class followed by a memory reference. Method `toString` follows the instructions precisely specified in the `Object` class.

Example 14.1

```
public class Example141
{
    public static void main (String args[])
    {
        int number = 100;
        Student student = new Student("Tom",21);
        System.out.println(number + "    " + student);
    }
}

class Student
{
    private String name;
    private int age;

    public Student(String n, int a)
    {
        name = n;
        age = a;
    }
}
```

Program Output
100   Student@19821f

Make sure that you do not get confused. The program in **Example 14.2** shows an `ArrayList` object `names` and this object displays without difficulty. The four names stored in the object are shown without any memory reference. This program actually reminds you of the whole *re-definition* point. The `toString` method is re-defined for the `ArrayList` class or at least some superclass of the `ArrayList` class.

Example 14.2

```
public class Example142
{
    public static void main (String args[])
    {
        ArrayList<String> names = new ArrayList<String>();
        names.add("Sue");
        names.add("Tom");
        names.add("Joe");
        names.add("Ann");
        System.out.println(names);
    }
}
```

Program Output
[Sue, Tom, Joe, Ann]

Method toString Notes

print and **println** request display instructions from the **toString** method.

The **toString** method, as defined by the **Object** class, returns the actual string representation values of all the primitive types like **int** and **double**.

toString returns the class name followed by the memory reference of any variable object.

Many classes, such as the **ArrayList** class, use a re-defined **toString** method.

If **toString** is not re-defined in any class you declare, the output of your class object will be the class name followed by a memory reference.

Class `Student` is rewritten in **Example 14.3**. This time method `toString` is re-defined. It is a short method without many details. The only requirement is that a string is returned. In this case a format is used to mimic the style of output that is used by the `ArrayList` class.

Example 14.3

```
class Student
{
    private String name;
    private int age;

    public Student(String n, int a)
    {
        name = n;
        age = a;
    }

    public String toString()
    {
        return "[" + name + ", " + age + "]";
    }
}
```

The new, and improved, `Student` class can now be used and tested. Program **Example 14.3 Continued** shows that the output does in fact have the same output format as an `ArrayList` object, including square brackets and commas.

Example 14.3 Continued

```
public class Example143
{
    public static void main (String args[])
    {
        Student student = new Student("Tom",21);
        System.out.println(student);
    }
}
```

Program Output
`[Tom, 21]`

Method `equals` is not very practical with its original definition. Like `toString`, `equals` is re-defined for many Java standard classes, like the `String` class. When you create your own classes make sure that you consider the equality issue. The program in **Example 14.4** compares students and checks equality according to GPA.

Example 14.4

```
public class Example144
{
    public static void main (String args[])
    {
        Student student1 = new Student("Tom",21,3.575);
        Student student2 = new Student("Sue",23,2.925);
        Student student3 = new Student("Ann",19,3.575);
        if (student1.equals(student2))
            System.out.println("student1 equals student2");
        else
            System.out.println("student1 does not equal student2");
        if (student1.equals(student3))
            System.out.println("student1 equals student3");
        else
            System.out.println("student1 does not equal student3");
    }
}

class Student
{
    private String name;
    private int age;
    private double gpa;

    public Student(String n, int a, double g)
    {
        name = n;
        age = a;
        gpa = g;
    }

    public String getName()    { return name; }
    public int getAge()        { return age; }
    public double getGPA()     { return gpa; }

    public boolean equals(Object obj)
    {
        Student temp = (Student) obj;
        return temp.getGPA() == gpa;
    }
}
```

Program Output

```
student1 does not equal student2
student1 equals student3
```

Method equals Notes

The **equals** method, as defined by the **Object** class, compares the immediate, *shallow*, values of two objects.

Many classes, such as the **String** class and the **ArrayList** class, use a re-defined **equals** method.

If method **equals** is not re-defined in any class you create, equality will be tested according the shallow or memory references of your objects.

Redefining toString and equals Pitfalls

It is not necessary to have a special pitfall section for this chapter. There are no subtle problems. You need to know the exact method headings and make sure that they are properly re-defined.

The primary concern is knowing where `toString` and `equals` are defined. Every class you use in a program has a definition for `toString` and `equals`. It will either be the original definition started in the `Object` class or re-defined in some other class. If it is the original definition in the `Object` class, it means that `toString` returns shallow memory values and `equals` compares shallow memory values.

If `toString` and `equals` are re-defined there are two possibilities. First, the re-definition occurred in one of the Java standard classes. In such a case you must find out the details of the re-definition from Java documentation. The second possibility is that you are creating a new class and then you decide how to re-define `toString` and/or `equals`.

Chapter 14 Questions
Re-defining Methods toString and equals

01. Consider the following code segment.

```
ArrayList<String> names = new ArrayList<String>();
names.add("Astrid");
names.add("Leon");
names.add("Ingrid");
names.add("Remy");
System.out.println(names);
```

What is printed as a result of executing the code segment?

(A) `ArrayList@<some hexadecimal number>` like `ArrayList@18d107f`
(B) `[Astrid, Leon, Ingrid, Remy]`
(C) `Astrid`
(D) `Astrid Leon Ingrid Remy`
(E) `Remy Ingrid Leon Astrid`

02. Consider the following code segment.

```
ArrayList<Student> students = new ArrayList<Student>();
students.add(new Student(25,3.575));
students.add(new Student(23,2.225));
System.out.println(students);

class Student
{
    private int age;
    private double gpa;

    public Student(int age, double gpa)
    {
        this.age = age;
        this.gpa = gpa;
    }
}
```

What is printed as a result of executing the code segment?

(A) `[Student@e9f784d, Student@7930ebb]`
(B) `Student@e9f784d, Student@7930ebb`
(C) `students@b8d34be`
(D) `[[25, 3.575], [23, 2.225]]`
(E) `[25,3.575], [23, 2.225]`

03. Consider the following code segment.

```
ArrayList<String> cats = new ArrayList<String>();
cats.add("Lions");
cats.add("Tigers");

ArrayList<String> swimmers = new ArrayList<String>();
swimmers.add("Whales");
swimmers.add("Dolphins");

ArrayList<String> primates = new ArrayList<String>();
primates.add("Gorillas");
primates.add("Chimpanzees");

ArrayList<ArrayList<String>> mammals = new ArrayList<ArrayList<String>>();
mammals.add(cats);
mammals.add(swimmers);
mammals.add(primates);

System.out.println(mammals);
```

What will be printed as a result of executing the code segment?

(A) [cats@e9f784d, swimmers@7930ebb, primates@a7dc234]
(B) [mammals@7930ebb]
(C) [[Lions, Tigers], [Whales, Dolphins], [Gorillas, Chimpanzees]]
(D) [Lions], [Tigers], [Whales], [Dolphins], [Gorillas], [Chimpanzees]
(E) [Lions, Tigers, Whales, Dolphins, Gorillas, Chimpanzees]

04. Consider the following code segment.

```
ArrayList<Student> students = new ArrayList<Student>();
students.add(new Student(25,3.575));
students.add(new Student(23,2.225));
System.out.println(students);


class Student
{
    private int age;
    private double gpa;
    public Student(int age, double gpa)
    {
        this.age = age;
        this.gpa = gpa;
    }

    public String toString()
    {
        return age + " " + gpa;
    }
}
```

What is printed as a result of executing the code segment?

(A) [Student@e9f784d, Student@7930ebb]
(B) Student@e9f784d, Student@7930ebb
(C) students@b8d34be
(D) [[25 3.575], [23 2.225]]
(E) [25 3.575, 23 2.225]

05. Consider the following code segment and `Widget` class.

```
Widget w = new Widget(50);
System.out.println(w);                  // Output-1
System.out.println(w.toString());       // Output-2
System.out.println(w.getWidgets());     // OutPut-3


class Widget
{
    private int numWidgets;

    public Widget(int nW)
    {
        numWidgets = nW;
    }

    public int getWidgets()
    {
        return numWidgets;
    }

    public void setWidgets(int nW)
    {
        numWidgets = nW;
    }

    public String toString()
    {
        return "" + numWidgets;
    }
}
```

Which of the following three `// Output-x` statements will display the number of `widgets` stored?

(A) `Output-1` only
(B) `Output-2` only
(C) `Output-3` only
(D) `Output-1` and `Output-3` only
(E) `Output-1`, `Output-2` and `Output-3`

06. Consider the following code segment and `IntList` class.

```
IntList list = new IntList(10);
System.out.println(list);


class IntList
{
    private int size;
    private int[] numbers;

    public IntList(int n)
    {
        size = n;
        numbers = new int[size];
        for (int k = 0; k < n; k++)
            numbers[k] = (int) (Math.random() * 100);
    }

    /** Postcondition: returns the members of the numbers array
     *                 in the format [32, 56, 42, 78, 82, 31]
     */
    public String toString()
    {
        /* missing code */
    }
}
```

Which of the following three implementations of /* **missing code** */ will make method `toString` work as intended?

Implementation 1
```
String temp = "[";
for (int k = 0; k < size-1; k++)
    temp += numbers[k] + ", ";
temp += numbers[size-1] + "]";
return temp;
```

Implementation 2
```
System.out.print("[");
for (int k = 0; k < size-1; k++)
    System.out.print(intArray[k] + ", ");
System.out.println(intArray[size-1] + "]");
```

Implementation 3
```
return "[" + intArray + "]";
```

(A) Implementation 1 only
(B) Implementation 2 only
(C) Implementation 3 only
(D) Implementations 1 and 2 only
(E) Implementations 1 and 3 only

07. Consider the following code segment and Student class.

```
Student tom = new Student(25,3.215);
Student sue = new Student(19,2.975);
System.out.println(tom);
System.out.println(sue);


class Student
{
    private int age;
    private double gpa;

    public Student(int age, double gpa)
    {
        this.age = age;
        this.gpa = gpa;
    }

    public int getAge()
    {
        return age;
    }

    public double getGPA()
    {
        return gpa;
    }

    public String toString()
    {
        return getAge() + getGPA();
    }
}
```

What is printed as a result of executing the code segment?

(A) 253.215
     192.975

(B) 253.215 192.975

(C) [25, 3.215], [19, 2.975]

(D) Student@e9f784d Student@7930ebb

(E) A compile error message indicating incompatible types

08. Consider the following code segment and `Student` class.

```
Student tom = new Student(25,3.215);
Student sue = new Student(25,3.215);
Student meg = new Student(25,2.575);
System.out.println(tom == sue);
System.out.println(tom == meg);


class Student
{
    private int age;
    private double gpa;

    public Student(int age, double gpa)
    {
        this.age = age;
        this.gpa = gpa;
    }

    public int getAge()
    {
        return age;
    }

    public double getGPA()
    {
        return gpa;
    }
}
```

What is printed as a result of executing the code segment?

(A) true
    true

(B) true
    false

(C) false
    true

(D) false
    false

(E) A compile error message indicating incompatible types

09. Consider the following code segment and `Student` class.

```java
Student tom = new Student(25,3.215);
Student sue = new Student(25,3.215);
Student meg = new Student(25,2.575);
System.out.println(tom.equals(sue));
System.out.println(tom.equals(meg));


class Student
{
    private int age;
    private double gpa;

    public Student(int age, double gpa)
    {
        this.age = age;
        this.gpa = gpa;
    }

    public int getAge()
    {
        return age;
    }

    public double getGPA()
    {
        return gpa;
    }

    public boolean equals(Student obj)
    {
        return (this.gpa == obj.gpa);
    }
}
```

What is printed as a result of executing the code segment?

(A) `true`
`true`

(B) `true`
`false`

(C) `false`
`true`

(D) `false`
`false`

(E) A compile error message indicating incompatible types

10. Consider the following code segment and `Student` class.

```
Student tom = new Student(25,3.215);
Student sue = new Student(24,3.215);
Student meg = new Student(25,2.575);
System.out.println(tom.equals(sue));
System.out.println(tom.equals(meg));


class Student
{
    private int age;
    private double gpa;

    public Student(int age, double gpa)
    {
        this.age = age;
        this.gpa = gpa;
    }

    public int getAge()
    {
        return age;
    }

    public double getGPA()
    {
        return gpa;
    }

    public boolean equals(Student obj)
    {
        return (this.gpa == obj.gpa || this.age == obj.age);
    }
}
```

What is printed as a result of executing the code segment?

(A) true
    true

(B) true
    false

(C) false
    true

(D) false
    false

(E) A compile error message indicating incompatible types

11. Consider the following code segment and List class.

```
int[] numbers1 = {10,10,10,10,10,10,10};
int[] numbers2 = {10,20,30,40,50,60,70};
int[] numbers3 = {40,40,40,40,40,40,40};
List list1 = new List(numbers1);
List list2 = new List(numbers2);
List list3 = new List(numbers3);
System.out.println(list1.equals(list2));
System.out.println(list1.equals(list3));
System.out.println(list2.equals(list3));


class List
{
    private int size;
    private int[] numbers;
    private double x;

    public List(int[] numbers)
    {
        size = numbers.length;
        this.numbers = numbers;
        int temp = 0;
        for (int n: numbers)
            temp += n;
        x = (double) temp / size;
    }

    public boolean equals(List obj)
    {
        return this.x == obj.x;
    }
}
```

What is printed as a result of executing the code segment?

(A)	(B)	(C)	(D)	(E)
true	false	false	true	true
true	false	false	false	true
true	false	true	true	false

12. An Iron Man triathlon consists of 3 events: A 2.4 mile swim, a 112 mile bike, and a Marathon (26.2 mile) run. All 3 events are done on the same day, one right after the other. Each triathlete's time in each event is recorded in hours, minutes, and seconds. The total time of all 3 events is used to determine a triathlete's standing.

Consider the following code segment and 2 classes.

```
Time tomSwim    = new Time(1,4,28);   // 1 hour, 4 minutes and 28 seconds
Time tomBike    = new Time(5,54,26);
Time tomRun     = new Time(4,32,2);
Triathlete tom = new Triathlete(tomSwim, tomBike, tomRun);

Time joeSwim    = new Time(1,6,42);
Time joeBike    = new Time(6,3,44);
Time joeRun     = new Time(4,20,30);
Triathlete joe = new Triathlete(joeSwim, joeBike, joeRun);

System.out.println(tom.equals(joe));
```

```
class Time
{
   private int sec;

   public Time (int h, int m, int s)
   {
      sec  =  h * 3600 + m * 60 + s;
   }

   public int getSec()
   {
      return sec;
   }

   public boolean equals(Time that)
   {
      return this.sec == that.sec;
   }
}
```

```
class Triathlete
{
   private Time swimTime;
   private Time bikeTime;
   private Time runTime;

   public Triathlete(Time sT, Time bT, Time rT)
   {
      swimTime = sT;
      bikeTime = bT;
      runTime  = rT;
   }

   public boolean equals(Triathlete that)
   {
      /* missing code */
   }
}
```

Which of the following implementations of /* **missing code** */ will make the `equals` method of the `Triathlete` class work as intended?

(A) `return this.equals(that);`

(B) `int thisTime = this.swim.getSec() + this.bike.getSec() + this.run.getSec();`
     `int thatTime = that.swim.getSec() + that.bike.getSec() + that.run.getSec();`
     `return (thisTime == thatTime);`

(C) `return this.swim.equals(that.swim) && this.bike.equals(that.bike) &&`
     `                                       this.run.equals(that.run);`

(D) `return this.swim.getH() == that.swim.getH() &&`
     `         this.swim.getM() == that.swim.getM() &&`
     `         this.swim.getS() == that.swim.getS() &&`
     `         this.bike.getH() == that.bike.getH() &&`
     `         this.bike.getM() == that.bike.getM() &&`
     `         this.bike.getS() == that.bike.getS() &&`
     `         this.run.getH()  == that.run.getH()  &&`
     `         this.run.getM()  == that.run.getM()  &&`
     `         this.run.getS()  == that.run.getS();`

(E) All of the above

Chapter 15 Review
Algorithms and Informal Algorithmic Analysis

The point of algorithmic analysis is not to reinvent the wheel, but to know which wheel to use. Computer Science has many established algorithms. The biggest job of computer programs is data processing and data needs to be continuously searched and sorted. If there exist many algorithms, and these algorithms are conveniently available in some library, there is still the question about which algorithm to pick. This is where algorithmic analysis assists and helps you to decide the best algorithm for the job.

Analysis starts by understanding execution frequency of various control structures. The next five program examples, **Example 15.1 – Example 15.5** show various loop situations. In each program a `count` variable is initialized to 0. With each iteration of the loop the `count` is incremented by 1. At the conclusion, the program displays the number of times that the loop or loops repeated, as indicated by the `count` value. With each program example there is also a *generalized* statement of how many times `count` increased based on variable n.

Example 15.1

```
public class Example151
{
    public static void main(String[] args)
    {
        int count = 0;
        for (int k = 1;  k <= 10;  k++)
            count++;
        System.out.println("Count: " + count);
    }
}
```

Program Output
Count: 10

Example 15.2

```
public class Example152
{
    public static void main(String[] args)
    {
        int n = 100;
        int count = 0;
        for (int k = 1;  k <= n;  k++)
            count++;
        System.out.println("Count: " + count);
    }
}
```

Program Output
Count: 100
General count: **n**

Example 15.3

```
public class Example153
{
    public static void main(String[] args)
    {
        int n = 100;
        int count = 0;
        for (int k = 1; k <= n/2; k++)
            count++;
        System.out.println("Count: " + count);
    }
}
```

Program Output
Count: 50

General count:	n/2

Example 15.4

```
public class Example154
{
    public static void main(String[] args)
    {
        int n = 10;
        int count = 0;
        for (int p = 1; p <= n; p++)
            for (int q = 1; q <= n; q++)
                count++;
        System.out.println("Count: " + count);
    }
}
```

Program Output
Count: 100

General count:	n x n or n^2

Example 15.5

```
public class Example155
{
    public static void main(String[] args)
    {
        int n = 10;
        int count = 0;
        for (int p = 1; p < n; p++)
            for (int q = 1; q < n; q++)
                count++;
        System.out.println("Count: " + count);
    }
}
```

Program Output
Count: 81

General count:	(n-1) x (n-1) or $(n-1)^2$ or $n^2 - 2n + 1$

You can expect questions that present program segments with loop structures that ask how many times a method is called or what value is returned. Such program segments, like the first five examples shown here, do not perform a practical function, but it helps to analyze algorithms. Informal analysis also involves recognizing why one algorithm implementation is more efficient than another implementation. Several implementations will be shown of search algorithms following by a variety of sort algorithms. At each level, advantages and disadvantages will be pointed out.

All the methods that will be shown are meant to be part of an `IntList` class. **Example 15.6** shows the initial class with its attributes and constructor. The constructor generates a list of random integers in a specified number range. The size of the list and range is provided by the constructor parameters.

Example 15.6

```
class IntList
{
    private int intArray[];   // stores array elements
    private int size;         // number of elements in the array
    private int minInt;       // smallest random integer
    private int maxInt;       // largest random integer

    public IntList(int s, int min, int max)
    {
        Random rndInt = new Random(12345);
        minInt = min;
        maxInt = max;
        size = s;
        intArray = new int[size];
        int range = maxInt - minInt + 1;
        for (int k = 0; k < size; k++)
            intArray[k] = rndInt.nextInt(range) + minInt;
    }

}
```

All the methods could be presented as if they stand alone, but then the storing data structure would become one of the parameters in very poor Object Oriented Design. The `IntList` class is meant to store and process an array of integers. The integers are stored in a static `int` array, called `intArray`. As you look at the methods that follow, you must realize that they belong inside the `IntList` class. Some methods will have several iterations. They are presented intentionally with some poor features. As you observe different implementations, you can analyze features that are bad and appreciate improvements.

The first `linearSearch` method, shown in **Example 15.7**, is inefficient. Each array element is compared to the search number, `sn`. Variable `found` becomes `true` when a match is found, but the search still continues to make comparisons even after the search number has already been found.

Example 15.7

```
public boolean linearSearch(int sn)
{
    boolean found = false;
    for (int k = 0; k < size; k++)
        if (intArray[k] == sn)
            found = true;
    return found;
}
```

The next example is an improvement. The `linearSearch` method in **Example 15.8** checks a compound condition, which exits the loop when the search number is found. The third `linearSearch` method, in **Example 15.9**, returns the location of the search number.

Example 15.8

```
public boolean linearSearch(int sn)
{
    boolean found = false;
    int k = 0;
    while (k < size && !found)
    {
        if (intArray[k] == sn)
            found = true;
        else
            k++;
    }
    return found;
}
```

Example 15.9

```
public int linearSearch(int sn)
{
    boolean found = false;
    int k = 0;
    while (k < size && !found)
    {
        if (intArray[k] == sn)
            found = true;
        else
            k++;
    }
    if (found)
        return k;
    else
        return -1;
}
```

Example 15.10 presents a `bubbleSort` method. This implementation also uses a `swap` method. In the bubble sort, adjacent elements in the array are compared and exchanged if they are out of order. This implementation sorts in ascending order.

Example 15.10

```
    private void swap(int x, int y)
    {
        int temp = intArray[x];
        intArray[x] = intArray[y];
        intArray[y] = temp;
    }


    public void bubbleSort()
    {
        for (int p = 1; p < size; p++)
            for (int q = 0; q < size-p; q++)
                if (intArray[q] > intArray[q+1])
                    swap(q,q+1);
    }
```

The first bubble sort implementation can be improved by stopping the comparison process when the list is sorted. The `bubbleSort` in **Example 15.11** checks to see if any `swap` method calls are made. Anytime that an entire iteration pass occurs, without any `swap` calls, it can be concluded that the list must be sorted. This implementation is often called the *smart* bubble sort. The `swap` method is not included, but it is identical to the `swap` method of the previous example.

Example 15.11

```
    public void bubbleSort()
    {
        boolean sorted;
        int p = 1;
        do
        {
        sorted = true;
            for (int q = 0; q < size-p; q++)
                if (intArray[q] > intArray[q+1])
                {
                    swap(q,q+1);
                    sorted = false;
                }
            p++;
        }
        while (!sorted);
    }
```

You will probably not see any questions about the *bubble sort* on the APCS Exam. The bubble sort is not that popular in the computer science community. It is considered an inefficient sort, which can be replaced by better sorts. It is included here, because it helps to demonstrate the analysis process and the goal to seek better implementations.

The bubble sort does much processing. Comparisons are made every step along the way and a `swap` routine of three program statements must be executed whenever data is in the wrong order. The `selectionSort` method, shown in **Example 15.12**, eliminates the majority of the swapping. Each array element must still be compared, but now there is a comparison with the smallest (or largest if you prefer) element found so far. At the end of each pass, the smallest element is swapped and placed at the beginning of the list. There only one swap made for each comparison pass.

Example 15.12

```
public void selectionSort()
{
    int p, q, smallest;
    for (p = 0; p < size-1; p++)
    {
        smallest = p;
        for (q = p+1; q < size; q++)
            if (intArray[q] < intArray[smallest])
                smallest = q;
        if (intArray[p] != intArray[smallest])
            swap(p,smallest);
    }
}
```

The `binarySearch` method, in **Example 15.13**, goes to the midpoint of a list and makes a comparison. If the search item is not found, half the list is discarded and a midpoint is found in the remaining segment. This process continuous very efficiently until the item is found.

Example 15.13

```
public int binarySearch(int sn)
{
    boolean found = false;
    int lo = 0;
    int hi = size-1;
    int mid = 0;
    while (lo <= hi && !found)
    {
        mid = (lo + hi) / 2;
        if (intArray[mid] == sn)
            found = true;
        else
        {
            if (sn > intArray[mid])
                lo = mid + 1;
            else
                hi = mid - 1;
        }
    }
    if (found)
        return mid;
    else
        return -1;
}
```

The binary search is not just a little faster than the linear search. Consider a list with one million elements. A linear search could take as many as 1,000,000 comparisons to find the search item. On average, the linear search still takes 500,000 comparisons. The efficient binary search takes no more than 20 comparisons in a worst case scenario. Do keep in mind that the binary search requires that the list is sorted.

Another sort to consider is the insertion sort. At first glance this sort, which keeps adding new elements in their correct location, is no faster than the selection sort. That is true, but the selection sort must sort the entire list. An insertion sort can take a few new elements and insert them into an existing, sorted list.

For the APCS Exam you are not required to know many details about advanced sorts like the *quick sort, merge sort, binary tree sort* and *heap sort*. You are expected to know something about one of these sorts, the *Merge Sort*. Imagine that you have two separate lists, which are already sorted. Now bring these two lists together and merge them together, somewhat like a zipper. If you have two sets of index cards, each already alphabetized, you have an easier time creating one large alphabetized set than with two sets of random index cards.

However, if you have one list, and this list is not sorted. Split your list in two and two again and continue to split the list until you have a whole bunch of little lists. Each tiny list has precisely one element. Now work yourself back up.

Merge two 1-element lists to get a sorted 2-element list.
Merge two 2-element lists to get a sorted 4-element list.
Merge two 4-element lists to get a sorted 8-element list.
Continue this process until the entire list is sorted.

APCS Examination Alert

The APCS Exam is not overly concerned with memorizing the precise source implementation of an algorithm. The primary concern is to understand the logic and the pseudo code of the algorithm in a language-independent manner.

Students need to have knowledge of the linear search, binary search, selection sort, insertion sort and a realization that more advanced sorts exist. In particular, students need a fundamental understanding of the merge sort algorithm.

Chapter 15 Questions
Algorithms and Informal Algorithmic Analysis

01. Consider the following code segment and method.

```
int[] list = {100,110,120,130,140,150,160,170,180,190,200};
int number = 150;
System.out.print(algorithm(list,number) + "  ");
number = 999;
System.out.print(algorithm(list,number));


/** Precondition: x is a non-empty array of int values.
 */
public static int algorithm(int[] x, int n)
{
    boolean temp = false;
    int size = x.length;
    int k = 0;
    while (k < size && !temp)
    {
        if (x[k] == n)
            temp = true;
        else
            k++;
    }
    if (temp)
        return k;
    else
        return -1;
}
```

What is printed as a result of executing the code segment?

(A) 6   0
(B) true   false
(C) false   true
(D) 5   -1
(E) -1   5

02. Consider method `tango` below.

```
/** Precondition: list is a non-empty array of int values.
 *                list is a member of the same class as tango.
 */
public static void tango()
{
    int n = list.length-1;
    for (int q = 0; q < n; q++)
        if ( list[q] < list[q+1])
        {
            int temp = list[q];
            list[q] = list[q+1];
            list[q+1] = temp;
        }
}
```

Assume that `list` stores a random list of integers prior to calling method `tango`. How will the numbers be arranged in the `list` array after a call to method `tango`?

(A) The data will be arranged in ascending order.
(B) The data will be arranged in descending order.
(C) The largest integer will be stored in the last array element.
(D) The smallest integer will be stored in the last array element.
(E) The data order will remain unchanged.

03. Consider method `mambo` below.

```
/** Precondition: list is a non-empty array of int values.
 *                list is a member of the same class as mambo.
 */
public static void mambo()
{
    for (int p = 0; p < list.length-1; p++)
    {
        int temp = p;
        for (int q = p+1; q < list.length; q++)
            if (list[q] > list[temp])
                temp = q;
        if (list[p] != list[temp])
            rumba(p,temp);
    }
}

public static void rumba(int a, int b)
{
    int temp = list[a];
    list[a] = list[b];
    list[b] = temp;
}
```

Assume that `list` stores a random list of integers prior to calling method `mambo`.
How will the numbers be arranged in the `list` array after a call to method `mambo`?

(A) The data will be arranged in ascending order.
(B) The data will be arranged in descending order.
(C) The largest integer will be stored in the last array element.
(D) The smallest integer will be stored in the last array element.
(E) The data order will remain unchanged.

04. When using a binary search, what is the MAXIMUM number of comparisons necessary
to locate a specific item in a SORTED list of 2500 elements?

(A) 7
(B) 11
(C) 12
(D) 13
(E) 1250

05. Which of the following is true about comparing the linear search to a binary search for searching efficiency?

   (A) Both searches have roughly the same execution speed.
   (B) The linear search is always faster than the binary search.
   (C) The binary search is always faster than the linear search.
   (D) The linear search works with any type of data; the binary search does not.
   (E) The binary search works with any type of data; the linear search does not.

06. Consider the following code segment.

```
int n = <positive, odd integer>
int count = 0;
for (int p = 1; p < n; p++)
    for (int q = p; q < n; q++)
        count++;
System.out.println(count);
```

What value is stored by `count` after the code segment executes?

   (A) `((n-1)/2) * n`
   (B) `(n/2) * (n-1)`
   (C) `n * (n-1)`
   (D) `((n-1)/2) * (n-1)`
   (E) `(n * (n + 1)) / 2`

07. There are many algorithms to compute the Greatest Common Factor (GCF).
More than 2000 years ago Euclid devised a GCF algorithm, explained below.

Step-1	Divide num1 by num2 and compute the remainder.
Step-2	Check if the remainder equals zero.
Step-3	If the remainder equals zero, the GCF equals num2. You are finished.
Step-4	If the remainder does not equals zero, continue num1 becomes num2. num2 becomes the remainder.
Step-5	Go back to Step-1

Consider the Java implementations below.
Which of these will compute the GCF using Euclid's algorithm?

```
public static int getGCF1 (int n1, int n2)
{
    int gcf = 1;
    int rem = 1;
    while (rem != 0)
    {
        rem = n1 % n2;
        if (rem == 0)
            gcf = n2;
        else
        {
            n1 = n2;
            n2 = rem;
        }
    }
    return gcf;
}
```

```
public static int getGCF2 (int n1, int n2)
{
    int temp = 0;
    int rem = 0;
    do
    {
        rem = n1 % n2;
        if (rem == 0)
            temp = n2;
        else
        {
            n1 = n2;
            n2 = rem;
        }
    }
    while (rem != 0);
    return temp;
}
```

```
public static int getGCF3(int n1, int n2)
{
    int rem = n1 % n2;
    if (rem == 0)
        return n2;
    else
        return getGCF3(n2,rem);
}
```

(A) getGCF1 only
(B) getGCF2 only
(C) getGCF3 only
(D) getGCF1 and getGCF2 only
(E) getGCF1, getGCF2 and getGCF3

08. The Least Common Multiple (LCM) of 2 numbers is equal to
     the product of those 2 numbers divided by the GCF.

     Assume that a functional getGCF method is available,
     Consider the Java implementations below.
     Which of these will compute the LCM properly?

```java
public static int getLCM1(int n1, int n2)
{
    int gcf = getGCF(n1,n2);
    int lcm = (n1 + n2) * gcf;
    return lcm;
}

public static int getLCM2(int n1, int n2)
{
    int gcf = getGCF(n1,n2);
    int lcm = n1 / gcf * n2;
    return lcm;
}

public static int getLCM3(int n1, int n2)
{
    return n1 / getGCF(n1,n2) * n2;
}
```

(A) getLCM1 only
(B) getLCM2 only
(C) getLCM2 and getLCM3 only
(D) getLCM1 and getLCM2 only
(E) getLCM1, getLCM2 and getLCM3

09. Consider a business where a computer program handles client processing.
     Such a business can be a doctor's office, a dental office, a bank, a
     car dealership or many others.

     For ease of access, the client data needs to be sorted. Assume that
     this business has all its existing client records already sorted and
     adds a small number of new clients on a daily basis. Which of the following
     sort routines will give maximum time efficiency for keeping the entire
     client database sorted as there is a steady addition of new records?

(A) Regular Bubble sort
(B) Smart Bubble sort
(C) Selection sort
(D) Insertion sort
(E) Merge sort

10. Consider the method `mystery` below.

```
public int mystery(int n)
{
    boolean temp = false;
    int lo = 0;
    int ho = size-1;
    int mid = 0;
    while (lo <= hi && !temp)
    {
        mid = (lo + hi) / 2;
        if (list[mid] == n)
            temp = true;
        else
        {
            if (n > list[mid])
                lo = mid + 1;
            else
                hi = mid - 1;
        }
    }
    if (temp)
        return mid;
    else
        return -1;
}
```

This Java code implements which of the following algorithms?

(A) Binary search
(B) Bubble sort
(C) Selection sort
(D) Insertion sort
(E) Linear search

Questions 11-12 refer to the following merge method.

```java
public static int[] merge(int[] l1, int[] l2)
{
    int end1 = l1.length-1;
    int end2 = l2.length-1;
    int[] l3 = new int[l1.length + l2.length];
    int k1 = 0;
    int k2 = 0;
    int k3 = 0;
    while (k1 <= end1 && k2 <= end2)
    {
        if (l1[k1] < l2[k2])
        {
            l3[k3] = l1[k1];
            k1++;
        }
        else
        {
            l3[k3] = l2[k2];
            k2++;
        }
        k3++;
    }
    if (k1 > end1)
    {
        while (k2 <= end2)
        {
            l3[k3] = l2[k2];
            k2++;
            k3++;
        }
    }
    if (k2 > end2)
    {
        while (k1 <= end1)
        {
            l3[k3] = l1[k1];
            k1++;
            k3++;
        }
    }
    return l3;
}
```

11. Assume that the `merge` method executes with two arrays, which store the following values:

```
l1 = {11,22,33,44,55,66,77,88,95,97,98,99}
l2 = {23,32,39,45,47,63,65,86,88,93}
```

What values will be stored in the third `int` array returned by the `merge` method?

(A) 11 22 23 32 33 39 44 45 47 55 63 65 66 77 86 88 88 93 95 97 98 99

(B) 99 98 97 95 93 88 88 86 77 66 65 63 55 47 45 44 39 33 32 23 22 11

(C) 11 22 33 44 55 66 77 88 95 97 98 99 23 32 39 45 47 63 65 86 88 93

(D) 23 32 39 45 47 63 65 86 88 93 11 22 33 44 55 66 77 88 95 97 98 99

(E) 11 22 33 44 55 66 77 88 93 88 86 65 63 47 45 39 32 23 95 97 98 99

12. Assume that the merge method executes with two arrays, which are storing the following values:

```
l1 = {11,22,33,44,55,66,77,88,95,97,98,99}
l2 = {93,88,86,65,63,47,45,39,32,23}
```

What values will be stored in the third `int` array returned by the `merge` method?

(A) 11 22 23 32 33 39 44 45 47 55 63 65 66 77 86 88 88 93 95 97 98 99

(B) 99 98 97 95 93 88 88 86 77 66 65 63 55 47 45 44 39 33 32 23 22 11

(C) 11 22 33 44 55 66 77 88 95 97 98 99 23 32 39 45 47 63 65 86 88 93

(D) 23 32 39 45 47 63 65 86 88 93 11 22 33 44 55 66 77 88 95 97 98 99

(E) 11 22 33 44 55 66 77 88 93 88 86 65 63 47 45 39 32 23 95 97 98 99

Chapter 16 Review
Recursion

The computer science concept of recursion is easily stated. *Recursion is the process whereby a method calls itself.* The actual understanding of recursive methods and creating recursive methods is another story. Please be aware that recursion is an important topic and it will be tested.

APCS Examination Alert

Recursion is an important topic on the AP Computer Science Examination. The APCS Exam requires that students can <u>use</u> and <u>evaluate</u> recursive methods. The APCS Exam does not require that students can <u>create</u> their own recursive methods.

The program in **Example 16.1** shows fundamental recursion. The `main` method calls method `count` and `count` calls itself as long as `k < 99`.

Example 16.1

```
public class Example161
{
    static int k = 10;

    public static void main(String args[])
    {
        count();
    }

    public static void count()
    {
        k++;
        System.out.print(k + "  ");
        if (k % 10 == 0)
            System.out.println();
        if (k < 99)
            count();
    }
}
```

```
                        Example 16.1 Program Output

11   12   13   14   15   16   17   18   19   20
21   22   23   24   25   26   27   28   29   30
31   32   33   34   35   36   37   38   39   40
41   42   43   44   45   46   47   48   49   50
51   52   53   54   55   56   57   58   59   60
61   62   63   64   65   66   67   68   69   70
71   72   73   74   75   76   77   78   79   80
81   82   83   84   85   86   87   88   89   90
91   92   93   94   95   96   97   98   99
```

Example 16.1 is a comfortable example. Method `count` has no parameters and there are no other complexities to consider. This first example does demonstrate the first rule of recursion.

Recursion Rule

All recursive methods require an *exit* or *base case* that stops the recursive process.

It does not take long to fall into a variety of recursive pitfalls. Some text books state that recursion is elegant and easier than iteration. There are certain complex problems where recursion is simpler than iteration, but that is not true for most situations.

Remember that the computer has an internal stack. This stack is used not just for recursion. Anytime a method is called, the computer will jump to that method, but it will first store the current IP (Index Pointer, not Internet Protocol) address so it has a way to get back. If method A calls method B, the computer will store the IP address of where it was in method A on the stack, jump to method B, then retrieve the IP address from the stack and return to method A. Sounds simple. But what if method A calls method B, and method B calls method C, and C calls D, and D calls E? How does the computer keep track of where to return to? A stack operates in a LIFO (Last In First Out) sequence. The last IP address placed on the stack will be the first to be removed. This allows the computer to return to each of the calling methods in reverse order.

With recursion, the same exact process occurs. The only difference is now the method being called is the same as the method it was called from. The current IP address is still placed on the stack. This happens for each recursive call. When the base case is finally reached, the IP addresses can be removed from the stack. The computer will return back to the calling method – even though it is the same as the method that was called – again and again until the entire process unwinds. This LIFO sequence explains why the output of some recursive methods is in reverse order. With these ideas in mind you need to look at the common pitfalls of recursion.

Recursion Pitfalls

The first common pitfall occurs easily with a method shown in the previous program example. **Example 16.2** shows the method only to observe the potential problem. The base case, which occurs when k is no longer less than 99 is easily misunderstood. Students look at the statement and conclude that the largest number displayed is 98. Recursion stops when k equals 99. When k equals 98 method count is called for the last time and 99 is printed before the method stops.

Example 16.2

```
public static void count()
{
    k++;
    System.out.print(k + "   ");
    if (k < 99)
        count();
}
```

In a typical method it is common to see a variable with a starting value. In a recursive method, this type of statement can result in a computer crash. If you look at **Example 16.3** you will see a method that has a base case, but this exit is never reached, because the value of k is restarted each time that method count is called. It is true that the k++; statement increases k each time that the method is called, but it is equally true that the statement int k = 0; forces k to start over each time.

Example 16.3

```
public static void count()
{
    int k = 0;
    System.out.print(k + "   ");
    if (k < 99)
    {
        k++
        count();
    }
}
```

Methods count1 and count2, in **Example 16.4**, both display numbers in the [a . . b] integer value range. Both methods will display the exact same numbers. Method count1 uses *post-recursion*. In this case the recursive calls comes after the method action of printing values. Method count2 uses *pre-recursion*. Recursive calls are made before any method action occurs.

With pre-recursion there are many unfinished method calls. Printing is not possible, because every arrival at the method results in a departure on a new recursive call. All the print statements are stored for later execution. Since unfinished method business is stored on a stack, which behaves like a LIFO, the number will be displayed in reverse order. Method `count1` prints in forward order because it uses post-recursion.

Example 16.4

```
public static void count1(int a, int b)
{
    if (a <= b)
    {
        System.out.print(a + "  ");
        count1(a+1,b);                    // Post-Recursion
    }
}


public static void count2(int a, int b)
{
    if (a <= b)
    {
        count2(a+1,b);                    // Pre-Recursion
        System.out.print(a + "  ");
    }
}
```

Post-recursion methods do not cause much trouble. The trouble making occurs with pre-recursion when it is easy to forget that unfinished recursive calls must eventually be accounted for. Consider the `booHiss` method in **Example 16.5**.

Example 16.5

```
public int booHiss(int n)
{
    if (n == 1)
        return 25;
    else
        return n + booHiss(n-1);
}
```

Suppose that method `booHiss` is called with the statement `System.out.println(booHiss(5));` It is possible that you consider the result at the time when the base case is reached. At that time `n  is  2` and added to 25 equals 27. Returning 27 is the wrong answer and ignores all the values that have patiently been waiting to be used. Each time when the method is called, the value of n is stored and must be added when the exit is finally reached as shown in the **Example 16.5 Table**.

Example 16.5 Table

What value is returned by the call **booHiss(5) ?**		
CALL #	n	Method booHiss returns
1	5	5 + booHiss(4)
2	4	4 + booHiss(3)
3	3	3 + booHiss(2)
4	2	2 + booHiss(1)
5	1	25
m3(5) == 25 + 2 + 3 + 4 + 5 == 39		

Perhaps the easiest mistake to make is the case where multiple recursive calls occur on the same line. The hissBoo method in **Example 16.6** is an example of a method with two recursive calls in one program statement. The **Example 16.6 Table** calculates the value as it was done in the previous example. It may seem correct, but the answer is wrong.

Example 16.6

```
public int hissBoo(int n)
{
    if (n == 1 || n == 0)
        return 0;
    else
        return n + hissBoo(n-1) + hissBoo(n-2);
}
```

Example 16.6 Table

What value is returned by the call **hissBoo(6) ?**		
CALL #	n	Method hissBoo returns
1	6	6 + hissBoo(5) + hissBoo(4)
2	5	5 + hissBoo(4) + hissBoo(3)
3	4	4 + hissBoo(3) + hissBoo(2)
4	3	3 + hissBoo(2) + hissBoo(1)
5	2	2 + hissBoo(1) + hissBoo(0)
6	1	0
hissBoo(6) == 0 + 2 + 3 + 4 + 5 + 6 == 20		

Keep in mind that each recursive call executes a statement that makes two recursive calls. The binary tree below demonstrates how this happens. It also shows that the correct answer is the sum of the values stored by each recursive call.

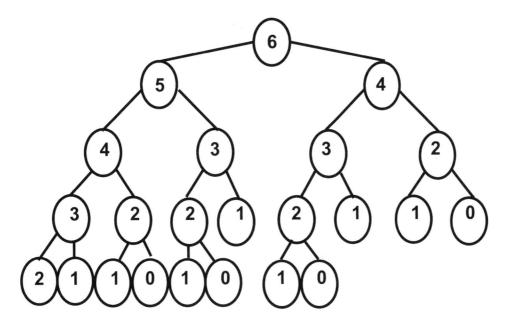

This shows that the correct answer is **6 + 5 + 4 + 4 + 3 + 3 + 2 + 3 + 2 + 2 + 2 + 2 = 38**.

NOTE: The **1**s in the above binary tree are not added because the base case states that if n equals 1 (or 0) then 0 will be returned.

Chapter 16 Questions
Recursion

01. Consider the following method.

```
/** Precondition: x > 0 and y > x
 */
public static void method1601(int x, int y)
{
    if (x < y)
    {
        System.out.print(x + "   ");
        method1601(x+1,y);
    }
}
```

What is printed as the result of calling `method1601(2,7)` ?

(A) 2   3   4   5   6   7
(B) 7   6   5   4   3   2
(C) 2   3   4   5   6
(D) 6   5   4   3   2
(E) Program crashes due to too many recursive calls

02. Consider the following method.

```
/** Precondition: x > 0 and y > x
 */
public static void method1602(int x, int y)
{
    if (x <= y)
    {
        method1602(x+1,y);
        System.out.print(x + "   ");
    }
}
```

What is printed as the result of calling `method1602(2,7)` ?

(A) 2   3   4   5   6   7
(B) 7   6   5   4   3   2
(C) 2   3   4   5   6
(D) 6   5   4   3   2
(E) Program crashes due to too many recursive calls

03. Consider the following method.

```
/** Precondition: x > 0 and y > x
 */
public static void method1603(int x, int y)
{
    if (x <= y)
    {
        method1603(x-1,y);
        System.out.print(x + "  ");
    }
}
```

What is printed as the result of calling `method1603(2,7)` ?

(A) 2 3 4 5 6 7
(B) 7 6 5 4 3 2
(C) 2 3 4 5 6
(D) 6 5 4 3 2
(E) Program crashes due to too many recursive calls

04. Consider the following method.

```
public static int method1604(int n)
{
    if (Math.sqrt(n) > n/2)
        return n;
    else
        return method1604(n - 1);
}
```

What value is returned as a result of the call `method1604(10)` ?

(A) 6
(B) 5
(C) 4
(D) 3
(E) Program crashes due to too many recursive calls

05. Consider the following method.

```
public static int method1605(int x, int y)
{
    if (x == 0)
        return y;
    else
        return y + method1605(x-1, y);
}
```

What value is returned as a result of the call `method1605(5,3)` ?

(A) 10
(B) 12
(C) 15
(D) 18
(E) 20

06. Consider the following method.

```
public static int method1606(int n)
{
    if (n == 0)
        return n;
    else if (n % 2 == 0)
        return n + method1606(n-1);
    else
        return n - method1606(n-1);
}
```

What value is returned as a result of the call `method1606(10)`?

(A) 11
(B) 8
(C) 7
(D) 4
(E) Program crashes due to too many recursive calls

07. Consider the following method.

```
public static int method1607(int n)
{
    if (n == 0 || n == 1)
        return 1;
    else
        return method1607(n-1) + method1607(n-2);
}
```

What value is returned as a result of the call method1607(8) ?

(A) 1
(B) 8
(C) 34
(D) 89
(E) Program crashes due to too many recursive calls

08. Consider the following method.

```
public static int method1608(int n)
{
    if (n == 0 || n == 1)
        return 1;
    else
        return method1608(n) + method1608(n-1);
}
```

What value is returned as a result of the call method1608(7) ?

(A) 1
(B) 17
(C) 23
(D) 39
(E) Program crashes due to too many recursive calls

09. Consider the following two methods.

```
public static int method1(int n)
{
    if (n == 0)
        return 1;
    else
        return n + method2(n-1);
}

public static int method2(int n)
{
    return method1(n-1);
}
```

What value is returned as a result of the call `method1(10)` ?

(A) 31
(B) 55
(C) 28
(D) 43
(E) Program crashes due to too many recursive calls

10. Consider the following two methods.

```
public static int method1(int n)
{
    if (n == 0)
        return 1;
    else
        return n + method2(n-1);
}

public static int method2(int n)
{
    if (n == 0)
        return 1;
    else
        return method1(n-1);
}
```

What value is returned as a result of the call `method1(10)` ?

(A) 31
(B) 55
(C) 28
(D) 43
(E) Program crashes due to too many recursive calls

11. Consider the following four methods.

```
public static int gcf1(int n1, int n2)
{
    int rem = 1;
    int gcf = 1;
    while (rem != 0)
    {
        rem = n1 % n2;
        if (rem == 0)
            gcf = n2;
        else
        {
            n1 = n2;
            n2 = rem;
        }
    }
    return gcf;
}
```

```
public static int gcf2(int n1, int n2)
{
    int rem = n1 % n2;
    if (rem == 0)
        return n2;
    else
        return gcf2(n2,rem);
}
```

```
public static int gcf3(int n1, int n2)
{
    if (n1 % n2 == 0)
        return n2;
    else
        return gcf3(n2,n1%n2);
}
```

```
public static int gcf4(int n1, int n2)
{
    int rem = n1 % n2;
    if (rem == 0)
        return n2;
    else
    {
        n1 = n2;
        n2 = rem;
    }
    return gcf4(n1,n2);
}
```

Which of the *recursive* gcf methods performs the same actions as the *iterative* gcf1 method?

(A) gcf2 only
(B) gcf3 only
(C) gcf4 only
(D) gcf2 and gcf3 only
(E) gcf2, gcf3 and gcf4

12. Consider the following four methods.

```
public static String reverse1(String str)
{
    String temp = "";
    for (int k = str.length()-1; k >= 0; k--)
        temp += str.substring(k,k+1);
    return temp;
}
```

```
public static String reverse2(String str)
{
    int n = str.length();
    if (n == 0)
        return "";
    else
        return str.substring(0,1) + reverse2(str.substring(1,n));
}
```

```
public static String reverse3(String str)
{
    int n = str.length();
    if (n == 0)
        return "";
    else
        return str.substring(n-1,n) + reverse3(str.substring(0,n-1));
}
```

```
public static String reverse4(String str)
{
    int n = str.length();
    if (n == 0)
        return "";
    else
        return str.substring(n-1,n) + reverse4(str.substring(1,n));
}
```

Which of the *recursive* reverse methods performs the same actions as the *iterative* reverse1 method?

(A) reverse2 only
(B) reverse3 only
(C) reverse4 only
(D) reverse2 and reverse3 only
(E) reverse2, reverse3 and reverse4

Chapter 17 Review
Java Standard Library Methods

The College Board has selected a subset of the Java standard library methods to be tested for the APCS examination. The greater majority of these methods have been reviewed in other chapters. The intention of this chapter is to consolidate all the standard library methods for the course in one location.

Since the methods in this section are explained in other chapters, they will only be summarized here. The information you see is similar to the review sheets that you will receive at the actual APCS Exam. These summaries are important, because most students have learned many concepts and classes that will not be tested. The whole intention of this study guide is to focus only on computer science topics and Java features that will be tested.

The heading of each class include the Java package that contains the method which follow. This is the style that is used on the Java Quick Reference that will be provided during the exam. that will be provided during the exam. The reference guide also provides a short description of the functionality for each method, which has been provided in earlier chapters that focused on the specific class that are summarized here.

---

class java.lang.Object

boolean equals (Object other)

String toString ( )

---

class java.lang.Integer

Integer (int value)

int intValue ( )

Integer.MIN_VALUE

Integer.MAX_VALUE

---

class java.lang.Double

Double (double value)

double doubleValue ( )

class java.lang.String

int length ( )

String substring (int from, intg to)

String substring (int from)

int indexOf (String str)

int compareTo (String other)

class java.lang.Math

static int abs (int x)

static double abs (double x)

static double pow (double base, double exponent)

static double sqrt (double x)

static double random ( )

interface java.util.List<E>

int size ( )

boolean add (E obj)

void add (int index, E obj)

E get (int index)

E set (int index, E obj)

E remove (int index)

```
class java.util.ArrayList<E> implements java.util.List<E>

    int size ( )

    boolean add (E obj)

    void add (int index, E obj)

    E get (int index)

    E set (int index, E obj)

    E remove (int index)
```

Chapter 17 Questions
Java Standard Libraries

01. Consider the following code segment.

```
int randomInt = (int) (Math.random() * 900 + 100);
System.out.println(randomInt);
```

After the code segment executes, what is the possible value range [smallest..largest] of randomInt ?

(A) [100..999]
(B) [100..900]
(C) [100..1000]
(D) [0..99]
(E) [0..899]

02. Consider the following code segment.

```
for (int k = 1; k <= 100; k++)
{
    double rndDouble = Math.random();
    int rndInt =   (int) /* Missing Code */ ;
    System.out.print(rndInt + "   ");
}
```

Which of the following implementations of /* **Missing Code** */ will generate a sequence of integers in the [-5 ... +5] range?

(A) (rndDouble * 10 + 5)
(B) (rndDouble * 11 + 5)
(C) (rndDouble * 10 - 5)

(D) (rndDouble * 11 - 5)
(E) (rndDouble * 6 - 5)

03. Consider the following two code segments.

Code Segment 1
```
for (int k = 1; k <= 10; k++)
{
    double rnd1 = (int) Math.random() * 100;
    System.out.print(rnd1 + "   ");
}
```

Code Segment 2
```
for (int k = 1; k <= 10; k++)
{
    double rnd2 = (int) (Math.random() * 100);
    System.out.print(rnd2 + "   ");
}
```

Which of the following statements is true about the execution comparison of
Code Segment 1 and **Code Segment 2**?

I.   Code Segment 1 and Code Segment 2 will display different numbers.
II. Code Segment 1 and Code Segment 2 will display numbers in the same range.
III. Code Segment 1 and Code Segment 2 will display numbers in different ranges.

(A) I only
(B) II only
(C) III only
(D) I and II
(E) I and III

04. Consider the following program statement.

```
System.out.print(Math.pow(Math.sqrt(100),-Math.sqrt(4)));
```

What is printed as a result of executing the program statement?

(A) 0.01
(B) 0.1
(C) 5
(D) 20
(E) 50

05. Consider the following code segment.

```
for (int k = -9; k < 0; k++)
{
    if (k % 2 == 0 || k % 3 == 0)
        System.out.print(Math.sqrt(Math.abs(k)) + "  ");
    else
        System.out.print(Math.sqrt(k) + "  ");
}
```

What is printed as a result of executing the code segment?

(A) 3.0   2.8284271247461903   NaN   2.449489742783178   NaN   2.0
1.7320508075688772   1.4142135623730951   NaN

(B) 3.0   2.8284271247461903   0.0   2.449489742783178   0.0   2.0
1.7320508075688772   1.4142135623730951   0.0

(C) NaN   NaN   NaN   NaN   NaN   NaN   NaN   NaN   NaN

(D) A compile error message, indicating nesting functions are not allowed

(E) An `ArithmeticException` error message

06. Consider the following code segment.

```
System.out.println(Integer.MAX_VALUE);
```

What is printed as a result of executing the code segment?
What is the binary representation in memory for Integer.MAX_VALUE?

(A) 32767
Binary representation: 1111 1111 1111 1111

(B) 32767
Binary representation: 0111 1111 1111 1111

(C) 2147483647
Binary representation: 1111 1111 1111 1111 1111 1111 1111 1111

(D) 2147483647
Binary representation: 0111 1111 1111 1111 1111 1111 1111 1111

(E) An `ArithmeticException` error message

07. Consider the following code segment.

```java
int n1 = Integer.MAX_VALUE;
int n2 = Math.abs(Integer.MIN_VALUE+1);

if (n1 < n2)
    System.out.println("Less Than");
else if (n1 == n2)
    System.out.println("Equals");
else
    System.out.println("Greater Than");
```

What is printed as a result of executing the code segment?

(A) Less Than
(B) Equals
(C) Greater Than
(D) A compile error due to memory overflow
(E) An ArithmeticException error message

08. Consider the following code segment.

```java
ArrayList<Integer> list = new ArrayList<Integer>();
for (int k = 0; k < 10; k++)
    list.add(new Integer(k));
int sum = 0;
for (Integer n: list)
{
    sum += n.intValue();
    System.out.print(sum);
}
```

What is printed as a result of executing the code segment?

(A) 45
(B) 0 1 3 6 10 15 21 28 36 45
(C) 0136101521283645
(D) An IndexOutOfBoundsException error message
(E) A compile error, indicating that method intValue cannot be used here

09. Java methods `toString` and `equals` are originally defined in a standard Java superclass. What is the name of this superclass and which of the following describes the similarity between the original definitions of `toString` and `equals`?

(A) Original class: `System`
Similarity: Both methods process strings only

(B) Original class: `Object`
Similarity: Both methods access immediate (shallow) memory values only

(C) Original class: `Java`
Similarity: Both methods process strings only

(D) Original class: `Language`
Similarity: Both methods access immediate (shallow) memory values only

(E) Original class: `System`
Similarity: Both methods handle input/output processes

10. Consider the following code segment.

```
String s1 = new String("Scheveningen");
int start = s1.indexOf("eve");
int end = s1.indexOf("gen");
String s2 = s1.substring(start);
String s3 = s1.substring(start,end);
System.out.println(s2);
System.out.println(s3);
```

What will be output when the code segment executes?

(A) eveningen
    evenin

(B) eveningen
    evening

(C) veningen
    venin

(D) veningen
    vening

(E) eveningen
    eveningen

11. Consider the following code segment.

```
String s1 = new String("Scheveningen");
String s2 = s1.substring(6,s1.length());
String s3 = s1.substring(6);
if (s2.compareTo(s3) != 0)
    System.out.println(s2.compareTo(s3));
else
    System.out.println("Equals");
```

What will be output when the code segment executes?

(A) Equals
(B) 1
(C) 0
(D) -1
(E) -2

12. Consider the following code segment.

```
double[] list = {1.1,2.2,3.3,4.4,5.5,6.6,7.7,8.8,9.9};
ArrayList<Double> reals = new ArrayList<Double>();
for (double real: list)
    reals.add(new Double(real));
for (int k = 1; k < reals.size(); k++)
{
    if (k % 2 == 0)
        reals.remove(k);
    else
        reals.set(k,reals.get(k-1));
}
for (Double real: reals)
    System.out.print(real.doubleValue() + "  ");
```

What is printed as a result of executing the code segment?

(A) 1.1 3.3 5.5 7.7 9.9
(B) 2.2 2.2 4.4 4.4 6.6 6.6 8.8 8.8
(C) 1.1 1.1 4.4 4.4 7.7 7.7
(D) 1.1 1.1 3.3 3.3 5.5 5.5 7.7 7.7 9.9 9.9
(E) An IndexOutOfBoundsException error message

Chapter 18 Review
Snooker Questions

This is the last chapter before the three sample AP Computer Science Examinations. Chapter 18 is not a single topic. The 30 questions of this chapter represent all the topics that are likely to be tested; however, this group of questions is more than a simple collection of questions from all the various topics. These are mostly *snooker questions*.

A *snooker question* is a question that a student, who knows the topic well, nevertheless gets wrong. It is also one reason why some good students get a surprisingly low scores So what is a snooker question?

Snooker Question Definition

A snooker question is a question that includes a subtle component that many students will overlook. Students will call such a question tricky, but the question is actually reasonable.

The problem is that some students judge the question as easy and quickly select the "obvious" answer. They get *snookered* and get the question wrong.

The AP Computer Science Examination is not a collection of snooker questions. Questions of different difficulty levels are selected and some snooker questions are part of every exam.

Some of the questions that follow may not be that tricky after students have completed the previous review chapters. Alert students may apply what they have learned from the *pitfalls* of each chapter and catch the subtle tricks.

Students also need to be aware that the very fact that these questions are advertised as snooker questions creates an awareness that does not exist during the actual AP Exam, where there are a wide variety of questions. In other words, do not underestimate a question.

Chapter 18 Questions
Snooker Questions

(Topic 01:   Control Structures)

01. Consider the following code segment.

```
int x = <some integer greater than zero>
int n = 0;
if (x < 500)
{
    if (x > 750)
        n = 100;
    else
        n = 200;
}
else
{
    if (x < 300)
        n = 300;
    else
        n = 200;
}
System.out.println(n);
```

What is printed as a result of executing the code segment?

(A) Unknown without the value of x   (D) 200

(B) 0   (E) 300

(C) 100

(Topic 01:   Control Structures)

02. Consider the following code segment.

```
int n = <some integer greater than zero>
int count = 0;
int p = 0;
int q = 0;
for (p = 1; p < n; p++)
    for (q = 1; q < n; q++)
        count++;
System.out.println(count);
```

What is the value of count when the code finishes executing?

(A) n^2

(B) $n^2 - 1$

(C) $(n - 1)^2$

(D) p * q

(E) both C and D

(Topic 02:   Methods and Parameters)
03.   Consider the following code segment and method.

```
int p = 10;
int q = 20;
swap(p,q);
System.out.println(p + "   " + q);

public static void swap(int x, int y)
{
    int temp = x;
    x = y;
    y = temp;
}
```

What is printed as a result of executing the program?

(A) 10   20
(B) 20   10
(C) 10   10
(D) 20   20
(E)   0   0

(Topic 02:   Methods and Parameters)
04.   Consider the following code segment and method.

```
int[] list = {1,2,3,4,5,6,7,8,9};
swap(list,3,4);
System.out.println(list[3] + "   " + list[4]);

public static void swap(int[] x, int p, int q)
{
    int temp = x[p];
    x[p] = x[q];
    x[q] = temp;
}
```

What is printed as a result of executing the program?

(A) 3   4
(B) 4   3
(C) 4   5
(D) 5   4
(E) An `ArrayIndexOutOfboundsException` error message

(Topic 03: Boolean Logic)

05. The Boolean expression

```
!((A < B) && (C > D))
```

is equivalent to which of the following expressions?

(A) `(A < B) || (C > D)`

(B) `(A >= B) && (C <= D)`

(C) `(A >= B) || (C <= D)`

(D) `(A > B) && (C < D)`

(E) `(A > B) || (C < D)`

(Topic 03: Boolean Logic)

06. Consider the following code segment.

```
for (int k = 1; k <= 100; k++)
{
    int n1 = (int) Math.random();
    int n2 = (int) Math.random() * 4;
    boolean bool = n1 == n2;
    System.out.print(bool + "  ");
}
```

What is printed as a result of executing the code segment?

(A) The code segment always prints `true`.
(B) The code segment always prints `false`.
(C) The code segment prints `true` roughly 25% of the time and prints `false` roughly 75% of the time.
(D) The code segment prints both `true` and `false`, but `true` more frequently.
(E) The code segment prints both `true` and `false`, but `false` more frequently.

(Topic 04: Inheritance)

07. Consider the following code segment and two classes.

```
Person sue = new Person(25);
Student tom = new Student(17,12);
System.out.println(sue.getAge());
System.out.println(tom.getGrade());


class Person
{
    private int age;

    public Person(int a)
    {
        age = a;
        System.out.println("Person Constructor");
    }

    public int getAge()   { return age;  }
}


class Student extends Person
{
    private int grade;
    public Student(int g, int a)
    {
        super(a);
        grade = g;
        System.out.println("Student Constructor");
    }

    public int getGrade() { return grade; }
}
```

What are the first 2 lines of program output?

(A) 25
     17

(B) Student Constructor
     Student Constructor

(C) Person Constructor
     Student Constructor

(D) Student Constructor
     Person Constructor

(E) Person Constructor
     Person Constructor

(Topic 04: Inheritance)

08. Consider the following code segment and three classes.

```
ClassA item1 = new ClassA();
ClassA item2 = new ClassB();
ClassA item3 = new ClassC();
item1.method2008(10);
item2.method2008(20);
item3.method2008(30);

class ClassA
{
    public ClassA() { }

    public void method2008(int a)
    {
        System.out.println("Class A " + a);
    }
}

class ClassB extends ClassA
{
    public ClassB() { }

    public void method2008(int b)
    {
        System.out.println("Class B " + b);
    }
}

class ClassC extends ClassB
{
    public ClassC() { }
}
```

What is printed as a result of executing the code segment?

(A) `Class A 10`
    `Class A 20`
    `Class A 30`

(B) `Class A 10`
    `Class B 20`
    `Class B 30`

(C) `Class A 10`
    `Class B 20`

(D) `Class A 10`
    `Class B 20`
    `Class B 20`

(E) An `Exception` error message

(Topic 05: 1D Static Arrays)

09. Consider the following code segment.

```
int[] list = {11,22,33,44,55,66,77,88,99};

for (int k = 0; k < list.length; k++)
    list[k] = list[k]/list[0];

for (int k = 0; k < list.length; k++)
    System.out.print(list[k] + "  ");
```

What is printed as a result of executing the code segment?

(A) 11   22   33   44   55   66   77   88   99
(B) 1   2   3   4   5   6   7   8   9
(C) 1   1   1   1   1   1   1   1   1
(D) 1   22   33   44   55   66   77   88   99
(E) 11   22   33   44   55   66   77   88   9

(Topic 05: 1D Static Arrays)

10. Consider the following code segment.

```
int[] list1 = {10,20,30,40,50,60,70,80,90};
int[] list2 = list1;
for (int k = 0; k < list2.length; k++)
    list2[k] = list1[0];
for (int k = 0; k < list1.length; k++)
    list1[k] *= list2[k];
for (int k = 0; k < list1.length; k++)
    System.out.print(list1[k] + "  ");
```

What is printed as a result of executing the code segment?

(A) 100   100   100   100   100   100   100   100   100
(B) 100   200   300   400   500   600   700   800   900
(C) 1   2   3   4   5   6   7   8   9
(D) 10
(E) 100

(Topic 06: 2D Static Arrays)

11. Consider the following code segment.

```
double [][] values = new double[10][15];
int sum = 0;
```

Each row in the array holds (in order) a student number, 10 homework grades of equal weight, and 4 exam grades.

Choose the code segment below that would sum the homework grades in the sixth row and place them in the integer variable `sum`.

```
(A) for (int j = 0; j < 15; j++)
        sum += values[6][j];

(B) for (int j = 0; j < 10; j++)
        sum += values[5][j];

(C) for (int j = 1; j < 11; j++)
        sum += values[j][6];

(D) for (int j = 0; j < 10; j++)
        sum += values[j][5];

(E) for (int j = 1; j < 11; j++)
        sum += values[5][j];
```

(Topic 06: 2D Static Arrays)

12. Consider the following code segment.

```
int[][] matrix;
matrix = {{1,1,1,1},{2,2,2,2},{3,3,3,3}};

for (int[] row: matrix)
{
    for (int number: row)
        System.out.print(number + "  ");
        System.out.println();
}
```

What is printed as a result of executing the code segment?

(A) A compile error message due to the `matrix` declaration
(B) A compile error message due to using a `<for..each>` loop with two-dimensional array
(C) `1  1  1  1  2  2  2  2  3  3  3  3`
(D) `1, 1, 1, 1, 2, 2, 2, 2, 3, 3, 3, 3`

```
(E) 1  1  1  1
    2  2  2  2
    3  3  3  3
```

(Topic 07: String Methods)

13. Consider the following method.

```
/** Precondition: str is a nonempty string of upper-case letters
 */
public static String mystery(String str)
{
    String temp = "";
    for (int k = 0; k < str.length(); k++)
    {
        String t = str.substring(k,k+1);
        if (t != "A" || t != "E" || t != "I" || t != "O" || t != "U")
            temp += t;
    }
    return temp;
}
```

Which of the following is a correct Postcondition, based on the return of method `mystery`?

(A) Postcondition: mystery returns str
(B) Postcondition: mystery returns str with all vowels removed
(C) Postcondition: mystery returns only the vowels in str
(D) Postcondition: mystery returns null
(E) It will generate a StringIndexOutOfBoundsException error message

(Topic 07: String Methods)

14. Consider the following method.

```
/** Precondition: str is a nonempty string of upper-case letters
 */
public static String mystery(String str)
{
    String temp = "";
    for (int k = 0; k < str.length(); k++)
    {
        String t = str.substring(k,k+1);
        if (t.equals("A")|| t.equals("E")|| t.equals("I")|| t.equals("O")|| t.equals("U"))
            temp += t;
    }
    return temp;
}
```

Which of the following is a correct Postcondition, based on the return of method mystery?

(A) Postcondition: mystery returns str
(B) Postcondition: mystery returns str with all vowels removed
(C) Postcondition: mystery returns only the vowels in str
(D) Postcondition: mystery returns null
(E) It will generate a StringIndexOutOfBoundsException error message

(Topic 08: Dynamic Arrays with ArrayList)

15. Consider the following code segment.

```
ArrayList<String> names = new ArrayList<String>();
names.add("Isolde");
names.add("John");
names.add("Greg");
names.add("Maria");
names.add("Heidi");
names.set(3,names.get(4));
names.set(4,names.get(3));
System.out.println(names);
```

What is printed as a result of executing the code segment?

(A) [Isolde, John, Greg, Maria, Heidi]
(B) [Isolde, John, Greg, Heidi, Maria]
(C) [Isolde, John, Greg, Heidi, Heidi]
(D) [Isolde, John, Greg, Greg, Maria]
(E) An IndexOutOfBoundsException error message

(Topic 08: Dynamic Arrays with ArrayList)

16. Consider the following method.

```
/** Precondition: list contains [13, 64, 42, 27, 77, 38, 11]
 */
public static void mystery(ArrayList<Integer> list)
{
    for (int k = 0; k < list.size(); k++)
    {
        if (list.get(k) % 2 == 0)
            list.remove(k);
    }
}
```

Which of the following describes the values stored in list after mystery executes?

(A) [13, 64, 42, 27, 77, 38, 11]
(B) [13, 27, 77, 11]
(C) [13, 42, 27, 77, 11]
(D) [64, 42, 38]
(E) An IndexOutOfBoundsException error message

(Topic 09:   Composition)

17.   Consider the following program statement and two classes.

```
Rumba r = new Rumba();

class Rumba extends Mambo
{
    private Mambo mambo;

    public Rumba()
    {
        mambo = new Mambo();
        System.out.println("Executing the Rumba constructor");
    }
}

class Mambo
{
    public Mambo()
    {
        System.out.println("Executing the Mambo constructor");
    }
}
```

What are the first two lines printed as the result of executing the program statement?

(A) Executing the Rumba constructor
     Executing the Rumba constructor

(B) Executing the Mambo constructor
     Executing the Mambo constructor

(C) Executing the Rumba constructor
     Executing the Mambo constructor

(D) Executing the Mambo constructor
     Executing the Rumba constructor

(E) A compile error message

(Topic 09:   Composition)

18. Consider the following code segment and two classes.

```
Mambo m = new Mambo();
Rumba r = new Rumba();

class Rumba
{
    private Mambo mambo;

    public Rumba()
    {
        System.out.println("Executing the Rumba constructor");
        mambo = new Mambo();
    }
}

class Mambo
{
    private Rumba rumba;

    public Mambo()
    {
        System.out.println("Executing the Mambo constructor");
    }
}
```

What are the last two lines printed as the result of executing the program statement?

(A) Executing the Rumba constructor
     Executing the Rumba constructor

(B) Executing the Mambo constructor
     Executing the Mambo constructor

(C) Executing the Rumba constructor
     Executing the Mambo constructor

(D) Executing the Mambo constructor
     Executing the Rumba constructor

(E) A StackOverflowException error message

(Topic 10: Polymorphism)

19. Consider the following class definitions and code segment

```
ClassA item1 = new ClassA();
ClassA item2 = new ClassB();
ClassA item3 = new ClassC();
ArrayList<ClassA> items = new ArrayList<ClassA>();
items.add(item1);
items.add(item2);
items.add(item3);

for (ClassA item: items)
    item.showClass();


class ClassA
{
    public ClassA() {}
    public void showClass(){System.out.println("Class A");}
}

class ClassB extends ClassA
{
    public ClassB(){}
    public void showClass(){System.out.println("Class B");}
}

class ClassC extends ClassB
{
    public ClassC(){}
}
```

What is printed as a result of executing the code segment?

```
(A)  Class A
     Class B
     Class C

(B)  Class A
     Class B
     Class B

(C)  Class A
     Class B
     Class A

(D)  Class A
     Class B


(E)  Class A
     Class A
```

(Topic 10: Polymorphism)

20. Consider the following class definitions and code segment.

```
ClassA item1 = new ClassA();
ClassA item2 = new ClassB(20);
ClassA item3 = new ClassC(30);
ArrayList<ClassA> items = new ArrayList<ClassA>();
items.add(item1);
items.add(item2);
items.add(item3);

for (ClassA item: items)
    item.showClass();

class ClassA
{
    private int value;
    public void showClass() {System.out.println("Class A " + value);}
}

class ClassB extends ClassA
{
    private int value;
    public ClassB(int v)    { value = v; }
    public void showClass() {System.out.println("Class B " + value);}
}

class ClassC extends ClassA
{
    private int value;
    public ClassC(int v) { value = v; }
}
```

What is printed as a result of executing the code segment?

(A) ```
    Class A 10
    Class B 20
    Class C 30
```

(B) ```
    Class A 10
    Class B 20
    Class A 30
```

(C) ```
    Class A 0
    Class B 20
    Class A 0
```

(D) ```
    Class A 10
    Class B 20
```

(E) ```
    Class A 0
    Class B 20
```
```

(Topic 11: Interfaces and Abstract Classes)

21. Consider the following code segment, interface and class.

```
Acrobat ivan = new Acrobat();
ivan.performance();


interface CircusPerformer
{
    public String getPerformer();
    public String getAct();
    public void act();
    public void entrance();
    public void performance();
    public void exit();
}


class Acrobat implements CircusPerformer
{
    public void performance()
    {
        System.out.println("Flips forwards and backwards on trapeze");
    }
    public String getPerformer() { }
    public String getAct()       { }
    public void act()            { }
    public void entrance()       { }
    public void exit()           { }
}
```

What is printed as a result of executing the code segment?

(A) flips forwards and backwards on trapeze
(B) ivan flips forwards and backwards on trapeze
(C) ivan
(D) An Exception error message, indicating that the Acrobat class has no constructor.
(E) A compile error message, due to improper implementation of some interface methods.

(Topic 11: Interfaces and Abstract Classes)

22. Consider the following code segment, interface and classes.

```
ConcreteHiss x = new ConcreteHiss(10);
x.hissD();


interface Hiss
{
    public void hissA();
    public void hissB();
    public void hissC();
    public void hissD();
}


abstract class HissAdapter implements Hiss
{
    public void hissA() {}
    public void hissB() {}
    public void hissC() {}
    public void hissD() {}
}


class ConcreteHiss extends HissAdapter
{
    private int value;

    public ConcreteHiss(int v)
    {
        value = v;
    }

    public void hissD()
    {
        System.out.println("Method hissD " + value);
    }
}
```

What is printed as a result of executing the code segment?

(A) `Method hissD 10`
(B) `Method hissD`
(C) `10`
(D) A compile error message, due to not implementing three abstract methods
(E) A compile error message, due to extending `HissAdapter` in place of implementing

23. A data structure needs to store information in about 20,000 college student records. A variety of information needs to be stored in each student record, such as *name, age, gpa, date of birth, address* and *social security number*.

    The data structure is to be used in a program with the following two data processing requirements:
    [1] Frequent quick access to any student records to update student information.
    [2] End-of-semester access to print a student GPA list from highest to lowest.

    Consider the following two methods to implement the two processing requirements.

    Method 1 stores all the student records in a data structure that is sorted according to *GPA* so as to allow efficient processing of a GPA list, but a linear search is required to access any individual student information according to *social security number*.

    Method 2 stores all the student records in a data structure that is sorted according to student *social security number*. The data structure must be sorted according to *GPA* before a sorted *GPA* list can be printed.

    Which of the following statements is true about the manner in which **method 1** and **method 2** satisfy the two data processing requirements?

    (A) Method 1 is better, because it keeps the data sorted, such that all 20,000 records can be easily printed according to *GPA* order.

    (B) Method 1 is better, because it takes longer to sort records than it takes to search for one specific record.

    (C) Method 2 is better, because frequent searches take longer than occasional sorting.

    (D) Method 2 is better, because it takes longer to search for one record than to sort all the data.

    (E) Method 1 and method 2 are essentially identical and each works as efficiently as the other does.

(Topic 12: Program Design)

24. Consider the following code segment.

```
ArrayList<Integer> list1 = new ArrayList<Integer>();
    < program code that enters appropriate values to the list1 object >
ArrayList<Integer> list2 = list1;
    < code statements to perform various processing functions >
```

    The visible code has some potential problems that can negatively impact the later invisible code.

    Which of the following are potential problems with the visible code segment?

    I.   An `ArrayIndexOutOfBoundsException` will occur.
    II. `list2` makes a *shallow* copy of `list1`, which can result in unwanted changes to the state of `list1`.
    III. `list2` makes a *deep* copy of `list1`, which can result in unwanted changes to the state of `list2`.

    (A) I only   (C) III only   (E) I and III only
    (B) II only   (D) I and II only

(Topic 13:   toString and equals)

25.   Consider the following code segment and `Widget` class.

```
Widget w = new Widget(50);
System.out.println(w);                  // Output-1
System.out.println(w.toString());       // Output-2
System.out.println(w.getWidgets());     // OutPut-3


class Widget
{
    private int numWidgets;

    public Widget(int nW)
    {
        numWidgets = nW;
    }

    public int getWidgets()
    {
        return numWidgets;
    }

    public void setWidgets(int nW)
    {
        numWidgets = nW;
    }

    public String toString()
    {
        return numWidgets;
    }
}
```

Which of the following three `// Output-x` statements will display the number of widgets stored?

(A) Output-1 only
(B) Output-2 only
(C) Output-3 only
(D) Output-1 and Output-3 only
(E) Output-1, Output-2 and Output-3

(Topic 13: toString and equals)

26. Consider the following code segment and `Student` class.

```
Student tom1 = new Student("Tom",25);
Student sue = new Student("Sue",25);
Student tom2 = new Student("Tom",32);
System.out.println(tom1.equals(sue));
System.out.println(tom1.equals(tom2));


class Student
{
    private String name;
    private int age;
    public Student(String  n, int a)
    {
        name = n;
        age = a;
    }
    public String getName() { return name; }
    public int getAge()     { return age; }

    public boolean equals(Student obj)
    {
        return name == obj.getName();
    }
}
```

What is printed as a result of executing the code segment?

(A) true
    true

(B) false
    true

(C) true
    false

(D) false
    false

(E) A compile error message indicating incompatible types

(Topic 14:   Algorithms)

27. Consider method `tango` below.

```
/** Precondition: list is a non-empty array of int values.
 *                list is a member of the same class as tango.
 */
public static void tango()
{
    int n = list.length-1;
    for (int q = 0; q < n; q++)
        if ( list[q] == list[q+1])
        {
            int temp = list[q];
            list[q] = list[q+1];
            list[q+1] = temp;
        }
}
```

Assume that `list` stores a random list of integers prior to calling method `tango`. How will the numbers be arranged in the `list` array after a call to method `tango`?

(A)   The data will be arranged in ascending order.
(B)   The data will be arranged in descending order.
(C)   The largest integer will be stored in the last array element.
(D)   The smallest integer will be stored in the last array element.
(E)   The data will appear unchanged.

(Topic 14:   Algorithms)

28. When using a binary search, what is the MAXIMUM number of comparisons necessary to locate a specific item in a list of 2049 elements?

(A)   7
(B)   11
(C)   12
(D)   13
(E)   1024

29. Consider the following method.

```
public static int mystery(int n)
{
    if (Math.sqrt(n) > n/4)
        return n;
    else
        return mystery(n - 1);
}
```

What value is returned as a result of the call mystery(21)?

(A) 19
(B) 18
(C) 17
(D) 16
(E) 15

30. Consider the following method.

```
public static int mystery(int n)
{
    if (n == 0)
        return n;
    else if (n % 2 == 0)
        return n + mystery(n-3);
    else
        return n - mystery(n+1);
}
```

What value is returned as a result of the call mystery(10)?

(A) 11
(B) 9
(C) 7
(D) 5
(E) Program crashes due to too many recursive calls.

Chapter 19
The Three AP Labs

You are looking at the 9th edition of the D&S Marketing AP Exam preparation book for AP Computer Science. This edition is specifically aimed at the examination that starts with May, 2015. Most AP Computer Science teachers know that the GridWorld Case Study is out and some AP Labs are in. So what does that exactly mean? Let's start by looking at the information that the College Board provides on their web site.

New Computer Science A Lab Requirement

As of the 2014-15 school year, the GridWorld case study has been replaced by a required lab component consisting of a minimum of 20 hours of hands-on lab experiences.

Computer Science A Labs for 2014-15

New Computer Science A Lab Resource Page
Computer Science A Course Home Page
Frequently Asked Questions
AP Computer Science A Teacher Community

Three new AP Computer Science A labs are available as exemplars to support the implementation of at least 20 hours of hands-on lab work in the classroom. Teacher guides with solutions are available through teachers' AP Course Audit accounts, and student guides are available on the AP Computer Science A Lab Resource Page.

Teachers will have the flexibility to modify and implement these new labs according to the needs of their students and to use other, comparable labs and resources to meet the 20-hour lab requirement.

The 2015 AP Computer Science A Exam will not have specific questions that focus on the new AP Computer Science A labs and will continue to assess the concepts and skills outlined in the Course Description. In addition, there will no longer be any GridWorld case study questions. A practice exam is available for teachers through their AP Course Audit accounts.

Taken from AP Computer Science home page posted on the College Board web site at http://apcentral.collegeboard.com/home 11-22-2014.

It may assist teachers new to AP Computer Science to get some AP Computer Science background. The first exam was given May, 1984 and during the Eighties the exam focused on multiple choice questions and free response questions. Free-response in computer science mostly means writing methods below provided headings. Students did well on those exams and compared favorably to college students taking the same examinations. A university survey was conducted in the Eighties and found that the average lab assignment in a college-level computer science course was considerable larger than the average lab assignment in a high school course. This concerned computer science departments in colleges and created a reluctance to grant college credit to high school students.

The College Board then started including a "Case Study" in the curriculum. The case study involved a sizable program and this program was tested on the AP Examination with five multiple choice questions and one free response questions. The first case study was the *Directory Manager*, followed by the *Long Integer*. Both programs were considered duller than dirt and then came the more interesting *Marine Biology Case Study*.

With the switch to Java, the *Marine Biology Case Study* stayed, but received a very attractive graphics makeover. Then came the switch to *GridWorld*, a more generalized program similar to *Marine Biology*, but open to a greater variety of interesting problems.

After many years of *GridWorld* there were rumors of multiple programs; there would not be a switch to a new case study, but multiple ones. And sure enough three programs were introduced. This in itself is not much of a surprise. If there can be one program to study, then why not have three? The surprise and confusion for many teachers arrived after reading the sentence below. OK, something is required, but then it is not going to be tested. How exactly does that work?

> The 2015 AP Computer Science A Exam will not have specific questions that focus on the new AP Computer Science A labs and will continue to assess the concepts and skills outlined in the Course

For many years and now many decades I have conducted APSIs in AP Computer Science. Somewhere during the workshop I ask the question: *Is the topic of input/output with files part of the AP Computer Science Curriculum?* Answers come quickly, and firmly. *No, that is not part of the curriculum.* On that cue I take teachers to a section in the College Board Course Description, shown below, that addresses input and output.

II. Program Implementation

There are topics not included in the course outline that will be part of any introductory course. For example, input and output must be part of a course on computer programming. However, in a modern object-oriented approach to programming, there are many ways to handle input and output. Consequently, the AP Computer Science A course does not prescribe any particular approach and will not test the details of input and output (except for basic text output using `System.out.print` and `System.out.println`), so that teachers may use an approach that fits their own style and whatever textbook and other materials they use.

Taken from AP Computer Science Course Description posted on the College Board web site at http://apcentral.collegeboard.com/home 11-22-2014.

It states in black and white - and has for many years now - that input/output (file handling) *must be part of any introductory course.* The same paragraph continues and also states *will not test the details of input and output.*

In other words the College Board indicates that there are requirements in the curriculum that will not be explicitly tested on the AP Exam. AP schools and AP teachers indicate during their annual AP Audit that they will teach the AP course according to the current course description.

The 2014 AP Computer Science A Course Description describes early in its publication that there will be important revisions that involve **New AP Computer Science A Labs**.

AP Computer Science A Course Description

Important Revisions to This Course Description

- New *AP Computer Science A Labs* can be found on the AP Computer Science home page, http://apcentral.collegeboard.com/apc/public/courses/teachers_corner/222163.html

- Lab Requirements and the new *AP Computer Science Labs.*

- Sample Search and Sort algorithms (Appendix C)

Taken from AP Computer Science Course Description posted on the College Board web site at http://apcentral.collegeboard.com/home 11-22-2014.

Later the course description specifies that the course must include a minimum of 20 hours of hands-on structured-lab experiences. Note that 20 hours is meant to be the minimum requirement.

The AP Computer Science A course must include a minimum of 20 hours of hands-on structured-lab experiences to engage students in individual or group problem solving. Thus, each AP Computer Science A course must include a substantial laboratory component in which students design solutions to problems, express their solutions precisely (i.e., in the Java programming language), test their solutions, identify and correct errors (when mistakes occur), and compare possible solutions.

Taken from AP Computer Science Course Description posted on the College Board web site at http://apcentral.collegeboard.com/home 11-22-2014.

The course description then continues and provides some detail on each of the three AP labs.

> Three exemplar labs, the AP Computer Science A Labs, have been developed for teachers to use in the AP Computer Science A course. AP Computer Science A teachers will be able to access all instructional resources for each lab (Teacher and Student Guides, solutions and code files) through their AP Course Audit accounts. The first lab (Magpie) can be incorporated early in the course and involves simple string processing and conditional execution. The second lab (Picture Lab) involves 2-dimensional array manipulation in the context of image processing. The third lab (Elevens) provides an example of larger object-oriented program design. The AP Computer Science Labs include
>
> **Taken from AP Computer Science Course Description posted on the College Board web site at http://apcentral.collegeboard.com/home 11-22-2014.**

If this material is not actually tested on the AP Exam, what does it mean for exam preparation? First, it means precisely what it states. Students require a minimum of 20 hours of hands-on lab experience.

What happens next is *indirect testing*. The **Magpie** lab involves string processing, and compound Boolean conditions. The **Picture** lab involves 2-dimensional array manipulation. The **Elevens** lab concentrates on Object Oriented Design.

Each one of the labs addresses important computer science topics, and these topics will be tested on both the multiple-choice section and the free-response section of the AP Exam. In other words, studying the AP Labs and doing lab assignments on the labs will increase knowledge in many topics that will be tested.

This AP Exam preparation book has specific chapters in each one of the topics handled by the AP Labs. This includes *string processing* and *Boolean conditions* that are part of the **Magpie** lab. There are also three chapters on arrays, including *two-dimensional arrays* that are covered in the **Picture** lab. Finally, there are a total of five chapters on *Object Oriented Programming* and *program design* that are the focus of the **Elevens** lab.

However, none of the questions will be based on actual AP Labs program code. This is not what will happen on the AP Exam and neither will be questions in this preparation book be taken directly from the AP Labs materials.

Chapter 20 Questions
Sample AP Examination I

Section I

    Time - 1 hour and 15 minutes

    Number of questions - 40

    Percent of total grade - 50

01. Consider the following method.

```
/** Precondition: p > 0 and q > p
 */
public static int colombia(int p, int q)
{
    int n = 0;
    while (n < p)
    {
        while (p < q)
            p++;
        n++;
    }
    return n;
}
```

What value is returned as a result of the call `colombia(12,11)` ?

(A) 10
(B) 11
(C) 12
(D) 13
(E) 14

---

02. Consider the following two methods.

```
/** Precondition: q > 0 and p > q
 */
public static int burma(int p, int q)
{
    int temp = laos(p,q);
    return p * temp / q;
}

/** Precondition: p > 0 and q > 0
 */
public static int laos(int p, int q)
{
    if (p % q == 0)
        return p;
    else
        return q;
}
```

What value is returned as a result of the call burma(5,3)?

(A) 5
(B) 6
(C) 7
(D) 8
(E) 9

03. Consider the following method.

```
public static void italy(ArrayList<Integer> list)
{
    for (int k = 0; k < list.size(); k++)
    {
        Integer n = list.get(k);
        if (n.intValue() % 2 == 0)
            list.remove(k);
    }
}
```

Which of the following describes the result of the call italy(list)?

(A) All even integer values are deleted from the list array.
(B) All odd integer values are deleted from the list array.
(C) Only some even integer values are deleted from the list array.
(D) Only some odd integer values are deleted from the list array.
(E) Some even integer values and some odd integer values are deleted from the list array

04. Consider the following code segment.

```
String bigString1 = "";
String bigString2 = "";
String str = "Annapolis";

int k = 3;
while (k < str.length())
{
    bigString1 += str.substring(k,str.length());
    bigString2 += str.substring(k);
    k++;
}
System.out.println(bigString1);
System.out.println(bigString2);
```

What is printed as a result of executing the code segment?

(A) apolispolisolislisiss
     apolispolisolislisiss

(B) napolisapolispolisolis
     apolispolisolislisiss

(C) apolispolisolislisiss
     napolisapolispolisolis

(D) sislisolispolisapolis
     sislisolispolisapolis

(E) A StringIndexOutOFBoundsException error message

05. The mean of a list of numbers is the average computed by dividing the sum of the numbers by the quantity.
The median of a list of numbers is the average determined by the middle number in an ordered list.
If the list has an odd number of values then the median is the exact middle value.
If the list has an even number of values then the median is the mean of the two middle numbers.

Consider the following incomplete `getMedian` method.
Which of the following implementations of /* **Missing Code** */ will return the correct median?

```
public static double getMedian(double[] list)
{
    double median = 0.0;

    /* Missing Code */

    return median;
}
```

Implementation I
```
int max = list.length-1;
int n1 = max/2;
int n2 = n1+1;
if (list.length % 2 == 0)
    median = (list[n1] + list[n2]) / 2;
else
    median = list[n1];
```

Implementation II
```
int max = list.length-1;
int n1 = (max-1)/2;
int n2 = n1-1;
if (list.length % 2 == 0)
    median = (list[n1] + list[n2]) / 2;
else
    median = list[n1];
```

Implementation III
```
int n1 = list.length/2;
int n2 = n1+1;
if (list.length % 2 == 0)
    median = (list[n1] + list[n2]) / 2;
else
    median = list[n1];
```

(A) I only
(B) II only
(C) III only
(D) I and II only
(E) I and III only

06. Consider the following code segment and two methods.

```
holland(45,30);


public static void holland(int x, int y)
{
    System.out.println(x + "   " + y);
    belgium(x,y);
    System.out.println(x + "   " + y);
}


public static void belgium(int x, int y)
{
    int t = x;
    x = y;
    y = t;
}
```

What value is returned as a result of the call holland(45,30) ?

(A) 45   30
     45   30

(B) 45   30
     30   45

(C) 45   45
     30   30

(D) 30   30
     45   45

(E) 30   45
     45   30

07. Consider the following two methods.

```
public static int guess1(int n)
{
    if (n == 0)
        return 0;
    else if (n == 1)
        return 1;
    else
        return guess1(n-1) + guess1(n-2);
}
```

```
public static int guess2(int n)
{
    int t1 = 0;
    int t2 = 1;
    int t3 = 1;
    for (int k = 3; k <= n; k++)
    {
        t1 = t2;
        t2 = t3;
        t3 = t1 + t2;
    }
    return t3;
}
```

For which values of n do guess1(n) and guess2(n) return the same result?

(A) For all values of n
(B) For all values, such that n >= 0
(C) For all values, such that n > 0
(D) For all values, such that n >= 1
(E) For no values of n

08. Consider the following code segment and class.

```
Blip b1 = new Blip(100);
Blip b2 = new Blip(200);
System.out.println(b1);
System.out.println(b2);


class Blip
{
    private int numBlips;

    public Blip(int nB)
    {
        numBlips = nB;
        System.out.println("Constructing a Blip object");
    }
}
```

What is printed as a result of executing the code segment?

(A) ```
Constructing a Blip object
Constructing a Blip object
```

(B) ```
Constructing a Blip object
Constructing a Blip object
100
200
```

(C) ```
Constructing a Blip object
Constructing a Blip object
Blip@6350ed68
Blip@561279c8
```

(D) ```
Blip@6350ed68
Blip@561279c8
```

(E) ```
Blip@6350ed68
Blip@561279c8
100
200
```
```

09. Consider the following four classes.

```
class Person
{
    private String name;
    public Person (String n)   { name = n; }
}


class Student extends Person
{
    public Student (String n) { super(n); }
}


class Teacher extends Person
{
    public Teacher (String n) { super(n); }
}


class School
{
    private String name;
    private Student[] students;
    private Teacher[] teachers;

    public School (String n)
    {
        name = n;
        students = new Student[1000];
        teachers = new Teacher[100];
    }
}
```

What type(s) of relationship(s) is/are established among these classes?

(A) One example of inheritance only
(B) One example of composition only
(C) Two examples of inheritance and one example of composition
(D) One example of inheritance and two examples of composition
(E) Two examples of inheritance and two examples of composition

10. Consider the following code segment and `Student` class.

```
Student kathy = new Student(10);
System.out.println(kathy.getAge());


class Student
{
    private int age;

    public Student(int age)
    {
        this.age = age;
    }

    public int getAge()
    {
        return age;
    }
}
```

What is printed as a result of executing the code segment?

(A) `10`
(B) `0`
(C) `null`
(D) compile error message
(E) runtime exception message

11. Consider the following code segment and two methods.

```
for (int n = 1; n < 5; n++)
{
    if (method1(n) || method2(n))
        System.out.println("At least one method is true");
}


public static boolean method1(int n)
{
    System.out.println("Calling method 1");
    return n < 3;
}


public static boolean method2(int n)
{
    System.out.println("Calling method 2");
    return n < 4;
}
```

The output of executing the code segment is shown below.

```
Calling method 1
At least one method is true
Calling method 1
At least one method is true
Calling method 1
Calling method 2
At least one method is true
Calling method 1
Calling method 2
```

The output execution shows evidence of

(A) inheritance.
(B) composition.
(C) encapsulation.
(D) short-circuiting.
(E) polymorphism.

12. Consider the following code segment.

```
boolean trueFalse1 = true;
boolean trueFalse2 = false;
trueFalse1 = (trueFalse1 == true && !trueFalse2 == false);
trueFalse2 = (trueFalse1 == false && !trueFalse2 == true);
System.out.println(trueFalse1);
System.out.println(trueFalse2);
```

What is printed as a result of executing the code segment?

(A) false
    true

(B) true
    false

(C) true
    true

(D) false
    false

(E) BooleanException error message

13. Consider the code segment below.

```
int[] list = new int[40];
list[0] = 0;
list[1] = 1;
for (int k = 2; k < list.length; k++)
    list[k] = list[k-1] + list[k-2];

for (int k = 5; k <= 10; k++)
    System.out.print(list[k] + "  ");
```

What is printed as a result of executing the code segment?

(A) 5   8   13   21   34   55
(B) 3   5   8   13   21   34
(C) 8   13   21   34   55   89
(D) 3   6   10   15   21   28
(E) 4   8   16   32   64   128

14. Consider the following code segment, interface and class.

```
Acrobat dimitri = new Acrobat("Dimitri");
dimitri.entrance();


interface CircusPerformer
{
    public String getPerformer();
    public void act();
    public void entrance();
    public void performance();
    public void exit();
}


class Acrobat implements CircusPerformer
{
    private String performerName;
    public Acrobat(String pN)    { performerName = pN; }
    public void entrance()
    {
        System.out.println("Parades with performers");
    }
    public void performance()
    {
        System.out.println("Flips forwards and backwards on trapeze");
    }
    public void exit()
    {
        System.out.println("Lands in safety net");
    }
}
```

What is printed as a result of executing the code segment?

(A) Flips forwards and backwards on trapeze
    Parades with performers
    Lands in safety net

(B) Ivan Flips forwards and backwards on trapeze
    Ivan Parades with performers
    Ivan Lands in safety net

(C) Ivan
    Flips forwards and backwards on trapeze
    Parades with performers
    Lands in safety net

(D) Compile error message, due to implementing a method that was not declared in the interface.

(E) Compile error message, due to not implementing methods that were declared in the interface.

15. Consider the following code segment.

```
Worker tom = new Worker ("Tom",27,"Pilot",12);
Worker sue = new Worker ("Sue",29,"Doctor", 3);
Worker ann = sue;
sue.setName("Sue");
sue.setAge(33);
sue.setJob("Nurse");
sue.setYears(5);
```

This code segment may have a problem with program reliability.

A bad technique, called _____ is used, which can cause unwanted side effects.

(A) double instantiation
(B) dereferencing
(C) aliasing
(D) data conflict
(E) memory deallocation

16. A search item exists in a sorted array of 1000 elements.
How many comparisons, on average, will be made by a linear search method?

(A) 9
(B) 10
(C) 11
(D) 500
(E) 1000

17. Consider the following class with four incomplete methods.

```
class Sort
{
    public static void sortList (int[] list)
    {
        /* Sorting Code */
    }

    public static void sortList (double[] list)
    {
        /* Sorting Code */
    }

    public static void sortList (String[] list)
    {
        /* Sorting Code */
    }

    public static void sortList (Student[] list)
    {
        /* Sorting Code */
    }
}
```

Can a class work correctly with four methods that have the same sortList identifier?

(A) Yes, because the four sortList methods have different signatures.
(B) Yes, but only as long as the four methods have different source code.
(C) No, because overloaded methods may not use the same number of parameters.
(D) No, because overloaded methods may not have identical parameter identifiers.
(E) No, because overloaded methods may only use object data types.

18. Consider the following code segment.

```
for (int k = 1; k <= 100; k++)
{
    int n1 = (int) (Math.random() * 10);
    int n2 = (int) (Math.random() * 10);
    boolean bool = n1 == n2;
    System.out.print(bool + "  ");
}
```

What is printed as a result of executing the code segment?

(A) The code segment always prints true.
(B) The code segment always prints false.
(C) There is a 1 in 10 probability that the code segment prints true.
(D) The code segment prints both true and false, but roughly 10 % more times true.
(E) The code segment prints both true and false, but roughly 10 % more times false.

19. Consider the following code segment with a /* **Missing Code** */ statement.

```
ArrayList<Integer> numbers = new ArrayList<Integer>();
for (int k = 1; k <= 10; k++)
{
    /* Missing Code */
    numbers.add(new Integer(rndInt));
}

for (Integer number : numbers)
    System.out.println(number);
```

This code segment must print ten random integers x, such that $10 <= x <= 99$.
Which of the following statements, which will replace /* **Missing Code** */, will print the correct numbers?

(A) `int rndInt = (int) (Math.random() * 99);`
(B) `int rndInt = (int) (Math.random() * 99) + 10;`
(C) `int rndInt = (int) (Math.random() * 90) + 10;`
(D) `int rndInt = ((int) Math.random()) * 89 + 10;`
(E) `int rndInt = (int) (Math.random() * 89) + 10;`

20. Consider the following method

```
/** Precondition: list.length > 0
 */
public static int counter(int[] list)
{
    int count = 0;
    int p = 0;
    int q = list.length-1;
    int r = 0;
    while (p <= q)
    {
        r = (p + q) / 2;
        count++;
        if (count % 2 == 0)
            q = r - 1;
        else
            p = r + 1;
    }
    return count;
}
```

What value is returned by method counter if `list.length` equals 64 ?

(A) 32
(B) 63
(C) 5
(D) 6
(E) 7

21. Consider the following program segment and `List` class.

```
int[] x = {11,22,33,44,55,66,77,88,99};
List list = new List(x);
System.out.println(list);


class List
{
private int[] array;

public List(int[] x)
{
    array = x;
}

public String toString()
{
    String temp = "[";
    for (int k = 0; k < array.length; k++)
    {
        temp = temp + array[k];
        if (k < array.length-1)
            temp = temp + ", ";
    }
    temp += "]";
    return temp;
}
}
```

What is the output of executing the program segment?

(A) `[0, 0, 0, 0, 0, 0, 0, 0, 0]`
(B) `[11, 22, 33, 44, 55, 66, 77, 88, 99]`
(C) `[11, 22, 33, 44, 55, 66, 77, 88, 0]`
(D) `[0, 22, 33, 44, 55, 66, 77, 88, 99]`
(E) `ArrayIndexOutOfBoundsException message`

22. What is the output of the following code segment and methods?

```
System.out.println(method1(7));


public static int method1(int p)
{
    if (p < 5)
        return p;
    else
        return method2(p-1);
}

public static int method2(int q)
{
    return method1(q-1);
}
```

(A) 3
(B) 4
(C) 5
(D) 6
(E) No output. Recursive calls never stop.

23. Consider the following method.

```
/** Precondition list.length > 2
 **/
public static void mystery(int[] list)
{
    int n = list.length;
    for (int k = 0; k < n-1; k++)
    {
        int temp = list[k];
        list[k] = list[k+1];
        list[k+1] = temp;
    }
}
```

How are number in the `list` array altered after a call to method `mystery` ?

(A) Every two numbers have exchanged positions.
(B) All the numbers are in the same order, except the last number, which is in the first location.
(C) All the numbers are in the same order, except the first number, which is in the last location.
(D) All the numbers are in reverse order.
(E) The numbers are initially exchanged, but then exchanged again to remain in the original order.

24. Consider the following code segment and class.
    `Worker` objects are considered equal, if they have the same job title.

```
Worker jack = new Worker("Jack","Printer",45000.0,32);
Worker kate = new Worker("Kate","Printer",52000.0,36);
System.out.println(jack.equals(kate));


class Worker
{
    private String name;
    private String job;
    private double salary;
    private int age;

    public Worker (String n, String j, double s, int a)
    {
        name = n;
        job = j;
        salary = s;
        age = a;
    }

    public boolean equals (Object source)
    {
        /* Missing Code */
    }
}
```

Which of the following implementations of /* **missing code** */ makes method `equals` work as intended?

Implementation 1	Implementation 2

`Worker temp = source;`
`if (job.equals(temp.job))`
`    return true;`
`else`
`    return false;`
	`Worker temp = (Worker) source;`
	`if (job.equals(temp.job))`
	`    return true;`
	`else`
	`    return false;`

Implementation 3	
`Worker temp = (Worker) source;` `return (job.equals(temp.job));`	(A) Implementation 1 only (B) Implementation 2 only (C) Implementation 3 only (D) Implementations 1 and 2 only (E) Implementations 2 and 3 only

25. Consider the following code segment and `Matrix` class.

```
int[][] square = {{1,2,3},{4,5,6},{7,8,9}};
Matrix matrix = new Matrix(square);
System.out.println(matrix);


class Matrix
{
    int[][] mat;

    public Matrix (int[][] m)
    {
        mat = m;
    }

    public String toString()
    {
        String temp = "";
        for (int r = 0; r < mat.length; r++)
        {
            for (int c = 0; c < mat.length; c++)
                temp += mat[r][c] + "   ";
            temp += "\n";
        }
    }
}
```

What is printed as a result of executing the code segment?

(A) 1   2   3   4   5   6   7   8   9

(B) 1   2   3
    4   5   6
    7   8   9

(C) {{1,2,3},{4,5,6},{7,8,9}}

(D) {{1,2,3},
    {4,5,6}
    {7,8,9}}

(E) A compile error message indicating a missing `return` statement

26. Consider the following method.

```
public static String bizarre (String str)
{
    String temp1 = "";
    String temp2 = "";
    String temp3 = "";
    for (int k = 0 ; k < str.length(); k++)
    {
        temp1 = str.substring(k);
        temp2 = str.substring(k,k+1);
        if (temp1.equals(temp2))
            temp3 += temp1;
    }
    return temp3;
}
```

What value is returned as a result of the call `bizarre ("HOLLAND")` ?

(A) D
(B) ND
(C) AND
(D) LAND
(E) LLAND

27. Consider the following code segment.

```
int n1 = (int) (Math.random() * 4) + 1;
int n2 = (int) (Math.random() * 4) + 1;
int n3 = Math.abs(n2 - n1);
double n4 = Math.pow(n1,n3);
```

What is the range of smallest to largest values that is stored by `n4`?

(A) [1.0 .. 9.0]
(B) [4.0 .. 16.0]
(C) [1.0 .. 64.0]
(D) [4.0 .. 128.0]
(E) [1.0 .. 256.0]

Questions 28-29 refer to the following information.

Your software company has been contracted to create a Gradebook program for a large school district.

Currently the design team has created a set of classes with a brief explanation of the functionalities for each class.

The classes are as follows:

`Student` class
>   Stores all personal information for each student.
>   Stores all school courses and grades.
>   Processes all data at the student level, such as GPA.

`Freshman, Sophomore, Junior` and `Senior` classes
>   Stores individual student information and processes that are unique to each class.
>   For instance, a 9th grader takes English-1, a 10th grader English-2, etc.

`School` class
>   This is a large class which stores information about all the students.
>   This class also computes student ranking.

28. Class interaction with inheritance and/or composition is an important
    concern. Which of the following shows proper class interaction?

    I.   The four grade classes (9, 10, 11, 12) extend the `Student` class.
    II. The `School` class extends each one of the grade (9, 10, 11, 12) classes.
    III. The School class uses composition by containing four array data structures,
          each storing objects of the grade classes.

    (A) I only
    (B) II only
    (C) III only
    (D) I and II only
    (E) I and III only

29. Correct use of inheritance and composition insures reliability of individually
    tested classes. Polymorphism also assists with reliability. Where might be
    a good opportunity to take advantage of Polymorphism in this program design?

    (A) The methods defined in the `Student` class should be polymorphic.
    (B) The methods in the `School` class computing class rank should be polymorphic.
    (C) Some methods in the grade classes, unique to each grade, like registration,
          should be polymorphic methods.
    (D) The methods from a superclass that are not re-defined should be polymorphic.
    (E) The gradebook program does not have any opportunities to benefit from polymorphism.

30. Consider the following code segment.

```
ArrayList<Double> numbers1 = new ArrayList<Double>();
numbers1.add(new Double(1.1));
numbers1.add(new Double(1.2));
numbers1.add(new Double(1.3));
numbers1.add(new Double(1.4));

ArrayList<Double> numbers2 = numbers1;
numbers2.add(new Double(2.1));
numbers2.add(new Double(2.2));
numbers2.add(new Double(2.3));
numbers2.add(new Double(2.4));

System.out.println(numbers1);
System.out.println(numbers2);
```

What is printed as a result of executing the segment?

(A) [1.1, 1.2, 1.3, 1.4]
     [2.1, 2.2, 2.3, 2.4]

(B) [2.1, 2.2, 2.3, 2.4]
     [2.1, 2.2, 2.3, 2.4]

(C) [1.1, 1.2, 1.3, 1.4, 2.1, 2.2, 2.3, 2.4]
     [1.1, 1.2, 1.3, 1.4, 2.1, 2.2, 2.3, 2.4]

(D) [1.1, 1.2, 1.3, 1.4]
     [1.1, 1.2, 1.3, 1.4]

(E) [1.1, 1.2, 1.3, 1.4, 2.1, 2.2, 2.3, 2.4]
     [2.1, 2.2, 2.3, 2.4, 1.1, 1.2, 1.3, 1.4]

31. Consider the following program statement and three classes

```
Employee juan = new Employee("Plumber",45000,"Juan",29,14,"Associates");

class Car
{
    private int year;
    private String make;
    public Car (int y, String m)
    {
        year = y;
        make = m;
        System.out.println("Car is instantiated");
    }
}

class Person
{
    private String name;
    private int age;
    private Car car;
    public Person(String n, int a, int y, String m)
    {
        name = n;
        age = a;
        car = new Car(y,m);
        System.out.println("Person is instantiated");
    }
}

class Employee extends Person
{
    private String job;
    private double salary;
    public Employee(String j, double s, String n, int a, int y, String m)
    {
        super(n,a,y,m);
        job = j;
        salary = s;
        System.out.println("Employee is instantiated");
    }
}
```

What is printed as a result of executing the program statement?

(A) `Car is instantiated`
`Person is instantiated`
`Employee is instantiated`
	(B) `Person is instantiated`
	`Employee is instantiated`

(C) `Employee is instantiated`
`Person is instantiated`
`Car is instantiated`
	(D) `Employee is instantiated`
	`Person is instantiated`

(E) `Employee is instantiated`	

32. What value is returned after calling `texas(4)` ?

```
public static int texas(int p)
{
    if (p < 1)
        return p;
    else
        return p + texas(p-1) + texas(p-1);
}
```

(A) 0
(B) 11
(C) 26
(D) 57
(E) Runtime Exception. Recursive calls never stop.

33. Consider the following code segment.

```
for (int k = 1; k <= 10; k++)
{
    int rndInt = (int) (Math.random() * 10);
    System.out.print(rndInt + "   ");
}
```

What is printed as a result of executing the code segment?

(A) A set of 10 zeros for each separate execution.
(B) A different set of random integers in the `[0..10]` range for each separate execution.
(C) A different set of random integers in the `[0..9]` range for each separate execution.
(D) An identical set of random integers in the `[0..10]` range for each separate execution.
(E) An identical set of random integers in the `[0..9]` range for each separate execution.

34. Consider the following abstract `Worker` interface declaration.

```
interface Worker
{
    public void getResume();
    public void setInterview();
    public void SetBenefits();
    public void getBackgroundCheck();
    public void JobDescription();
    public void JobTraining;

    // Additional methods to process employees
}
```

A large corporation is creating a new program for managing its employees.
The following concrete classes will be used to process different categories of workers.

class `Engineer`
class `Secretary`
class `Manufacturer`
class `Accounting`
class `Research`
.... additional classes for other worker categories ....

Keep in mind that this is a large corporation with every conceivable category of worker.
Even though there are different worker categories, all employees do share common procedures.
Examples of common procedures are *getting hired*, *setting up benefits*, *getting a background check* and others.

What is a logical next step in the sequence of creating this program?

(A) Design and implement the classes that hire an employee first.
(B) Write an abstract class that implements the `Worker` interface common procedures only.
(C) Set up a concrete class for each worker category that implements `Worker`.
(D) Design the methods in the `Worker` interface.
(E) Determine the input/output requirements of the program.

35. A magic square is a square matrix of consecutive integers that are stored in a two-dimensional array, such that every row, column and diagonal have the same sum. For instance, the 3 X 3 matrix below is a magic square and every sum equals 15.

Consider the two incomplete methods below.

```
/** Precondition:   sqr is a non-empty two-dimensional array
 *                  sqr.length equals sqr[0].length
 *                  sqr is possibly a magic square
 *   Postcondition: returns an array of sums for each row,
 *                  column and diagonal in sqr
 */
public static int[] computeSums(int[][] sqr)
{
    /* Missing Code */
}


/** Precondition:   sums is a non-empty array
 *   Postcondition: returns true if every value in sums is equal
 *                  and returns false otherwise
 */
public static boolean isMagic(int[] sums)
{
    /* Missing Code */
}
```

Which of the following statements uses methods computeSums and isMagic such that the execution of the statement prints true if the square is a magic square?

(A) System.out.println(computeSums(isMagic(square)));
(B) System.out.println(isMagic(computeSums(square)));
(C) System.out.println(isMagic(sums) = computeSums(square));
(D) System.out.println(computeSums(sums) = isMagic(square));
(E) Both B and C

36. What is the output of the following code segment?

```
ArrayList<ArrayList<Integer>> matrix = new ArrayList<ArrayList<Integer>>();
ArrayList<Integer> x = new ArrayList<Integer>();
ArrayList<Integer> y = new ArrayList<Integer>();
ArrayList<Integer> z = new ArrayList<Integer>();
for (int k = 1; k <= 5; k++)
{
    x.add(new Integer(k));
    y.add(new Integer(k * 10));
    z.add(new Integer(k * 100));
}
matrix.add(x);
matrix.add(y);
matrix.add(z);
System.out.println(matrix);
```

(A) [x, y, z]
(B) [[1, 2, 3, 4, 5], [10, 20, 30, 40, 50], [100, 200, 300, 400, 500]]
(C) [three memory references separated by commas]
(D) a single Memory reference
(E) ArrayIndexOutOfBoundsException message

37. Consider the following method.

```
public static int spain(int n)
{
    if (n == 0 || n == 1)
        return n;
    else
        return n + spain(n-1) + spain(n-2);
}
```

What value is returned as a result of the call spain(4) ?

(A) 3
(B) 5
(C) 8
(D) 14
(E) 26

38. Consider the following method.

```
public static void count(int p, int q)
{
    if (p < q)
    {
        count(p+1,q);
        System.out.print(p + "  ");
    }
}
```

Which of the following is printed as a result of the call `count(5,10)` ?

(A) 5 6 7 8 9
(B) 5 6 7 8 9 10
(C) 9 8 7 6 5
(D) 10 9 8 7 6 5
(E) Stack overflow runtime error due to infinite recursion

39. Consider the following code segment with a /* **Missing Code** */ statement.

```
ArrayList<Integer> numbers = new ArrayList<Integer>();
for (int k = 1; k <= 100; k++)
{
    /* Missing Code */
    int rndInt = (int) (Math.random() * 21) - 10;
    numbers.add(new Integer(rndInt));
}

for (Integer number : numbers)
System.out.print(number + "  ");
```

This code segment must print ten random integers x, such that $-10 <= x <= 10$.
Which of the following statements, which will replace /* **Missing Code** */ will print the correct numbers?

(A) `int rndInt = (int) (Math.random() * 11);`
(B) `int rndInt = (int) (Math.random() * 20) - 10;`
(C) `int rndInt = (int) (Math.random() * 10) - 21;`
(D) `int rndInt = ((int) Math.random()) * 21 + 10;`
(E) `int rndInt = (int) (Math.random() * 21) - 10;`

40. Consider following code segment and classes.

```java
Animal lucky = new Pet(3,"Cat",7);
System.out.println(lucky);


class Animal
{
    private int age;

    public Animal (int age)    { this.age = age; }
    public int getAge()        { return age; }
}


class Pet extends Animal
{
    private String type;
    private int weight;

    public Pet(int a, String t, int w)
    {
        super(a);
        type = t;
        weight = w;
    }

    public String toString()
    {
        return type + ", " + getAge() + ", " + weight;
    }
}
```

What is printed as a result of executing the code segment?

(A) `Animal@fa4cd82, Pet@7930ebb`
(B) `Pet@7930ebb`
(C) `type Cat, age 3, weight 7`
(D) `Cat, 3, 7`
(E) An Exception error message

Section II
   Time - 1 hour and 45 minutes
   Number of questions - 4
   Percent of total grade - 50

Question 1.

A *Latin Square* is a square matrix of consecutive integers. There exist different types of *Latin* Squares. One type is used for this question. The sequence of integers is repeated and never exceeds the size of the matrix. A **3 x 3** square matrix is size **3** and the sequence of integers in the *Latin Square* is **1 2 3** in the pattern shown below. Whenever number **3** is reached the sequence starts over with **1**.

1	2	3
2	3	1
3	1	2

Assume the existence of a `Latin` class, which creates and displays Latin Squares. Now consider the following code segment. Execution of this code segment results in the display of two matrixes. The matrix below on the left is displayed after the construction of the `Latin` object and the matrix on the right is displayed after calling method `makeLatin`.

```
Latin square = new Latin(3);
System.out.println(square);
square.makeLatin();
System.out.println(square);
```

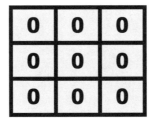

Consider the following incomplete declaration of the `Latin` class.

```
class Latin
{
    private int size;
    private int[][] square;

    public Latin(int n)
    {
        /* implemented in part (a) */
    }

    public void makeLatin()
    {
        /* implemented in part (b) */
    }

    public String toString()
    {
        /* implemented in part (c) */
    }

}
```

Part (a).

Complete constructor `Latin` below.

```
/** precondition:  n > 1
  *  postcondition: n x n space is allocated for object square
  */
public Latin(int n)
```

Part (b).

Complete method `makeLatin` below.

```
/** precondition:  n x n space is allocated for square
 *  postcondition: integers are stored in square to form a Latin square
 */
public void makeLatin()
```

Part (c).

Complete method `toString` below.

```
/** postcondition: toString returns a string of integers stored
 *                 in square with linefeeds to display a square matrix
 */
public void toString()
```

Question 2.

Consider the following incomplete declaration of a `Random1` class. Class `Random1` could be an implementation of the standard Java class `Random`.

```
class Random1
{
    double currentNr;

    public Random1()
    {
        double seed = System.currentTimeMillis();
        currentNr = seed;
    }

    public Random1(double seed)
    {
        currentNr = seed;
    }

    /** postcondition: returns a double x, such that 0 <= x < 1
     */
    public double getRandom()
    {
        double nextNr = currentNr + Math.PI;
        nextNr = nextNr * nextNr;
        int temp = (int) nextNr;
        currentNr = nextNr = nextNr - temp;
        return nextNr;
    }

    public int nextInteger(int n)      {/* implemented in part (a) */}
}
```

Part (a).

Complete method `nextInteger` below.

```
/** precondition:  n > 1
 *  postcondition: returns an int x, such that 0 <= x < n
 */
public int nextInteger(int n)
```

Part (b).

Consider the following incomplete class `Random2`, which is a sub class of `Random1`.

```
class Random2 extends Random1
{
    public Random2 (double seed)                    {/* implemented in part (b) */ }

    public int nextInteger (int start, int end)  {/* implemented in part (c) */}
}
```

Complete constructor `Random2` below.

```
/** precondition:  seed > 0
  *  postcondition: seed is passed to the super class constructor
  */
public Random2 (double seed)
```

Part (c).

Complete method `nextInteger` below.

```
/** precondition:  start is an integer
  *                end is an integer such that end > start
  *  postcondition: returns a random integer x such that for all x,
  *                start <= x <= end
  */
public int nextInt (int start, int end)
```

Question 3.

Encrypting data is an important tool in computer science. A simplistic approach in encoding a message is to shift characters by a number of spaces with wraparound. If the shift is four characters forward then a word like **SATURDAY** becomes **WEXYVHEC**. The coded message looks unreadable, but a consistent pattern of shifting characters is quickly broken by programs designed to decode messages.

A better approach is to shift characters in a manner that is not consistent by using a special key. Each character in the original message is still shifted to another character, but the shifting is determined by the character shift-value of a key. The actual shift value is not important. This value can be the Unicode value of the character or it can be some value determined by a special key-value-code. The point is that the original message is now altered in an irregular pattern. Consider the following example with intentionally, small shift values in the key MONDAY.

Key Characters	M	O	N	D	A	Y
Shift Value	9	2	0	1	7	5

Now imagine that this key is applied to the source message *DISCOMBOBULATED*. The coding process goes through the following steps:

1. Get Unicode value of each character in the source message.
    (Unicode values and ASC values are the same for alpha-numeric characters)

2. Get the shift values for each character in the key.

3. Add the shift value of the key to each corresponding character in the message to get the coded value.

4. The coded message is the set of characters that is associated with the coded values.

Message	D	I	S	C	O	M	B	O	B	U	L	A	T	E	D
ASC value	68	73	83	67	79	77	66	79	66	85	76	65	84	69	68
Key	M	O	N	D	A	Y	M	O	N	D	A	Y	M	O	N
Shift value	9	2	0	1	7	5	9	2	0	1	7	5	9	2	0
Coded value	77	75	83	68	86	82	75	81	66	86	83	70	93	71	68
Coded message	M	K	S	D	V	R	K	Q	B	V	S	F	]	G	D

Consider the following incomplete declaration of the `Cryptic` class. The constructor initializes the `keyCode` field, which determines shift values. Private method `getCode` converts a single character of a source message into a coded character. Private method `getSource` converts a single character of a coded message into a character that is part of the source message. Method `enCrypt` converts a message into a coded message and method `deCrypt` converts a coded message back into a readable source message.

```
class Cryptic
{
    private String keyCode;

    public Cryptic ()
    {
        /* initializes the keyCode */
    }

    private String getCode(String sourceChar, String keyChar)
    {
        /* code to convert source message character into code */
    }

    private String getSource(String codedChar, String keyChar)
    {
        /* code to convert coded character into source message */
    }

    public String enCrypt(String source, String key)
    {
        /* implemented in part (a) */
    }

    public String deCrypt(String coded, String key)
    {
        /* implemented in part (b) */
    }
}
```

The code segment below is part of a client program that constructs a Cryptic object, converts the source message DISCOMBOBULATED into a coded message, and then converts the coded message back into the original message.

Code segment in client program using the `Cryptic` class	Execution Output

`Cryptic secret = new Cryptic();`
`String source = "DISCOMBOBULATED";`
`String key = "MONDAY";`
`System.out.println("source: " + source);`
`System.out.println();`
`String coded = secret.enCrypt(source,key);`
`System.out.println("coded:   " + coded);`
`System.out.println();`
`source = secret.deCrypt(coded,key);`
`System.out.println("source: " + source);`
	source: DISCOMBOBULATED
	
	coded: MKSDVRKQBVSF]GD
	
	source: DISCOMBOBULATED

Part (a).

Write method enCrypt as described earlier. In writing method enCrypt you may call method getCode specified below.

```
/** precondition:  sourceChar is not null and is a one-character String
 *                 member of some message to be coded.
 *                 keyChar is not null and is a one-character String
 *                 member of a coding key used to alter sourceChar
 *  postcondition: returns a one-character String, which is the
 *                 encrypted character of sourceChar
 */
private String getCode(String sourceChar, String keyChar)
```

Complete method enCrypt below.

```
/** precondition:  source is not null and represents the source message
 *                 to be encrypted
 *                 key is not null and represents the key string that    *
             is used to encrypt source
 *   postcondition: returns the encrypted version of source
 */
public String enCrypt(String source, String key)
```

Part (b).

Write method deCrypt as described earlier. In writing method deCrypt you may call method getSource specified below.

```
/** precondition:  codedChar is not null and is a one-character String
 *                 member of an encrypted message to be decoded.
 *                 keyChar is not null and is a one-character String
 *                 member of a coding key used to alter codedChar
 *   postcondition: returns a one-character String, which is the
 *                 decrypted character of codedChar
 */
private String getSource(String codedChar, String keyChar)
```

Complete method deCrypt below.

```
/** precondition:  coded is not null and represents the encrypted
 *                 message to be decoded
 *                 key is not null and represents the key string that    *
              is used to decrypt coded
 *    postcondition: returns the decrypted version of coded
 */
public String deCrypt(String coded, String key)
```

Question 4.

Consider the following incomplete declaration of the `Rational` class. The purpose of the `Rational` class is to facilitate arithmetic operations between rational numbers. Operations between fractional numbers are handled by Java in decimal format, like **0.25 + 0.375 = 0.625**. The rational class will be able to add and display the same operations in the form of common fractions, like **1/4 + 3/8 = 5/8**.

The `Rational` class has a constructor for rational numbers that are 0, rational numbers that are integers like 5, and rational numbers in the format num/den, where den != 0. The `toString` method needs to be re-defined so that `Rational` objects can be displayed as a common fraction in lowest terms. A `Rational` class would have all the customary arithmetic operations. For this question only the `add` method needs to be implemented.

```
class Rational
{
    private int num;
    private int den;
    public Rational ()              { num = 0;    den = 1;    }
    public Rational (int nr)        { num = nr;   den = 1;    }
    public Rational (int n, int d)  { num = n;    den = d;    }

    /** precondition:  num and den are initialized; den != 0
     *  postcondition: returns 0 if num equals 0
     *                 returns num if den equals 1
     *                 returns value-of-num/value-of-den if both
     *                 num and den are non-zero
     */
    public String toString()
    {
        /* implemented in part (a) */
    }

    /** precondition:  n and d are integers greater than 0
     *  postcondition: returns the greatest common factor of n and d
     */
    private int getGCF (int n, int d)
    {
        /* implemented in part (b) */
    }

    /** precondition:  r1 and r2 are Rational objects
     *  postcondition: r1 is added to r2 according to the common rules
     *                 of arithmetic for rational numbers and the final
     *                 object is in lowest terms.
     *                 The resulting num and den values are stored by
     *                 the current object
     */
    public void add(Rational r1, Rational r2)
    {
        /* implemented in part (c) */
    }

    /** additional arithmetic methods */

}
```

Part (a).

Write method `toString`, which is described as follows. Method `toString` is redefined to display `Rational` objects in the form of common fractions, **0** is displayed as **0**, integers are displayed with numbers only, like **5** and fractions are displayed like **7/6**. The table below demonstrates the result of redefining the `toString` method for the `Rational` class.

Code segment in client program using the `Rational` class	Execution Output
| ```
Rational nr1 = new Rational();
Rational nr2 = new Rational(5);
Rational nr3 = new Rational(3,4);
Rational nr4 = new Rational(5,10);
System.out.println(nr1);
System.out.println(nr2);
System.out.println(nr3);
System.out.println(nr4);
nr1.add(nr3,nr4);
System.out.println(nr1);
``` | 0<br>5<br>3/4<br>5/10<br>5/4 |

Complete method `toString` below.

```
/** precondition: num and den are initialized; den != 0
 *  postcondition: returns 0 if num equals 0
 *                 returns num if den equals 1
 *                 returns value-of-num/value-of-den if both
 *                 num and den are non-zero
 */
public String toString()
```
```

Part (b).

Write method `getGCF` as described earlier. There exist many implementations for computing the Greatest Common Factor. *Euclid's Algorithm* is a 2000-year-old GCF algorithm that is suited very well for the sequential instructions required by a computer program. In the example below, Euclid's Algorithm is used to compute the GCF of **120** and **108**. The result is **12**.

Algorithm Steps	Sample Problem
Step 1: Start with two integers	integer1 is 120 integer2 is 108
Step 2: Divide integer1 by integer2 and compute the remainder.	120 / 108 = 1 The remainder = 12
Step 3: If the remainder equals 0, you are finished. The GCF is integer2.	The remainder is not 0 You are not finished.
Step 4: If the remainder is not 0 then integer1 becomes integer 2 and integer2 becomes the remainder	integer1 is now 108 integer2 is now 12
Step 5: Go to **Step2** below:	
Step 2: Divide integer1 by integer2 and compute the remainder. Continue with **Step 3** below.	108 / 12 = 9 The remainder = 0
Step 3: If the remainder equals 0, you are finished. The GCF is integer2.	The remainder is 0 You are finished and the GCF = 12

Complete method `getGCF` below.

```
/** precondition:  n and d are integers greater than 0
 *  postcondition: returns the greatest common factor of n and d
 */
private int getGCF (int n, int d)
```

Part (c).

Write method `add` as described earlier. Method `add` not only adds two Rational objects, it also reduces the resulting rational number before it is assigned to the current object. In writing method `add`, you may call method `getGCF` specified in part (b). Assume that `getGCF` works as specified, regardless of what you wrote in part (b).

Complete method `add` below.

```
/** precondition:  r1 and r2 are Rational objects
 *  postcondition: r1 is added to r2 according to the common rules
 *                 of arithmetic for rational numbers and the final
 *                 object is in lowest terms.
 *                 The resulting num and den values are stored by the
 *                 current object
 */
public void add(Rational r1, Rational r2)
```

Chapter 21 Questions
Sample AP Examination II

Questions 01-02 refer to the following classes and code segment.

```
interface Language
{
    public void greeting();
}

class German implements Language
{
    public void greeting() {System.out.println("In German you say Guten Tag");}
}

class Dutch implements Language
{
    public void greeting() {System.out.println("In Dutch you say Goeden Dag");}
}

class French implements Language
{
    public void greeting() {System.out.println("In French you say Bonjour");}
}


ArrayList<Language> countries = new ArrayList<Language>();
countries.add(new German());
countries.add(new Dutch());
countries.add(new French());
for (Language country: countries)
    country.greeting();
```

01. What is printed as a result of executing the code segment?

(A)   In German you say Guten Tag
       In Dutch you say Goeden Dag
       In French you say Bonjour

(B)   Guten Tag
       Goeden Dag
       Bonjour

(C)   German
       Dutch
       French

(D)   A compile error message, because an abstract class was not used to implement the Language interface

(E)   A compile error message, because the for loop structure does not access array elements properly

02. If another language is added to this program, what must be done to alter the program?

I.   Create a new language class.
II.   Change the Language interface.
III.   Add the new Language object to the countries array in the main method.
IV.   Change the loop that displays the languages.

(A)   I only
(B)   II only
(C)   III only
(D)   I and III only
(E)   II only IV only

03. Consider the following code segment and method.

```
int[] list = {90,80,70,60,50,40,30,20,10};
mystery(list);

public static void mystery(int[] x)
{
    int n = x.length-1;
    for (int k = n; k >= 0; k--)
        x[k] = x[k]/x[n];
}
```

Assume that integer array contains the following values: {90,80,70,60,50,40,30,20,10}
Which of the following represents the contents of list as a result of calling method mystery?

(A) {90,80,70,60,60,40,30,20,10}
(B) {9,8,7,6,6,4,3,2,1}
(C) {9,8,7,6,6,4,3,2,10}
(D) {90,80,70,60,60,40,30,20,1}
(E) An ArrayIndexOutOfBoundsException error message

04. Consider the following two mystery methods. If both methods mystery1 and mystery2 are called with an identical integer array of n consecutive integers, starting at 1, like 1,2,3,4,5...n, what can be stated about the arrays at the conclusion of the execution?

```
public static void mystery1(int[] x1)
{
    for (int k = 1; k < x1.length; k++)
    x1[k] = x1[k] + x1[k-1];
}

public static void mystery2(int[] x2)
{
    int increase = 2;
    for (int k = 1; k < x2.length; k++)
    {
        x2[k] = x2[k-1] + increase;
        increase++;
    }
}
```

(A) Nothing can be stated with knowing the size of the arrays.
(B) Both arrays will be identical.
(C) Both arrays start with 1 and then they store different values.
(D) Both arrays store identical values, except for the first element.
(E) An ArrayIndexOutOfBoundsException error message

05. Consider the following program segment and `List` class.

```
int[] x = {11,22,33,44,55,66,77,88,99};
List list = new List(x);
x[x.length] = 0;
System.out.println(list);


class List
{
    private int[] array;

    public List(int[] x)
    {
        array = x;
    }

    public String toString()
    {
        String temp = "[";
        for (int k = 0; k < array.length; k++)
        {
            temp = temp + array[k];
            if (k < array.length-1)
                temp = temp + ", ";
        }
        temp += "]";
        return temp;
    }
}
```

What is the output of executing the program segment?

(A) `[0, 0, 0, 0, 0, 0, 0, 0, 0]`
(B) `[11, 22, 33, 44, 55, 66, 77, 88, 99]`
(C) `[11, 22, 33, 44, 55, 66, 77, 88, 0]`
(D) `[0, 22, 33, 44, 55, 66, 77, 88, 99]`
(E) `ArrayIndexOutOfBoundsException` message

06. Consider the following method.

```
/** Precondition: str is a nonempty string of upper-case letters
 */
public static String oddString(String str)
{
    String temp = "";
    for (int k = 0; k < str.length(); k++)
    {
        String t = str.substring(k,k+1);
        System.out.print(t + "   ");
        if (t != "A" && t != "E" && t != "I" && t != "O" && t != "U")
            temp += t;
    }
    return temp;
}
```

Which of the following is a correct Postcondition, based on the return of method oddString?

(A) Postcondition: oddstring returns str
(B) Postcondition: oddstring returns str with all vowels removed
(C) Postcondition: oddstring returns only the vowels in str
(D) Postcondition: oddstring returns null
(E) It will generate a StringOutOfBoundsException error message

07. Consider the following code segment.

```
int p = <some int > 0>
int q = <some int > p>
int temp = q - p + 1;
int rndNum = (int) (Math.random() * temp) + p;
```

What is the range of random numbers that can be assigned to rndNum?

(A) [0 .. q]
(B) [p .. q]
(C) [q .. p]
(D) [0 .. p+q]
(E) [p .. q-1]

08. Imagine that you are creating a graphics program that involves rotating 3d objects. The program requires complex mathematical operations. All these mathematical operations have been placed in a special Math3d class.

Consider the following Math3d class information.

I. The preconditions and postconditions of each public method.
II. The method's heading signature.
III. The mathematical logic and implementation source code of each method.

Using the Math3d class effectively only requires I and II.
The implementation of the source code is not required to use the Math3d class.

This type of program design philosophy is called

(A) encapsulation.
(B) information hiding.
(C) divide and conquer
(D) class interaction
(E) program enhancement

09. Consider the following two methods.

```
/** Precondition: x > 0 and y > 0
 */
public static int mango(int x, int y)
{
    int temp = papaya(x,y);
    return (x * y) / temp;
}

public static int papaya(int a, int b)
{
    int temp = a % b;
    if (temp == 0)
        return b;
    else
    {
        a = b;
        b = temp;
    }
    return papaya(a,b);
}
```

What value is returned as a result of the call mango(45,60) ?

(A) 15
(B) 90
(C) 180
(D) 1350
(E) 2700

10. Consider the following code segment.

```
ArrayList<Integer> numbers1 = new ArrayList<Integer>();
numbers1.add(new Integer(100));
numbers1.add(new Integer(200));
numbers1.add(new Integer(300));
numbers1.add(new Integer(400));
numbers1.add(new Integer(500));

ArrayList<Integer> numbers2 = numbers1;
numbers2.set(2,numbers2.get(3));
numbers2.set(3,numbers2.get(2));
System.out.println(numbers1);
System.out.println(numbers2);
```

What is printed as a result of executing the segment?

(A) [100, 200, 300, 400, 500]
    [100, 200, 400, 300, 500]

(B) [100, 200, 400, 400, 500]
    [100, 200, 400, 400, 500]

(C) [100, 200, 400, 300, 500]
    [100, 200, 400, 300, 500]

(D) [100, 200, 300, 500, 500]
    [100, 200, 400, 500, 500]

(E) [100, 200, 300, 500, 400]
    [100, 200, 300, 500, 400]

11. Consider the following program statement and two classes.

```
CamperVan superSleeper = new CamperVan("Chrysler","SuperCaravan",4,6);


class Van
{
    private String companyName;
    private String carType;

    public Van(String cN, String cT)
    {
        companyName = cN;
        carType = cT;
        System.out.println("Van object is constructed");
    }
}

class CamperVan extends Van
{
    private int sleepingSpaces;
    private int captainSeats;

    public CamperVan(String cN, String cT, int sS, int cS)
    {
        sleepingSpaces = sS;
        captainSeats = cS;
        System.out.println("CamperVan object is constructed");
    }
}
```

What is printed as a result of executing the program statement?

(A) CamperVan is constructed

(B) CamperVan object is constructed
    Van object is constructed

(C) Van object is constructed
    CamperVan object is constructed

(D) Van object is constructed

(E) Compile error message indicating problems with the Van constructor

12. Consider the following code segment.

```
int[][] matrix = {{11,22,33},{44,55,66},{77,88,99}};
for (int k = 0; k < 3; k++)
{
    matrix[k][k] = matrix[0][0];
}
```

Which of the following describes the contents of matrix after the code segment executes?

(A) All of the integers in the left-top to bottom-right diagonal are the same.
(B) All of the integers in the left-bottom to top-right diagonal are the same.
(C) All of the integers in the top row are the same.
(D) All of the integers in the bottom row are the same.
(E) All of the integers in the entire matrix are the same.

13. Consider the following code segment.

```
int n1 = Integer.MAX_VALUE;
int n2 = Integer.MIN_VALUE;
int result = n1 + n2;
System.out.println(result);
```

What will be printed as a result of printing the segment?

(A) −1
(B) 0
(C) 1
(D) compile error indicating that the integer number is too large
(E) An ArithmeticException error message

14. Consider the following code segment and classes.

```
Student tom = new Student();
System.out.println(tom);


class Person
{
    private int age;
    private int grade;
    private String gender;

    public Person ()
    {
        age = 16 ;
        grade = 10;
        gender = "Female";
    }

    public String toString()
    {
        String temp = "[" + age + ", " + grade + ", " + gender + "]";
        return temp;
    }
}

class Student extends Person
{
}
```

What is executed as a result of executing the code segment?

(A) Compile error message, indicating the `Student` class constructor is not defined
(B) `InheritanceException` error message
(C) Program compiles, but there is no output, since the `Student` class is empty.
(D) `Student@78fd4a0` or other memory reference address
(E) `[16, 10, Female]`

15. What is the output of the following code segment and methods?

```
System.out.println(method1(7));

public static int method1(int p)
{
    if (p < 5)
        return p;
    else
        return method2(p);
}

public static int method2(int q)
{
    return method1(q-1);
}
}
```

(A) 3
(B) 4
(C) 5
(D) 6
(E) There is no output. Recursive calls never stop.

16. The primary benefit of *Object Oriented Programming* is greater program reliability.
Which of the following programming features are used by OOP in achieving this reliability benefit?

I. *Encapsulation*, which keeps data and accessing methods in the same module

II. *Class interaction*, which is divided up into inheritance and composition class relationships

III. *Polymorphism*, which manages methods with identical signatures to behave according to their own class implementation.

IV. *Separation*, which keeps data and accessing methods in separate modules

(A) IV only
(B) I and II only
(C) I and III only
(D) II, III and IV only
(E) I, II and III only

17. High school students register for 9th, 10th, 11th and 12th grade classes.
    All students must register before attending classes.
    The registration process is handled differently for 9th, 10th 11th and 12th graders.

    This registration processes can be compared to _____ in Object Oriented Programming.

    (A) encapsulation
    (B) inheritance
    (C) composition
    (D) class interaction
    (E) polymorphism

18. Consider the following code segment.

    ```
    int grade = < an int value, such that 0 <= grade <= 100 >
    if (grade < 70)
        System.out.println(grade + " F Student");
    else if (grade < 80)
        System.out.println(grade + " C Student");
    else if (grade < 90)
        System.out.println(grade + " B Student");
    else
        System.out.println(grade + " A Student");
    ```

    Which grades will print correctly?

    (A) For all student grades
    (B) A students only
    (C) A and B students only
    (D) A, B and C students only
    (E) F students only

19. Consider the following code segment and classes.

```
Apple apple = new Apple("Red Delicious",1000);
apple.showData();


class Fruit
{
    private int quantity;

    public Fruit(int q)
    {
        quantity = q;
    }

    public void showData()
    {
        System.out.println(quantity + " pieces of fruit");
    }
}

class Apple extends Fruit
{
    private String name;

    public Apple(String n, int q)
    {
        super(q);
        name = n;
    }

    public void showData()
    {
        super.showData();
        System.out.println(name + " Apples");
    }
}
```

What is printed as a result of executing the code segment?

(A) Red Delicious Apples

(B) null pieces of fruit
    Red Delicious Apples

(C) 1000 pieces of fruit
    Red Delicious Apples

(D) 0 pieces of fruit
    Red Delicious Apples

(E) 0 pieces of fruit
    1000 Red Delicious Apples

20. Consider the following two methods

```
/** Precondition: nr > 0
 */
public static String monkey(int nr)
{
    String temp = "";
    while (nr > 0)
    {
        temp = nr % 2 + temp;
        nr /= 2;
    }
    return temp;
}
```

What string is returned as a result of the call `monkey(n)`?

(A) A string displaying the binary numbers of `nr`, like [1 2 4 8 16 ...]
(B) A string containing the sum of the binary numbers of `nr`, like [1+2+4+8+16+...]
(C) A string containing the base-2 representation of `nr`
(D) A string containing the reverse of the base-2 representation of `nr`
(E) A string containing all the factors of `nr`

21. Consider the following method

```
/** Precondition: p > 0 and p < q
 */
public static int toad(int p, int q)
{
    int n = 1;
    while (n < p)
    {
        while (p < q)
        {
            n++;
            p++;
        }
    }
    return n;
}
```

What value is returned as a result of the call `toad(3,5)`?

(A) 3
(B) 4
(C) 5
(D) 6
(E) No value; the program is stuck in a non-ending loop

22. Consider the following method.

```
/** Precondition: p > 0
 */
public static boolean foxtrot(int p)
{
    int temp = 1;
    for (int k = 2; k < p; k++)
    {
        if (p % k == 0)
            temp += k;
    }
    return p == temp;
}
```

For which values of p is true returned by method foxtrot?

(A) For all odd values of p
(B) For all even values of p and q
(C) For all binary (1, 2, 4, 8, 16, etc.) values of p
(D) For all values of p
(E) Only for all values of p, such that the sum of the factors equals p, like 6 and 28

23. Consider the following method.

```
/** Precondition: list contains [23, 39, 42, 28, 99, 57]
 */
public static void mystery(ArrayList<Integer> list)
{
    for (int k = 0; k < list.size(); k++)
    {
        if (list.get(k) % 2 != 0)
            list.remove(k);
    }
}
```

Which of the following describes the values stored in list after mystery executes?

(A) [39, 42, 28, 57]
(B) [42, 28]
(C) [23, 39, 99, 57]
(D) [23, 39, 42, 28, 99, 57]
(E) An IndexOutOfBoundsException error message

24. Consider the following code segment and `Student` class.

```
ArrayList<Student> students = new ArrayList<Student>();
Student tom = new Student("Tom",17,2.785);
Student ann = new Student("Ann",16,3.025);
Student liz = new Student("Liz",15,3.765);
students.add(tom);
students.add(ann);
students.add(liz);
System.out.println(students);


class Student
{
    private String name;
    private int age;
    private double gpa;

    public Student(String name, int age, double gpa)
    {
        this.name = name;
        this.age = age;
        this.gpa = gpa;
    }

    public String toString() {return "[" + name + ", " + age + ", " + gpa + "]";}
}
```

What is printed as a result of executing the code segment?

(A) `Student@6e818805, Student@7a0938f0, Student@73795327`
(B) `[Student@6e818805, Student@7a0938f0, Student@73795327]`
(C) `[Tom, 17, 2.785], [Ann, 16, 3.025], [Liz, 15, 3.765]`
(D) `[[Tom, 17, 2.785], [Ann, 16, 3.025], [Liz, 15, 3.765]]`
(E) `[Tom, 17, 2.785, Ann, 16, 3.025, Liz, 15, 3.765]`

25. Consider the following code segment and method.

```
ArrayList<Double> list = new ArrayList<Double>();
double temp = 3.14159;
for (int k = 1; k <= 10; k++)
{
    list.add(new Double(temp));
    temp = mystery(temp);
}
System.out.println(list);

public static double mystery (double x)
{
    x = x + Math.PI;
    x = Math.sqrt(x);
    x = x - (int) x;
    return x;
}
```

What can correctly be stated about the second execution of the code segment?

(A) It will generate 10 random reals in the [0..0.99999] range different from the first set.
(B) It will generate the same set of reals as the first set.
(C) It will generate 10 random reals that could be the same or different from the first set.
(D) Each execution will store a set of 10 identical numbers.
(E) The program will generate an ArithmeticException error message during each execution.

26. Consider the following method.

```
/** Precondition: n > 1
 */
public static int method2126(int n)
{
    if (n == 1 || n == 2)
        return 1;
    else
        return n + method2126(n-1) + method2126(n-2);
}
```

What value is returned as a result of the call method2126(5) ?

(A) 5
(B) 10
(C) 20
(D) 36
(E) 63

27. Which one of the following statements is **FALSE**?

(A) A class can implement a single interface.
(B) A class can extend a single class.
(C) A class can implement one or more interfaces.
(D) A class can extend one or more classes.
(E) An abstract class can implement an interface.

28. Consider the following code segment.

```
Student tom = new Student("Tom",17,3.025);
Student ann = new Student("Ann",15,3.025);
Student liz = new Student("Liz",15,3.765);
System.out.println(tom.equals(ann));
System.out.println(tom.equals(liz));
System.out.println(liz.equals(ann));

class Student
{
    private String name;
    private int age;
    private double gpa;

    public Student(String name, int age, double gpa)
    {
        this.name = name;
        this.age = age;
        this.gpa = gpa;
    }

    public boolean equals(Student obj)
    {
        return this.age == obj.age;
    }
}
```

What is printed as a result of executing the code segment?

(A)	false	(B)	false	(C)	true	(D)	true	(E)	true
	false		true		false		false		true
	true		false		true		false		false

29. Consider the following two classes.

```
class Eye
{
    private Color color;
    private Person person;
    public Eye (Color c)
    {
        color = c;
        person = new Person(25);
    }
}

class Person
{
    private int age;
    private Eye eye;
    public Person (int a)
    {
        age = a;
        eye = new Eye(Color.red);
    }
}
```

These two classes are an example of _____ class definitions using _____

(A) improper   composition.
(B) proper   composition.
(C) improper   inheritance.
(D) proper   inheritance.
(E) improper   both composition and inheritance.

30. What value is returned after calling `texas(4)` ?

```
public static int texas(int p)
{
    if (p < 1)
        return p;
    else
        return p + texas(p-1) + texas(p+1);
}
```

(A) 0
(B) 11
(C) 26
(D) 57
(E) Runtime Exception. Recursive calls never stop.

31. Consider the following code segment and two methods.

```
for (int n = 3; n <= 6; n++)
{
    System.out.println("\nn = " + n);
    if (method1(n) && method2(n))
        System.out.println("Both methods returned true");
    else
        System.out.println("At least one method returned false");
}

public static boolean method1(int n)
{
    System.out.println("Calling method 1");
    return n % 2 == 0;
}

public static boolean method2(int n)
{
    System.out.println("Calling method 2");
    return n % 3 == 0;
}
```

The output below is the result of executing the code segment.

```
n = 3
Calling method 1
At least one method returned false

n = 4
Calling method 1
Calling method 2
At least one method returned false

n = 5
Calling method 1
At least one method returned false

n = 6
Calling method 1
Calling method 2
Both methods returned true
```

The output is evidence that the program used _____ during executing.

(A) short-circuiting
(B) inheritance
(C) composition
(D) polymorphism
(E) exception handling

32. Consider the following code segment.

```
for (int k = 1; k <= 100; k++)
{
    int n1 = (int) Math.random() * 2;
    int n2 = (int) Math.random() * 2;
    boolean bool = n1 == n2;
    System.out.print(bool + "  ");
}
```

What is printed as a result of executing the code segment?

(A) The code segment always prints `true`.
(B) The code segment always prints `false`.
(C) The code segment prints `true` roughly 50% of the time and prints `false` roughly 50% of the time.
(D) The code segment prints both `true` and `false`, but `true` more frequently.
(E) The code segment prints both `true` and `false`, but `false` more frequently.

33. Consider the following method.

```
/** Precondition: list is a non-empty array of int values.
 */
public static int merengue(int[] list)
{
    int temp = list[0];
    for (int p = 0; p < list.length; p++)
    {
        if (list[p] > temp)
            temp = list[p];
    }
    return temp;
}
```

What value is returned by method `merengue`?

(A) The largest `int` value of `list`.
(B) The smallest `int` value of `list`.
(C) The mean average value of `list`.
(D) The median average value of `list`.
(E) The last `int` value in `list`.

34. The linear search algorithm works on an ordered list or a random list.

    Can the linear search benefit from a list that is in descending or ascending order?

    (A) No, order makes no difference for a linear search.
    (B) Yes, it improves. Regardless of the sorting order, finding the requested data is faster.
    (C) Yes, it improves, but only if the list is sorted in ascending order.
    (D) Yes, it improves, but only if the list is sorted in descending order.
    (E) Yes, it improves, but only to identify that the search item does not exist.

35. Polymorphism can be functional with an "umbrella" interface or an "umbrella" superclass.

    Functional polymorphism requires that an interface is implemented or a superclass is extended. Some program designs place an abstract class between the "umbrella" interface and the concrete classes.

    What benefit is there in using an intermediate abstract class, which still requires extending concrete classes?

    (A) Java allows using abstract classes, but there is no noticeable benefit.
    (B) The abstract class can be used to implement common methods for greater efficiency.
    (C) The abstract class is only required when polymorphism is implemented.
    (D) The abstract class enables the use of multiple inheritance.
    (E) The abstract class is required for combining inheritance and composition.

36. Consider the following code segment.

```
CircusPerformer olga = new Equestrian("Olga");
CircusPerformer lizzy = new Equestrian("Lizzy");
CircusPerformer saskia = new Equestrian("Saskia");
CircusPerformer ivan = new TightRopeWalker("Ivan");
CircusPerformer bert = new TightRopeWalker("Bert");
ArrayList<CircusPerformer> performers = new ArrayList<CircusPerformer>();
performers.add(olga);
performers.add(lizzy);
performers.add(saskia);
performers.add(ivan);
performers.add(bert);

for (CircusPerformer performer: performers)
    performer.act();
```

This incomplete program show evidence that _____ is used.

I.   an interface or superclass
II. polymorphism
III. recursion

(A) I only
(B) II only
(C) III only
(D) I and II only
(E) II and III only

37. Consider the following classes.

```java
class List<E>
{
    private int size;
    private int index;
    private Object[] elements;

    public List(int s)
    {
        size = s;
        index = 0;
        elements = new Object[size];
    }

    public void add(E obj)
    {
        elements[index] = obj;
        index++;
    }

    public E remove()
    {
        index--;
        return (E) elements[index];
    }
}

class Student
{
    private int age;
    public Student(int a) { age = a; }
}
```

Which of the following statements uses the generic List array correctly?

(A) List<String> names = new List<String>(100);

(B) List<List<Integer>> matrix = new List<List<Integer>>(100);

(C) List<Double> numbers = new List<Double>(100);

(D) List<Student> students = new List<Student>(25);

(E) All of the above

38. What value is returned after calling texas(4) ?

```
int[] x = {10,20,30,40,50};
int[] y = {11,21,31,41,51};
int[] z = {12,22,32,42,52};
int[][] matrix = new int[3][5];
matrix[0] = x;
matrix[1] = y;
matrix[2] = z;
System.out.println(matrix);
```

(A) [x, y, z]

(B) [[10, 20, 30, 40, 50], [11,21,31,41,51], [12, 22, 32, 42, 52]]

(C) [10, 20, 30, 40, 50]
    [11, 21, 31, 41, 51]
    [12, 22, 32, 42, 52]

(D) Memory reference

(E) ArrayIndexOutOfBoundsException message

39. Consider the following code segment, which is used to store auto parts.

This is a code segment from an old program when only arrays could be used to store data.

```
int [][] parts = { {1,11,5,12,5,13,5,14,5},
                   {2,21,5,22,5,23,5,24,5},
                   {3,31,5,32,5,33,5,34,5} };
int numParts = 0;
```

Each row in the two-dimensional array represents an auto part category.
Each row category uses the columns to store the following elements:

The first column stores the category number.
The next 8 columns store 4 auto parts.
One column is used for the part number and the other column stores the part quantity.
This is done for 4 different auto parts in the same row category, as shown by the following table.

Category #	Auto part #1		Auto part #2		Auto part #3		Auto part #3	
	Part #	Quantity	Part #	Quantity	Part #	Quantity	Part #	Quantity
1	11	500	12	701	13	1213	14	5
2	21	123	22	634	23	3456	24	8
3	31	496	32	803	33	3216	34	6

Which of the following code segments will add up the quantities of all the auto parts and store them in the numParts variable?

Segment I
```
for (int row = 0; row < parts.length; row++)
   for (int col = 1; col < parts[0].length; col++)
      if (col % 2 == 0)
         numParts += parts[row][col];
```

Segment II
```
for (int row = 0; row < parts.length; row++)
   for (int col = 0; col < parts[0].length; col++)
      if (col % 2 != 0)
         numParts += parts[row][col];
```

Segment III
```
for (int row = 0; row < parts.length; row++)
   for (int col = 1; col < parts[0].length; col++)
      if (col > 1)
         numParts += parts[row][col];
```

(A) **Segment I** only
(B) **Segment II** only
(C) **Segment III** only
(D) **Segments I** and **II** only
(E) **Segments II** and **III** only

40. Consider the following ordered list of numbers and the provided binarySearch method.

`[11,22,33,44,55,66,77,88,99,111,222,333,444,555,666,777,888,999]`

```java
public int binarySearch(int sn)
{
    boolean found = false;
    int lo = 0;
    int hi = size-1;
    int mid = 0;
    int c = 0;
    while (lo <= hi && !found)
    {
        c++;
        System.out.println(c);
        mid = (lo + hi) / 2;
        if (intArray[mid] == sn)
            found = true;
        else
        {
            if (sn > intArray[mid])
                lo = mid + 1;
            else
                hi = mid - 1;
        }
    }
    if (found)
        return mid;
    else
        return -1;
}
```

How many comparisons, which are counted by variable c in the method, will be made by this binarySearch method to determine that number 100 is not in the list?

(A) 2
(B) 3
(C) 4
(D) 5
(E) 6

Chapter 21 Free Response Questions
Sample AP Examination II

Section II
    Time - 1 hour and 45 minutes
    Number of questions - 4
    Percent of total grade - 50

Question 1.

There are three measures of central tendency in statistics. One of the measures of central tendency is the arithmetic mean, which is calculated by adding all of the numbers and dividing by the quantity of the numbers. Another measure of central tendency is the mode, which is the number in the list with the highest frequency. A third measure of central tendency is the median, which is the middle value of a list of **n** ordered numbers. If **n** is even, the median is the mean of the two middle numbers.

Part (a).
    Write method `createList`, which constructs an `ArrayList` object, generates a set of random integers in the **[10..99]** range, stores these integers in the `ArrayList` object, and returns the array object.

Complete method `createList` below.

```
/** precondition:  n > 0
 *  postcondition: Returns an ArrayList object with n Integer values.
 *                 Each Integer object is created with a random int
 *                 in the [10..99] range.
public static ArrayList<Integer> createList (int n)
```

Part (b).

Write method `getMean`, which is described as follows. Method `getMean` returns the average, called the **mean**, of a set of numbers. The **mean** is computed by adding the numbers and dividing the sum by the quantity of the numbers.

For example:

The **mean** of {10, 18, 17} is **15**

The **mean** of {10, 15} is **12.5**

Complete method `getMean` below.

```
/** precondition:  list is a non-empty array with Integer objects.
 *  postcondition: Returns the mean of the int values stored
 *                 by the list array.
 */
public static double getMean (ArrayList<Integer> list)
```

Part (c).

Write method `getMedian`, which is described as follows. Method `getMedian` returns a measure, called the median, of a set of **n** numbers. The median is the middle number in a sorted list of numbers. If **n** is even, the median is the mean of the two middle numbers.

For example:

The **median** of {10, 13, 17, 18, 21} is **17**.

The **median** of {54, 60, 64, 68, 74, 81, 94} is **68**

The **median** of {10, 11, 13, 17, 19, 21} is **15**.

The **median** of {50, 60, 70, 80} is **65**

In writing method `getMedian` you may call method `sortList` specified below.

```
/** precondition: list is a non-empty ArrayList object of int elements.
 *  postcondition: The int values in list are sorted in ascending order.
 */
public static void sortList (ArrayList list)
```

Complete method `getMedian` below.

```
/** precondition: list is a non-empty ArrayList object of int elements.
 *                 The int elements in list are randomly ordered.
 *  postcondition: Returns the median value of list.
 */
public static double getMedian (ArrayList<Integer> list)
```

Question 2.

This question involves identifying palindromes. A *palindrome* is a string of characters that reads the same from front-to-back and back-to-front. Three examples of palindromes are **racecar**, **madam** and **123454321**.

These first three examples are <u>perfect</u> palindromes. It is possible to read the string of characters from either end with the exact same results, without any special conditions. There are other strings of characters, which can be considered palindromes, but they are not perfect. Three examples of imperfect palindromes are **Racecar**, **Madam I'm Adam** and **A man, a plan, a canal, Panama**. **Racecar** can be considered a palindrome if case-sensitivity is ignored. The other two examples are also palindromes if case-sensitivity, spaces and punctuation are ignored.

For this question a palindrome shall be defined as a *string of alpha-numeric characters that reads the same from front-to-back and back-to-front without case-sensitivity*. This definition means that strings like **Racecar** and **Madam** will be considered palindromes, but **Madam I'm Adam** is not a palindrome.

Consider the following incomplete declaration of a `Palindrome` class. The constructor determines if the parameter is a palindrome by using the `isPalindrome` method. The private method `isPalindrome` needs to return `true` if the string is a palindrome and `false` otherwise. The method `toString` needs to be re-defined to produce the output shown in the execution example.

```
class Palindrome
{
    private boolean palindrome;
    private String str;

    Palindrome(String s)
    {
        str = s;
        palindrome = isPalindrome();
    }

    public String toString()
    {
        /* implemented in part (a) */
    }

    private boolean isPalindrome()
    {
        /* implemented in part (b) */
    }
}
```

The code segment below is part of a client program that constructs and displays two `Palindrome` objects.

Code segment in client program using the `Palindrome` class	Execution Output

`Palindrome p1 = new Palindrome("Racecar");`
`System.out.println(p1);`
`Palindrome p2 = new Palindrome("Madam I'm Adam");`
`System.out.println(p2);`
	`String:    Racecar`
	`Palindrome: true`
	
	`String:    Madam I'm Adam`
	`Palindrome: false`

Part (a).

Redefine the `toString` method as discussed earlier. Method `toString` must return a string that will display two lines of output. The following table shows the result of several different calls made by `System.out.println(/* Palindrome Object */)` based on the argument of the constructor.

Constructor argument	toString returns
Racecar	`String:      Racecar` `Palindrome: true`
12345BOB54321	`String:      12345BOB54321` `Palindrome: true`
Madam I'm Adam	`String:      Madam I'm Adam` `Palindrome: false`

Complete method `toString` below.

```
/** precondition:  str is not null; palindrome is true or false;
 *  postcondition:Returns the value str and palindrome.
 */
public String toString()
```

Part (b).

Write method `isPalindrome` as described earlier. In writing method `isPalindrome` you may call the `String` method `toUpperCase` specified below.

```
/** precondition:  some String object s is constructed
 *  postcondition: returns s with all lower-case characters converted to
 *                 upper-case characters, if they exist
 */
public String toUpperCase()
```

Complete method `isPalindrome` below.

```
/** precondition:  str is not null
 *  postcondition: returns true if str is a palindrome, and false otherwise
 */
private boolean isPalindrome()
```

Question 3.

A *Magic Square* is a square matrix of consecutive integers, such that the integers in each row, each column and each diagonal add up to the same sum. For instance, the first **3 x 3** matrix below is a magic square and the rows, columns and diagonal add up to 15. The second **5 x 5** matrix has 25 consecutive integers - starting at 1 - where each row, column and diagonal has the sum of 65.

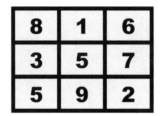

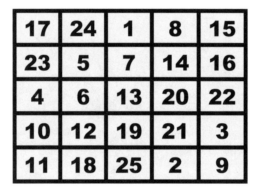

Magic squares have special algorithms that will create a magic square for any size. For the purpose of this question you are only concerned with odd-sized magic squares, like the two above. There are different algorithms for even-sided magic squares. The steps below describe the algorithm for any odd-sized magic square size **3** or larger.

1. Start number 1 in the top row, middle column.
2. If a number is a multiple of the matrix size, place the next number one row lower.
   In the **5 X 5** square above that happens to the numbers following 5, 10, 15 and 20.
3. Place the next number one row higher and one column to the right.
4. If the number is above the first row, drop it to the last row.
5. If the number is to the right of the last column, place it is the first column.

Consider the following incomplete declaration of the `Magic` class.

```
public class Magic
{
    private int size;
    private int[][] square;

    public Magic(int n)
    {
        /* implemented in part (a) */
    }

    public void makeMagic()
    {
        /* implemented in part (b) */
    }

    public String toString()
    {
        /* not required */
    }
}
```

Part (a).

Complete constructor `Magic` below.

```
/** precondition:  n is an odd integer > 2
 *   postcondition: n x n space is allocated for object square
 */
public Magic(int n)
```

Part (b).

Complete method makeMagic below, using the algorithm shown earlier, to form an odd magic square.

```
/** precondition:  n x n space is allocated for square
 *  postcondition: integers are stored in square to form a Magic Square
 */

public void makeMagic()
```

Question 4.

In mathematics, there exists the concept of a set. Some programming languages, including Java, implement this concept. Although Java has several standard classes that implement the set concept, this question concerns developing your own `MySet` class using only the `ArrayList` class. It will mimic one or more of the standard classes.

A set is similar to the `ArrayList` class and static arrays. However, members of a set cannot be accessed with an index, order is not important, and only unique values are stored in a set, which means a set will not have duplicate items.

Consider the following incomplete declaration of the `MySet` class. An `ArrayList` object is used to store the `MySet` elements. Method `contains` determines if the argument object is a member of the `MySet` object. Method `add` adds new elements to the `MySet` object, which are not already stored in the object. Method `remove` removes an element from the `MySet` object, if it exists.

```
class MySet
{
    private ArrayList<Object> set;
    private int numItems;

    public MySet()
    {
        set = new ArrayList<Object>();
        numItems = 0;
    }

    public int size()
    {
        return numItems;
    }

    private int contains (Object item)
    {
        /* implemented in part (a) */
    }

    public void add(Object item)
    {
        /* implemented in part (b) */
    }
    public void remove (Object item)
    {
        /* implemented in part (c) */
    }

    /** other methods to access and display MySet information */
}
```

Examples of `MySet` Operations

Example:

This is a set of digits [4,7,2,9,3,5]

This is not a set [4,7,2,9,3,5,7] because 7 is stored twice in this data structure.

Example:

`MySet` before `add(8)` [4,7,2,9,3,5]   `MySet` after `add(8)` [4,7,2,9,3,8,5]
`numItems` stores 6   `numItems` stores 7

`MySet` before `add(9)` [4,7,2,9,3,5]   `MySet` after `add(9)` [4,7,2,9,3,5]
`numItems` stores 6   `numItems` stores 6

Example:

`MySet` before `remove(2)` [4,7,2,9,3,5]   `MySet` after `remove(2)` [4,7,3,8,5]
`numItems` stores 6   `numItems` stores 5

`MySet` before `remove(6)` [4,7,2,9,3,5]   `MySet` after `remove(6)` [4,7,2,9,3,5]
`numItems` stores 6   `numItems` stores 6

Example:

`MySet` stores [4,7,2,9,3,5]   `contains(3)`   `returns 4`
`numItems` stores 6

`MySet` stores [4,7,2,9,3,5]   `contains(8)`   `returns -1`
`numItems` stores 6

Part (a).

Write method `contains`, which is described as follows. Method `contains` is a private helper method for other members of the `MySet` class. Method `contains` returns the index value if the parameter item exists in the current `MySet` object and returns -1 otherwise. Logically, `MySet` will behave like a set data structure, however since this is a private method the indexing will not be seen at the client level. The implementation may only use the operations available for the `ArrayList` class.

Complete method `contains` below.

```
/** precondition:  item is not null.
 *  postcondition: Returns index location in the set array if item exists,
 *                 and returns -1 otherwise.
 */
private int contains (Object item)
```

Part (b).

Write method `add`, which is described as follows. Method `add` checks to see if the parameter element is already present in the `MySet` object. The element is added to the `MySet` object if it is not yet present and `numItems` is incremented. In writing `add` you may call method `contains` specified in part (a). Assume that `contains` works as specified, regardless of what you wrote in part (a). Solutions that re-implement functionality by this method, rather than invoking this method, will not receive full credit.

Complete method `add` below.

```
/** precondition:  item is not null.
 *  postcondition: item is added to the set array, if item is not
 *                 contained in set and numItems is incremented.
 */
public void add (Object item)
```

Part (c).

Write method `remove`, which is described as follows. Method `remove` checks to see if the parameter element is present in the `MySet` object. The element is removed from the `MySet` object if it is present and `numItems` is decremented. In writing `remove` you may call method `contains` specified in part (a). Assume that `contains` works as specified, regardless of what you wrote in part (a). Solutions that re-implement functionality by this method, rather than invoking this method, will not receive full credit.

Complete method `remove` below.

```
/** precondition:  item is not null
 *  postcondition: item is removed from the set array, if item is
 *                 contained in set and numItems is decremented
 */
public void remove (Object item)
```

Chapter 22 Questions
Sample AP Examination III

01. Consider the following code segment.

```
ArrayList<Student> students = new ArrayList<Student>();
students.add(new Student(25,3.575));
students.add(new Student(23,2.225));
System.out.println(students);

class Student
{
    private int age;
    private double gpa;

    public Student(int a, double g)
    {
        age = a;
        gpa = g;
    }

    public String toString()
    {
        return "We Love Computer Science";
    }
}
```

What is printed as a result of executing the code segment?

(A) [We Love Computer Science, We Love Computer Science]

(B) [[We Love Computer Science], [We Love Computer Science]]

(C) [We Love Computer Science, 25, 3.575]
    [We Love Computer Science, 23, 2.225]

(D) [Student@7930ebb, Student@47ac1adf]

(E) Student@7930ebb
    Student@47ac1adf]

02. Consider the following method.

```
/** Precondition: m > 0
 */
public static int france(int m)
{
    int counter = 0;
    for (int p = 1; p < m; p++)
    {
        counter++;
        if (p % 2 == 0)
            p++;
    }
    return counter;
}
```

What value is returned as a result of the call `france(9)` ?

(A) 4
(B) 5
(C) 6
(D) 7
(E) 8

03. Consider the following method.

```
/** Precondition:  list is non-empty
 *                 list.length > 1
 */
public static void egypt(int[] list)
{
    for (int k = 1; k < list.length; k++)
        list[k] = list[k-1];
}
```

What `int` values are stored in `list` as a result of calling method `egypt`?

(A) All the values are shifted one index position higher.
(B) All the values are shifted one index position lower.
(C) All values are an identical, unknown integer.
(D) All values are equal to the integer value in `list[0]`.
(E) Without knowledge of the values in `list` before the method call, it is unknown.

04. Consider the following program segment.

```
String s1 = "MEXICO";
String s2 = "";
for (int k = 0; k < s1.length(); k++)
{
    s2 += s1.substring(k,k+1);
    if (s2 == "A" || s2 == "E" || s2 == "I" || s2 == "O" || s2 == "U")
        s2 += " ";
}
System.out.println(s2);
```

What will be output when the program segment executes?

(A) MEXICO
(B) ME XI CO
(C) A E I O U
(D) EIO
(E) E I O

05. Consider the following two code segments.

Segment long
```
long n1 = Integer.MAX_VALUE;
long n2 = Integer.MIN_VALUE;
long n3 = n1-n2;
System.out.println(n3);
```

Segment int
```
int n1 = Integer.MAX_VALUE;
int n2 = Integer.MIN_VALUE;
int n3 = n1-n2;
System.out.println(n3);
```

The intent of the code segment is to compute and display the range of int values from the minimum integer value to the maximum integer value.

An int variable stores its integer values in 4 bytes.
A long variable stores its integer values in 8 bytes.

Which of the following is correct about displaying the int range?

(A) Both Segment-long and Segment-int will display the correct int range.
(B) Only Segment-long will display the correct int range.
(C) Only Segment-int will display the correct int range.
(D) Both Segment-long and Segment-int will display the incorrect int range.
(E) The program does not compile and gives an ArithmeticException error message.

06. Consider the following code segment and class.

```
Student paul = new Student(15,3.000);
Student beth = new Student(15,3.999);
Student kate = new Student(16,3.999);
System.out.println(paul.equals(beth));
System.out.println(paul.equals(kate));
System.out.println(beth.equals(kate));


class Student
{
    private int age;
    private double gpa;
    public Student(int age, double gpa)
    {
        this.age = age;
        this.gpa = gpa;
    }
    public boolean equals(Student obj)
    {
        return (this.age == obj.age || this.gpa == obj.gpa || true || false);
    }
}
```

What is printed as a result of executing the code segment?

(A) true
    true
    true

(B) true
    true
    false

(C) false
    false
    true

(D) false
    true
    true

(E) false
    false
    false

07. Consider the following incomplete Student class.

```
public class Student
{
    private int age;

    /* missing constructor */

    public int getAge()
    {
        return age;
    }
}
```

Which of the following constructors will correctly assign the value of its parameter to the age attribute?

Constructor I
```
public Student(int a)
{
    age = a;
}
```

Constructor II
```
public Student(int age)
{
    age = age;
}
```

Constructor III
```
public Student(int age)
{
    this.age = age;
}
```

(A) I only
(B) II only
(C) III only
(D) I and II only
(E) I and III only

08. Consider the following two methods.

```
public static int spain(int x)
{
    int temp1 = italy(x);
    int temp2 = italy(x+1);
    return temp2/temp1;
}

public static int italy(int n)
{
    if (n == 1)
        return 1;
    else
        return n * italy(n-1);
}
```

What value is returned as a result of the call spain(q) ?

(A) 1
(B) q
(C) q + 1
(D) q factorial
(E) (q - 1) factorial

09. Consider the following code segment and Game class.

```
Game.setHighScore(10000);
for (int k = 1; k <= 5; k++)
{
    Game joe = new Game();
    joe.playGame();
    Game tom = new Game();
    tom.playGame();
    Game max = new Game();
    max.playGame();
    System.out.println("High Score: " + Game.getHighScore());
}


class Game
{
    public static int highScore;
    public void playGame()
    {
        int score = (int) (Math.random() * 100000);
        if (score > highScore)
            setHighScore(score);
    }
    public static void setHighScore(int hS) { highScore = hS; }
    public static int getHighScore()        { return highScore; }
}
```

Consider the following output as the result of executing the code segment.
What conclusions can be drawn after five rounds of game play?

```
High Score: 95610
High Score: 95610
High Score: 95610
High Score: 95610
High Score: 95610
```

(A) The high score must always be higher than the initial 10000 score.
(B) The high score is reset to 10000, each time a new Game object is instantiated.
(C) Joe earned the highest score.
(D) The first round was the best round.
(E) Since the game generates random scores, little can be concluded.

10. Consider the following class and re-defined `add` method.

```
class MyList<E> extends ArrayList<E>
{
    public boolean add(E obj)
    {
        if (this.contains(obj))
            return false;
        else
        {
            super.add(obj);
            return true;
        }
    }
}
```

The `MyList` class is a subclass of the `ArrayList` class with only one re-defined method.
How is the behavior of `MyList` different from `ArrayList`?

(A) The `MyList` class automatically sorts the object as new elements are added.
(B) The `MyList` class adds new element in the front of the list, not the end.
(C) The `MyList` class does not add any duplicate elements.
(D) The `MyList` class removes old "identical" elements, before adding new elements.
(E) The `MyList` class alerts the program user whenever there are duplicate elements stored.

11. Consider the following four classes.

```
class Foundation
{
    private String foundationType;
    public Foundation(String fT)        { foundationType = fT; }
    public String getFoundationType()   { return foundationType; }
}

class Frame
{
    private int numStories;
    public Frame(int nS)           { numStories = nS; }
    public int getNumStories()     { return numStories; }
}

class Roof
{
    private String roofType;
    public Roof(String rT)         { roofType = rT; }
    public String getRoofType()    { return roofType; }
}

class House
{
    private Foundation foundation;
    private Frame frame;
    private Roof roof;

    public House()
    {
        foundation = new Foundation("cement");
        frame = new Frame(2);
        roof = new Roof("composite shingles");
    }

    public void displayData()
    {
        System.out.println("Foundation: " + foundation.getFoundationType());
        System.out.println(frame.getNumStories() + " story frame");
        System.out.println("Roof: " + roof.getRoofType());
    }
}
```

Which of the following Object Oriented Features are used to create a House object?

I. Encapsulation II. Inheritance III. Composition IV. Polymorphism	(A) I and II only (B) I and III only (C) II and IV only (D) I, II and III only (E) II, III and IV only

12. Consider the following method

```
public static void change(int[][] matrix)
{
    int n = matrix.length - 1;
    for (int q = 0; q < matrix[0].length; q++)
    {
        int temp = matrix[0][q];
        matrix[0][q] = matrix[n][q];
        matrix[n][q] = temp;
    }
}
```

Which of the following correctly describes the integers stored by matrix after a call to method change ?

(A) The top row and bottom row are exchanged.
(B) The left column and right columns are exchanged.
(C) The top row and bottom row are identical.
(D) The left column and right column are identical.
(E) An ArrayIndexOutOfBoundsException error message

13. What is the output of the following code segment and methods?

```
System.out.println(method1(7));

public static int method1(int p)
{
    if (p < 5)
        return p;
    else
        return method2(p-1);
}

public static int method2(int q)
{
    return method1(q-1);
}
```

(A) 3
(B) 4
(C) 5
(D) 6
(E) There is no output. Recursive calls never stop.

14. Consider the following program segment and List class.

```
int[] x = {11,22,33,44,55,66,77,88,99};
List list = new List(x);
x[x.length-1] = 0;
System.out.println(list);


public class List
{
    private int[] array;

    public List(int[] x)
    {
        array = x;
    }

    public String toString()
    {
        String temp = "[";
        for (int k = 0; k < array.length; k++)
        {
            temp = temp + array[k];
            if (k < array.length-1)
                temp = temp + ", ";
        }
        temp += "]";
        return temp;
    }
}
```

What is the output of executing the program segment?

(A) [0, 0, 0, 0, 0, 0, 0, 0, 0]
(B) [11, 22, 33, 44, 55, 66, 77, 88, 99]
(C) [11, 22, 33, 44, 55, 66, 77, 88, 0]
(D) [0, 22, 33, 44, 55, 66, 77, 0, 99]
(E) ArrayIndexOutOfBoundsException message

15. Consider the following method.

```
/** precondition: strings is a non-empty array of String values.
 */
public static void peru(String[] strings)
{
    for (int p = 1; p < strings.length; p++)
    {
        for (int q = 0; q < strings.length-1; q++)
        {
            if (strings[q].compareTo(strings[q+1]) < 0)
            {
                String temp = strings[q];
                strings[q] = strings[q+1];
                strings[q+1] = temp;
            }
        }
    }
}
```

How are the elements arranged in strings, after a call to method `peru` ?

(A) The elements are reversed.
(B) The elements are returned to their original order.
(C) The elements are sorted in ascending order.
(D) The elements are sorted in descending order.
(E) The elements are rearranged in random order.

16. Object Oriented Programming has four important features, abbreviated to F1, F2, F3 and F4

F1: Encapsulation   F2: Inheritance   F3:   Composition   F4: Polymorphism

D1: Fx uses the object of an established class as a class attribute.
D2: Fx keeps the data and the methods that process the data in the same container.
D3: Fx creates new classes from established classes and only re-defines methods for required changes.
D4: Fx uses multiple classes with identical methods that each behave according to their own class definition.

Which of the following matches the OOP features correctly with the feature definitions?

(A) F1-D2   F2-D3   F3-D1   F4-D4

(B) F1-D1   F2-D3   F3-D4   F4-D2

(C) F1-D3   F2-D2   F3-D4   F4-D1

(D) F1-D4   F2-D1   F3-D3   F4-D2

(E) F1-D2   F2-D1   F3-D4   F4-D3

17. Which of the following features are required to make a large public airport function in an Object Oriented approach?

(A) Passengers enter a closed hallway restricted to their flight destination.
(B) Passengers check in their luggage with an agent who only handles one destination.
(C) The luggage is placed on a conveyer belt dedicated for one destination only.
(D) Airplanes stand at a gate that is dedicated to one destination only.
(E) All of the above

18. Consider the following code segment and method,

```
parser(100000);


public static void parser(int n)
{
    int d, h, m, s;

    d = n / 86400;
    n = n % 86400;

    h = n / 3600;
    n = n % 3600;

    m = n / 60;
    s = n % 60;

    System.out.println(d + "   " + h + "   " + m + "   " + s);

}
```

What is printed as a result of executing the code segment?

(A) 40   46   3   1
(B) 1   3   46   40
(C) 86400   3600   60
(D) 60   3600   86400
(E) An ArithmeticException error message

19. Consider the following code segment and three classes.

```
Apple apple = new Apple(3,1000,"McIntosh");
System.out.println(apple);


class Produce
{
    private int daysOld;
    public Produce (int dO)        { daysOld = dO; }
    public String toString()
    {
        return daysOld + " days old";
    }
}


class Fruit extends Produce
{
    private int quantity;
    public Fruit(int dO,int q)    { super(dO); quantity = q; }
    public String toString()
    {
        return super.toString() + " " + quantity + " ";
    }
}


class Apple extends Fruit
{
    private String name;
    public Apple(int dO,int q,String n) { super(dO,q); name = n; }
    public String toString()
    {
        return super.toString() + name + " apples";
    }
}
```

What is printed as a result of executing the code segment?

(A) McIntosh apples
(B) Compile error message, indicating that three-level inheritance is not allowed
(C) 3 1000 McIntosh
(D) 1000 3 days old McIntosh apples
(E) 3 days old 1000 McIntosh apples

20. Consider the following two methods.

```java
/** Precondition:  nr > 0
 */
public static String houston(int nr)
{
    String temp = "";
    while (nr > 0)
    {
        temp = (nr % 2) + temp;
        nr /= 2;
    }
    return temp;
}

public static String alter(String s)
{
    String temp = "[";
    int n = 4 - (s.length() % 4);
    if (n != 4)
    {
        for (int k = 1; k <= n; k++)
            temp += "0";
    }
    temp += s + "]";
    return temp;
}
```

What string is returned as a result of the call `alter(houston(6))` ?

(A) [6]
(B) 011
(C) [011]
(D) 0110
(E) [0110]

21. Consider the following code segment and method makeSquare.

```
int[] list = {11,12,13,14,15,16,17,18,19,20,21,22,23,24,25,26,27,28,29};
int[][] square = makeSquare(list);


/** Description:  Method makeSquare stores all the values from the 1D
 *                list array parameter into the smallest possible,
 *                square-shaped, 2D array.
 *
 *  Precondition: list is a non-empty array.
 *  Postcondition:1: Smallest possible square 2D array is returned.
 *                2: All list values are copied into the 2d array.
 *                3: 99 is stored into any leftover 2d spaces.
 */
public static int[][] makeSquare(int[] list)
{
    int n = (int) Math.sqrt(list.length) + 1;
    int[][] temp = new int[n][n];
    int count = 0;
    for (int r = 0; r < n; r++)
    {
        for (int c = 0; c < n; c++)
        {
            if (count < list.length)
            {
                temp[r][c] = list[count];
                count++;
            }
            else
                temp[r][c] = 99;
        }
    }
    return temp;
}
```

Which of the three Postconditions is satisfied by the makeSquare method?

(A) 1: only
(B) 2: only
(C) 1: and 2: only
(D) 2: and 3: only
(E) 1: , 2: and 3:

22. Consider the following classes.

```
class Eye {  }

abstract class Person
{
    private Eye eye;
    abstract public void getReady();
    public Eye getEye()  {  return eye;  }
}

class Student extends Person
{
    public void getReady() { System.out.println("Student is ready."); }
}

class Teacher extends Person
{
    public void getReady() { System.out.println("Teacher is ready."); }
}

class Pilot extends Person
{
    public void getReady() { System.out.println("Pilot is ready.");  }
}

class Nurse extends Person
{
    public void getReady() { System.out.println("Nurse is ready.");  }
}

class Roofer extends Person
{
    public void getReady() { System.out.println("Roofer is ready.");  }
}
```

Imagine that these "very incomplete" class declarations are part of a large program that manages the daily activities of all types of people.

Even though the program is incomplete, there is already evidence of certain Object Oriented features. Which of these OOP features are in the process of being set up?

(A) Inheritance
(B) Composition
(C) Encapsulation
(D) Polymorphism
(E) All of the above

23. Consider the following code segment.

```
ArrayList<Integer> numbers = new ArrayList<Integer>();
ArrayList<Integer> odds = new ArrayList<Integer>();
ArrayList<Integer> evens = new ArrayList<Integer>();
```

The intention of following code is to remove the integers from the numbers array and to transfer them into an array for even numbers and an array for odd numbers. After executing the following code how well did the code satisfy that intention?

```
for (int k = 0; k < numbers.size() ; k++)
{
    Integer temp = numbers.get(k);
    if (temp.intValue() % 2 == 0)
        evens.add(temp);
    else
        odds.add(temp);
    numbers.remove(k);
}
```

(A) The odds array will only store odd integers.
(B) The evens array will only store even integers.
(C) The numbers array will not be completely empty.
(D) The remove methods results in skipping certain numbers.
(E) All of the above

24. Consider the following code segment and method.

```
System.out.println(sillyString("1234567"));
System.out.println(sillyString("123456"));

public static String sillyString(String s)
{
    int n = s.length();
    String temp1 = s.substring(0,n/2);
    String temp2 = s.substring(n/2,n);
    String temp3 = temp1 + temp2;
    return temp3;
}
```

What is printed as a result of executing the code segment?

(A) 123567
     12356

(B) 1234567
     12356

(C) 123567
     123456

(D) 1234567
     123456

(E) A `StringIndexOutOfBoundsException` error message

25. Consider the following code segment and method.

```
double seed = 0.0;
for (int k = 1; k < 10; k++)
    seed = jack(seed);

public static double jack(double seed)
{
    seed = seed + Math.PI;
    seed = Math.sqrt(seed);
    seed = (int) seed - seed;
    return seed;
}
```

What values are returned as a result of executing the code segment?

(A) Ten double values such that for each x   0 < x < 1
(B) Ten double values such that for each x   -1 < x < 0
(C) Ten double values such that for each x   0 < x < Math.PI
(D) Ten double values such that for each x   -1 < x < Math.PI
(E) Ten double values such that for each x   -Math.PI < x < 0

26. Consider the following method.

```
/** Precondition:   q > 1
 *                   p > 1
 */
public static int canada(int p, int q)
{
    if (p < q)
        return canada(p+1,q-1);
    else
        return p + q;
}
```

What value is returned as a result of the call canada(a,b) ?

(A) b^a
(B) a^b
(C) a + b
(D) 1
(E) 0

Questions 27-29 refer to the following class and interface declarations.

```
class Person
{
    /* attributes and methods that process personal information */
}

class Sport
{
    /* attributes and methods that process one specific sport */
}

class Training
{
    /* attributes and methods that manage an athlete's training */
}

class Events
{
    /* attributes and methods that manage competitive events */
}

class Medical
{
    /* attributes and methods that manage an athlete's health */
}


interface Athlete
{
    public Person getData();
    public void setData(Person p);
    public Sport getSport();
    public void setSport(Sport s);
    public Training getTraining();
    public void setTraining(Training t);
    public Events getEvents();
    public void setEvents(Events e);
    public Medical getMedical();
    public void setMedical(Medical m);
}
```

27. The `Athlete` interface is the start of a large program that will manage every type of athlete for any kind of sporting event. What is a likely next step in the program design?

(A) Complete every one of `Person`, `Sport`, `Training`, `Events` and `Medical` classes.
(B) Implement each one of the abstract methods in a concrete class.
(C) Decide all the attributes needed for the Athlete's program.
(D) Create an abstract class that will implement common methods to all types of athletes.
(E) Test the interface thoroughly before implementing any abstract methods.

28. How will the `Person`, `Sport`, `Training`, `Events` and `Medical` classes interact with other classes?

(A) They will be used to implement the `Athlete` interface.
(B) They will be used to extend an abstract class that implements the `Athlete` interface.
(C) They will be used as attribute objects in classes that manage specific athletic categories.
(D) They will be utility classes with class methods that can be easily used anywhere.
(E) They are special classes designed to test the reliability of the program.

29. Consider the following `CommonAthlete` class, which implements the `Athlete` interface.

```
abstract class CommonAthlete
{
    public Person getData()              {/*statements to implement method*/}
    public void setData(Person p)        {/*statements to implement method*/}
    public Events getEvents()            {/*statements to implement method*/}
    public void setEvents(Events e)      {/*statements to implement method*/}
    public Medical getMedical()          {/*statements to implement method*/}
    public void setMedical(Medical m)    {/*statements to implement method*/}
}
```

Is it correct that not all the methods are implemented in the `CommonAthlete` class?

(A) Yes, but the remaining methods must be implemented by a subclass of `CommonAthlete`.
(B) Yes, as long as the remaining methods are listed in `CommonAthlete` as abstract methods.
(C) Yes, as long as the remaining methods are implemented in another abstract class
(D) No, because any class that implements an interface, must implement all methods.
(E) No, because an abstract class can only have abstract methods.

30. What value is returned after `calling texas(5)` ?

```
public static int texas(int p)
{
    if (p < 1)
        return p;
    else
        return texas(p-1) + texas(p-1);
}
```

(A) 0
(B) 1
(C) 3
(D) 4
(E) Runtime Exception. Recursive calls never stop.

31. Consider the following code segment.

```
boolean b3 = b1 && !( (b1 || b2) && !(b1 && b2) || (b1 || b2) );
System.out.println(b3);
```

What is printed as a result of executing the code segment?

(A) The code segment always prints `true`.
(B) The code segment always prints `false`.
(C) The code segment prints `true`, if `b1` is `true`.
(D) The code segment prints `false`, if `b1` is `false`.
(E) Nothing can be determined about the output since we do not know the value of `b2`.

32. Consider the following code segment.

```
boolean b3 = b1 || !( (b1 || b2) && !(b1 && b2) || (b1 || b2) );
System.out.println(b3);
```

What is printed as a result of executing the code segment?

(A) The code segment always prints `true`.
(B) The code segment always prints `false`.
(C) The code segment prints `true`, if `b1` is `true`.
(D) The code segment prints `false`, if `b1` is `false`.
(E) Nothing can be determined about the output since we do not know the value of `b2`.

33. Consider the following code segment and method.

```
int[] numbers = {66,22,77,11,44,55,33,99,88};
alter(numbers);
for (int number: numbers)
    System.out.print(number + "   ");

public static void alter(int[] list)
{
    for (int q = 0; q < list.length-1; q++)
    {
        if (list[q] < list[q+1])
        {
            int temp = list[q];
            list[q] = list[q+1];
            list[q+1] = temp;
        }
    }
}
```

What is printed as a result of executing the code segment?

(A) 66 77 22 44 55 33 99 88 11
(B) 99 88 77 66 55 44 33 22 11
(C) 11 22 33 44 55 66 77 88 99
(D) 22 66 11 44 55 33 77 88 99
(E) 66 22 77 11 44 55 33 99 88

34. Consider the following `selectionSort` and `BubbleSort` methods. Assume that a `swap` method is available in the same class as the methods.

```
public void selectionSort()
{
    int p,q;
    int smallest;
    for (p = 0; p < size-1; p++)
    {
        smallest = p;
        for (q = p+1; q < size; q++)
        {
            if (intArray[q] < intArray[smallest])
                smallest = q;
        }
        swap(p,smallest);
    }
}
```

```
public void bubbleSort()
{
    for (int p = 1; p < size; p++)
    {
        for (int q = 0; q < size-p; q++)
        {
            if (intArray[q] > intArray[q+1])
                swap(q,q+1);
        }
    }
}
```

What makes the Selection Sort more efficient than the Bubble Sort?

(A) The Selection Sort makes fewer comparisons than the Bubble Sort.
(B) The Selection Sort makes fewer `swap` calls than the Bubble Sort.
(C) The Selection Sort exits when it knows that the list is sorted.
(D) The Selection Sort insert each number in the correct location.
(E) The Selection Sort makes more efficient `swap` calls than the Bubble Sort.

35. Consider the following code segment and class.

```
int[] numbers1 = {10,10,10,10,10,10,10};
int[] numbers2 = {10,20,30,40,50,60,70};
int[] numbers3 = {40,40,40,40,40,40,40};
List list1 = new List(numbers1);
List list2 = new List(numbers2);
List list3 = new List(numbers3);
System.out.println(list1.equals(list2));
System.out.println(list1.equals(list3));
System.out.println(list2.equals(list3));


class List
{
    private int size;
    private int[] numbers;

    public List(int[] n)
    {
        size = n.length;
        numbers = n;
    }

    public boolean equals(List obj)
    {
        int x1 = this.numbers[size/2];
        int x2 = obj.numbers[size/2];
        return x1 == x2;
    }
}
```

What is printed as a result of executing the code segment?

(A) true	(B) false	(C) false	(D) true	(E) true
true	false	false	false	true
true	false	true	true	false

36. Consider the following `randomSearch` method.

```
/** Precondition: list is a non-empty array of int values.
 *                sn is an int value, which is not necessarily
 *                contained in list.
 *  Postcondition:returns index of sn in list if found,
 *                returns -1 otherwise.
 */
public static int randomSearch(int[] list, int sn)
{
    int max = list.length;
    boolean found = false;
    int guess = -1;
    while (!found)
    {
        guess = (int) (Math.random() * max);
        if (list[guess] == sn)
            found = true;
    }
    return guess;
}
```

What is wrong with the `randomSearch` method?

(A) It is not guaranteed that it will find the (`sn`) search number, if it exists.
(B) It will always be stuck in an infinite loop.
(C) The `while` loop will not exit if the (`sn`) search number does not exist.
(D) The method does not return the correct index for the (`sn`) search number.
(E) The method will generate an `ArrayIndexOutOfBoundsException` error message.

37. Consider the following method.

```
/** Precondition: mat is a non-empty two-dimensional array of int values.
  */
public static void alter (int[][] mat, int x, int y)
{
    for (int r = 0; r < mat.length; r++)
    {
        for (int c = 0; c < mat[0].length; c++)
        {
            if (c == x)
                mat[r][c] = 0;
            if (r == y)
                mat[r][c] = 0;
        }
    }
}
```

How is the mat array changed as a result of executing the alter method?

(A) Every value in the column with index [x] is altered to 0.
    Every value in the row with index [y] is altered to 0.

(B) Every value in the row with index [x] is altered to 0.
    Every value in the column with index [y] is altered to 0.

(C) Both the column with index [x] and the row with index [y] are removed.

(D) Both the row with index [x] and the column with index [y] are removed.

(E) Only the value at index [x][y] is changed to 0.

38. Imagine the following scenario in the life of a teenage student.

A student, Kate, wants to go on the spring break ski trip.
Her parents agree with the following conditions, all of which must be met 100%,
as a condition for going skiing during spring break.

All grades B or better
Room is kept clean
No school detentions
No fights with younger brother
Proper attitude towards parents

A week before the ski trip, Kate loses her temper and hits her little brother.
She tries to tell her parents that she met all of the other conditions, but the decision has already been made.
She is not allowed to go on the trip.
In computer science this type of situation is called ...

(A) short circuiting
(B) De Morgan's Law
(C) Boolean distribution
(D) Boolean inheritance
(E) Polymorphism

39. What is the output of the following code segment?

```
ArrayList matrix = new ArrayList();
int[] x = {10,20,30,40,50};
int[] y = {11,21,31,41,51};
int[] z = {12,22,32,42,52};
matrix.add(x);
matrix.add(y);
matrix.add(z);
System.out.println(matrix);
```

(A) [x, y, z]
(B) [[10, 20, 30, 40, 50], [11,21,31,41,51], [12, 22, 32, 42, 52]]
(C) [three memory references separated by commas]
(D) single Memory reference
(E) `ArrayIndexOutOfBoundsException`

40. Consider the following two-dimensional array declaration.

```
int[][] matrix = { {1,2,3,4},{2,3,4,1},{3,4,1,2},{4,1,2,3} };
```

Which of the following code segments displays the matrix using the enhanced for..each loop?

Loops I
```
for (int[] row: matrix)
{
    for (int number: row)
        System.out.print(number + "   ");
    System.out.println();
}
```

Loops II
```
for (int[][] row: matrix)
{
    for (int[] number: row)
        System.out.print(number + "   ");
    System.out.println();
}
```

Loops III
```
for (int r = 0; r < matrix.length; r++)
{
    for (int c = 0; c < matrix[0].length; c++)
        System.out.print(matrix[r][c] + "   ");
    System.out.println();
}
```

(A) Loop I only
(B) Loop II only
(C) Loop III only
(D) Loops I and Loops II only
(E) Loops II and Loops III only

Chapter 22 Free Response Questions
Sample AP Examination III

Section II
    Time - 1 hour and 45 minutes
    Number of questions - 4
    Percent of total grade - 50

Question 1.

This question involves converting numbers from Base16 to Base 10.

Part (a).

Write method `fromHexToBin`, which is described as follows. Method `fromHexToBin` converts the base-16 argument and converts the number to its base-2 equivalent. The base-2 number is returned. In completing method `fromHexToBin` you can use the following table, which details the unique relationship between base-16 and base-2 numbers. Every single base-16 digit corresponds to four base-2 digits.

Base 16	0	1	2	3	4	5	6	7	8	9	a	b	c	d	e	f
Base-2	0000	0001	0010	0011	0100	0101	0110	0111	1000	1001	1010	1011	1100	1101	1110	1111

Complete method `fromHexToBin` below.

```
/** precondition: hexNum is a String of characters, which represents
 *                a correct base-16 number.
 *  postcondition: returns a String of characters, which represents
 *                the base-2 number equivalent of hexNum.
 */
  public static String fromHexToBin(String hexNum)
```

Part (b).

Write method `fromBinToDec`, which is described as follows. Method `fromBinToDec` converts the base-2 argument and converts the number to its base-10 equivalent. The base-10 number is returned.

Complete method `fromBinToDec` below.

```
/** precondition:  binNum is a String of characters, which represents
 *                 a correct base-2 number.
 *  postcondition: returns an int value, which represents
 *                 the base-10 number equivalent of binNum.
 */
public static int fromBinToDec(String binNum)
```

Part (c).

Write method `fromHexToDec`, which is described as follows. Method `fromHexToDec` converts the base-16 argument and converts the number to its base-10 equivalent. The base-10 number is returned.

In writing method `fromHexToDec` you may call methods `fromHexToBin` and `fromBinToDec`, which are specified in Part (a) and Part(b), whether the methods are implemented correctly or not.

Complete method `fromHexToDec` below.

```
/** precondition: hexNum is a String of characters, which represents
 *  a correct base-16 number.
 *  postcondition: returns an int value, which represents
 *  the base-10 number equivalent of hexNum.
 */
public static int fromHexToDec(String hexNum)
```

Question 2.

This question involves examining *Pascal's Triangle*. *Pascal's Triangle* is a convenient way to compute the binomial coefficients of polynomials that are an expansion of $(x + y)^n$. Pascal's triangle can also be used for probability. The result of computing $(x + y)^5$ is shown below.

$$(x + y)^5 = x^5 + 5x^4y + 10x^3y^2 + 10x^2y^3 + 5xy^4 + y^5$$

Now consider the first 7 rows of *Pascal's Triangle*. Note that the numbers in row 6 correspond to the coefficients of the binomial expansion to the 5th power. Creating *Pascal's triangle* follows two rules:

1. The first and last number in each row are always 1.
2. All other numbers are the sum of two numbers in the previous row.
    The triangle below demonstrates this pattern and more formally it can be stated that:

$$\text{triangle[row][col] = triangle[row-1][col-1] + triangle[row-1][col]}$$

```
            1
           1 1
          1 2 1
         1 3 3 1
        1 4 6 4 1
      1 5 10 10 5 1
    1 6 15 20 15 6 1
```

Pascal's triangle can be viewed as a two-dimensional array. Since a two-dimensional array is in fact an array of arrays, it is not required that the array forms a square matrix. Each element of the array can be an array of a different size.

The number of rows in such an array, called `triangle`, is `triangle.length`.

The number of columns in each row is `triangle[row].length`.

Consider the following incomplete declaration of a `Pascal` class.

The intent of the Pascal class is to create *Pascal's Triangle*.

```
public class Pascal
{
    private int n;
    private int[][] triangle;

    public Pascal(int n)
    {
        /* implemented in part (a) */
    }

    public void makeTriangle()
    {
        /* implemented in part (b) */
    }

    public String toString()
    {
        /* not required */
    }
}
```

Part (a).

Complete constructor `Pascal` below.

```
/** precondition:  n is >= 0
 *  postcondition: space is allocated for a two-dimensional array, such
 *                 that row-0 has 1 element, row-1 has 2 elements, ...
 *                 and row-n has row+1 elements.
 */
public Pascal(int n)
```

Part (b).

Complete method `makeTriangle` below.

```
/**
 *  postcondition: Numbers are placed in n+1 rows of the triangle array
 *                 such that it represents Pascal's triangle.
 */
public makeTriangle()
```

Question 3.

Consider the following incomplete declaration of a `StringList` class. The intent of the `StringList` class is to facilitate data processing of string information stored in a `strings` array. For this question data processing will be limited to three actions, which are adding strings, sorting strings and displaying strings.

```
public class StringList
{

    private ArrayList<String> strings;
    private int size;

    public StringList()
    {
        strings = new ArrayList<String>();
        size = 0;
    }


    public void add(String str)
    {
        /* implemented by part (a) */
    }


    private void sortStrings()
    {
        /* implemented by part (b) */
    }

    public String toString()
    {
        /* implemented by part (c) */
    }

}
```

Part (a).

Write method `add`, which is described as follows. Method `add` adds new elements to the `strings` array. The `strings` array is a dynamic array implemented with an object of the `ArrayList` class.

Complete method `add` below.

```
/** postcondition: the String value of str is added to the strings
 *                  array.
 */
public void add(String str)
```

Part (b).

Write method `sortStrings`, which is described as follows. Method `sortStrings` arranges the elements of the `strings` array in ascending order.

Complete method `sortStrings` below.

```
/** precondition: strings is a non-empty dynamic array of String values
 *  postcondition: the strings array is sorted in ascending order
 */
private void sortStrings()
```

Part (c).

Write method `toString`, which is described as follows. Method `toString` enables the display of the `StringList` object.

If the strings array contains the following string value:

```
{Tom, Sue, Joe,Meg},
```
then method toString will return
```
[Tom, Sue, Joe, Meg]
```

In writing method `toString` you may call method `sortStrings`, which is specified in part (a), whether the method is implemented correctly or not.

Complete method `toString` below.

```
/** precondition:  strings is a non-empty dynamic array of String values.
 *  postcondition: the elements in the strings array are sorted in
 *                 ascending order.
 *                 returns a string in the format:
 *                 [string1, string2, string3, ........]
 */
private void toString()
```

Question 4.

Consider the following incomplete declaration of a `Matrix` class. The intent of the `Matrix` class is to facilitate mathematical operations performed on two-dimensional, rectangular arrays. `Matrix` objects can be constructed with row and column size information only or with a provided integer array parameter. A `Matrix` class can have many useful operations. For this question the focus will be on writing methods for matrix multiplication and matrix display.

Method `multiply` takes two `Matrix` objects and returns the product. Method `okSize` is a private helper method for method `multiply` and determines if the provided `Matrix` objects can be multiplied. You will also need to re-define the `toString` method to display the elements of a `Matrix` object.

```
public class Matrix
{
    private int twoD[][];
    private int numRows;
    private int numCols;

    public Matrix(int r, int c)
    {
        numRows = r;
        numCols = c;
        twoD = new int[numRows][numCols];
    }

    public Matrix(int array[][])
    {
        twoD = array;
        numRows = twoD.length;
        numCols = twoD[0].length;
    }

    public String toString()
    {
        /* not required */
    }

    private boolean okSize(Matrix m1, Matrix m2)
    {
        /* implemented by part (a) */
    }

    public void multiply(Matrix m1, Matrix m2)
    {
        /* implemented by part (b) */
    }

    // other methods used by the Matrix class

}
```

Part (a).

Matrix multiplication involves a process of adding the products of elements of rows in one matrix times corresponding elements of columns in a second matrix. This process is demonstrated by the matrix multiplication example below.

$$
\begin{matrix} a & b \\ c & d \end{matrix} \; * \; \begin{matrix} e & f \\ g & h \end{matrix} \; = \; \begin{matrix} ae + bg & af + bh \\ ce + dg & cf + dh \end{matrix}
$$

It is not necessary that matrices are square matrices or identical matrices. Two matrices can be multiplied as long as the number of columns in the first matrix is equal to the number of rows in the second matrix. The next example involves a **2 x 3** matrix and a **3 x 2** matrix.

$$
\begin{matrix} a & b & c \\ d & e & f \end{matrix} \; * \; \begin{matrix} g & h \\ i & j \\ k & l \end{matrix} \; = \; \begin{matrix} ag + bi + ck & ah + bj + cl \\ dg + ei + fk & dh + ej + fl \end{matrix}
$$

Observe that the **2 x 3** matrix is multiplied by a **3 x 2** matrix and creates a **2 x 2** matrix product. A general formula can be stated about the matrix multiplication, which is:

An **a x b** matrix times a **b x c** matrix becomes an **a x c** matrix.

This formula shows that there are special size requirements for all three matrices involved in the multiplication process. The column size (**b**) of the first matrix must be the same as the row size (**b**) of the second matrix. Furthermore, the product matrix must have row size (**a**) and column size (**c**).

Write method `okSize`, which is described as follows. Method `okSize` is used to see if the three matrices involved in multiplication follow the correct rules of row and column size. Method `okSize` returns `true` if the number of column of `m1` equals the number of rows of `m2` and the product matrix has the same number of rows as `m1` and the same number of columns as `m2`.

Complete method `okSize` below.

```
/** precondition:  m1 and m2 are not null
 *  postcondition: returns true if m1 columns equals m2 rows and
 *  m1 rows equals object's rows and m2 columns
 *  equals object's columns
 */
private boolean okSize(Matrix m1, Matrix m2)
```

Part (b).

Write method `multiply` as described earlier. In writing method `multiply`, you may call method `okSize`, as specified in part (b). Assume that `okSize` works as specified, regardless of what you wrote in part (a).

Complete method `multiply` below.

```
/** precondition:  m1 and m2 are not null
 *  postcondition: returns product of the m1 and m2 is stored in the
 *                 current object, if possible, otherwise the
 *                 current object remains unchanged.
 */
public void multiply(Matrix m1, Matrix m2)
```